# MUSLIM NARRATIVES

# AND THE

# DISCOURSE OF ENGLISH

# MUSLIM NARRATIVES

# AND THE

# DISCOURSE OF ENGLISH

AMIN MALAK

STATE UNIVERSITY OF NEW YORK PRESS

Cover art: Ahmad ibn al-Suhrawardi al-Bakri, Calligrapher (Baghdad, Iraq), *Folio from a Qur'an Manuscript*, 1307–1308/ A.H. 707; Ilkhanid period (1256–1353), Ink, colors, and gold on paper; H. 20 3/16 in. x W. 14 1/2 in. (51.3 cm x 36.8 cm). Courtesy of The Metrolopitan Museum of Art, Rogers Fund, 1955 (55.44). Photograph © 1955 The Metropolitan Museum of Art.

PUBLISHED BY
STATE UNIVERSITY OF NEW YORK PRESS,
ALBANY

© Amin Malak 2005

Printed in the United States of America

For information, address State University of New York Press,
90 State Street, Suite 700, Albany, NY 12207

Production, Laurie Searl
Marketing, Michael Campochiaro

**Library of Congress Cataloging-in-Publication Data**

Malak, Amin, 1946–
    Muslim narratives and the discourse of English / Amin Malak.
        p. cm.
    Includes bibliographical references (p. ) and index.
    ISBN 0-7914-6305-2 (alk. paper) — ISBN 0-7914-6306-0 (pbk. : alk. paper)
        1. English literature—Islamic influences.    2. English literature—Muslim authors—History and criticism.    3. Islam and literature—English-speaking countries.    4. Africa, North—In literature.    5. Middle East—In literature. 6. Muslims in literature.    7. Islam in literature.    8. Orientalism.    I. Title.

PR129.I75M35  2004
823'.910921297—dc22

                                                                    2004042982

10 9 8 7 6 5 4 3 2 1

For Baghdad, *Dar al-Salam,* my City, my Love

and

for the Memory of my Parents

# Contents

# Acknowledgments

I would like to thank Robert Merrett and Fred Radford, from the University of Alberta, for their constant support and encouragement during several years. Thanks also to Nancy Nanney, former head of the English Department at the International Islamic University in Kuala Lumpur, Malaysia, for inviting me to be a guest speaker at the university's conference "English and Islam: Creative Encounters" in December 1996. The university and many of its faculty were extremely warm and hospitable—I am grateful. Khaldoun al-Nu'aimi, Kavita Mathai, and Doireann MacDermott helped in different ways. Robert Einarsson, from Grant MacEwan College, patiently proofread the final version of the manuscript. Mustapha Marrouchi gave positive feedback and went well beyond the call of duty. James Peltz, from State University of New York Press, has been admirably prompt, professional, and encouraging throughout. Finally, special thanks to Louise Bohachyk who quite generously helped in numerous ways at several crucial stages of writing this book, especially with securing interlibrary loan materials—I owe her a deep debt of gratitude.

Segments of chapters 1, 2, 5, 6, and 8 appeared in the following periodicals: *Commonwealth Novel in English, Kunapipi, Ariel: A Review of International English Literature, World Literature Today, International Journal of Arabic-English Studies,* and *Alif: Journal of Comparative Poetics.* I would like to thank the editors of these journals for their interest in my work.

# Introduction

There is always the other side, always.

—Jean Rhys

## CONTEXTS AND REPRESENTATIONS

In a sweeping but significant statement, the Argentine writer Jorge Luis Borges once said, "A major event in the history of the West was the discovery of the East" (42). While one takes exception to the word *discovery*—the East exists in its own right and has never needed anyone to discover it—the statement nevertheless foregrounds the operative dynamics of the East–West encounter in which each pole, each party, becomes self-consciously aware of the weight and impact of the Other. Obviously, the relationship between these two heterogeneous conglomerates has not always been harmonious: the love–hate relationship has been characterized by cooperation and conflict, attraction and revulsion. It is perhaps axiomatic to state that any relationship involves a measure of power factored into it, because, as Michel Foucault has perceptively and repeatedly suggested, "power is everywhere, not because it embraces everything, but because it comes from everywhere" (93). In recent history, and by that I mean approximately the last three centuries, the balance of power has unmistakably shifted Westward, simply because the power equation has been, and still is, in favor of the technologized West. Apart from the political and economic spheres, the West's privileged position has manifested itself logocentrically, that is, in the discourse arena, whereby the West made normative judgments over the non-West under the guise of scholarly objectivity and scientific impartiality, while the East remained inarticulate or inaudible. As Edward Said has forcefully put it in his seminal work *Orientalism*: "The exteriority of the representation is always governed by some version of the truism that if the

1

Orient could represent itself, it would; since it cannot, the representation does the job, for the West, and *faute de mieux*, for the poor Orient" (21).

This book then has been prompted by an aching search for the voices that articulate the point of view of the disadvantaged and the marginalized, often silent, at times even invisible. (Glaring examples abound: the Kurds, the Dalits, the Palestinians, the Chechens, the Tibetans, the Roma, the natives and aborigines of the Americas and Australia, and countless other persecuted minorities denied their basic human rights.) In this highly mediatized, Internetted, wired/wireless world at the dawn of the twenty-first century, one searches for the alternative voices that speak the narratives of the submerged, silenced, or altogether erased Other. To put it simply, this book studies Muslim narrative writers who produce works in English, the world's latter-day lingua franca, and who project the culture and civilization of Islam from *within*. The focus is on novels, stories, and autobiographical narratives, which, for Muslim writers in English, are the most commonly practiced genres and are more easily disseminated beyond their locale than poetry or drama. Accordingly, three criteria evolved as the common denominator about the Muslim writers with whom I shall be dealing in the coming chapters: they have experienced Islam firsthand for an extended, formative period; they have been influenced by it to such a degree that it has represented a significant inspirational source for them; and they are producing their narratives in English.[1]

Obviously, the third point represents perhaps the most challenging aspect of the writing endeavor because it involves crossing boundaries and expressing ethos in an adopted language. Being associated with conquest and colonialism, English is seen as inherently inhospitable to Islam and as syntactically and discursively different from any of the major Islamic languages such as Arabic, Persian, Malay, Wolof, or Hausa. Here, the role of the India–Pakistan–Bangladesh subcontinent—for complex historical, political, and demographic reasons—becomes prominent: all the early Muslim writers in English and most of the current ones are either from there or have their roots there. Apart from the most famous and problematic of all, Salman Rushdie, one is indeed impressed to discover over thirty Muslim fiction writers in English from parts of the world as diverse as Australia, the Middle East, Africa, Britain, Canada, and the Caribbean.

Moving from geography to genesis, the first narrative ever published by a Muslim in English is a short story entitled "Sultana's Dream" written by Rokeya Sakhawat Hossain and published in 1905 in India. Deploying utopia as a strategy, the woman author reverses the gender roles and cleverly argues how our world would be a more peaceful and better place to live in if only women were to become the power wielders and men, secluded and shut indoors, were to do household chores. Hossain's landmark story was followed, over three decades later, by Ahmed Ali's impressive novel *Twilight in Delhi*. It was the first *major* work of fiction written by a Muslim ever to be published in English: thus a precedent is set and a tradition launched.

## ISLAM AS IDENTITY

The argument in this book is premised on the notion that many Muslims regard religion as a key component of their identity that could rival, if not supersede, their class, race, gender, or ethnic affiliation. Some, like the Egyptian writer and chief ideologue of the Muslim Brotherhood movement, Sayyid Qutb, go further and deem Islam to be their *sole* source of identity definition. During his trial by the Nasser regime—a process that led to his execution—Sayyid Qutb courageously took the stand in his own defense and unequivocally "set loyalty to the *Ummah* of Islam over obedience to the *Watan* of Egyptian nationalism, the whole 'nation' of Muslims everywhere above the citizenship of an individual state" (Cragg 53). A less categorical and more inclusivist stance than Sayyid Qutb's is articulated by Ahmed Ben Bella, the first president of independent Algeria: "I am Muslim first, Arab second and then Algerian. I am also proud to be an African" (Nkrumah). In the same interview with Kwame Nkrumah's journalist son, Ben Bella elaborates further:

> I am an Islamist Pan-Arabist before I am an Algerian. The West tried hard and long to obliterate our Arab and Islamic culture. We Algerians are only too aware of this historical fact. That is why being a Muslim is an essential, a sacrosanct component of our identity. (Nkrumah)

Of course, few can deny that after almost a millennium and a half from its emergence, Islam retains an identity-shaping valence that transcends signifiers of race, gender, class, and nationalism: "in this tight bonding of religion and identity, Muslims are like Jews" (Kabbani 9). In his comment on Arab and African Muslim writers' identification with Islam, Anouar Majid argues emphatically that

> [f]or authors such as Cheikh Hamidou Kane, Tayeb Salih, and, more recently, Ken Bugul (pseudonym for Mariétou M'Baye), identity is primarily rooted in Islamic consciousness, not in blackness, or some other colonial category. The Islamic continuum in Africa bridges temporal, spatial, and gender gaps remarkably well, and thus points to new cultural, economic, and political configurations that might serve as alternatives to the failed nation-state model that has brought the continent to the brink of ruin. Muslim African writers who underestimate this Islamic component and privilege either color or nation as better defining components of their identity tend to reiterate colonial prejudices, despite their best intentions and revolutionary rhetoric. (74–75)

Islam constitutes not only a cardinal component of Muslims' identity but also becomes a prominent feature in the identity of the non-Muslims (be they Hindus, Zoroastrians, Jews, or Christians) who happen to live in Muslim communities. In these cases the identification reflects a communal rather than a conversional attitude. It is not unusual to hear someone like Said—whom for years a well-read Canadian academic friend of mine assumed to be a Muslim—say "we as Arabs or as Muslims." In his attentive, if skewed and circumscribed, study of Said's meditations on religion and culture, William D. Hart raises pointed questions about Said's discursive strategy when defending Islam:

> If the Orientalist representation of Arabs is one pillar of Said's account, then the representation of Islam is the other. Why is this? Does it support the contention of some of his critics that he is "soft" on Islam, an apologist, a secret admirer? How does he manage the feat of criticizing religion and defending Islam? (Hart 76)

Hart answers his own questions but only partially: since Islam is the "constitutive feature of Arab or Oriental [sic] identity," then Said, though secular but for "pragmatic reasons," cannot defend one without the other:

> The reader should note well, in what follows, the specificity and sympathetic character of Said's account of Islam compared to his abstract and hostile depiction of religion. Here . . . Said engages in practices, where they suit his own purposes, that he otherwise calls Orientalist—namely, the use of abstract generalities, reified notions, and Manichaean logic. (Hart 76–77)

In order to put Said's championing the cause of Islam into a context, one needs to recall that Said is simply arguing for a sense of fair play when he observed that most of the Orientalists monopolized the power of describing Islam in their own terms and according to their own agendas. His represents a Voltairian stance: the fair-minded intellectual may not agree with another's viewpoint but is willing to die defending the other's right to express that viewpoint. Moreover, as an uprooted Palestinian, Said is quite aware that the majority of his people espouse a religion that is not unusual to see maligned at various levels of Western discourse, which assumed, in some quarters, a brazenly Islamophobic tone in the aftermath of the atrocious terrorist attack of September 11, 2001. Here the non-Muslim affiliation with Islam comes into play. A good example of this would be to compare Said with the case of many Lebanese Christian writers who wrote openly and admiringly about Islam, names such as Gibran Khalil Gibran, Mikhail Nu'ayma, Maroun Aboud, and George Jurdaq—the latter wrote a multivolume book entitled *Al-Imam 'Ali: Saut al-'Adalah al-Insaniyah* (al-Imam

'Ali: The Voice of Humane Justice) about the life and ideas of 'Ali, the Prophet's cousin and son-in-law.

Thus as "a Christian who is culturally a Muslim" (Majid 28), Said's commitment to Islam is at once sincere, secular, and strategic: his erudite, enthusiastic discourse has been instrumental in unmasking the subtle and not-so-subtle slurs that seem to permeate various levels of Euro-American political, social, literary, and scholarly descriptions of Muslims—referred to variably as "Moslems," "Mohammedans," "Turks," "Saracens," or, worse, "Infidels." When Said published *Orientalism* in 1978, he was championing a cause that was neither fashionable nor of pragmatic careerist glamour. Nevertheless, that principled piece of writing has provided many Muslims and "third worldists" with the tools to deconstruct power-backed assumptions of knowledge, transmitted from metropolitan institutions whose dominant discourses went unchallenged for decades and even centuries. Claims about Islam with racist or quasi-racist nuances can no longer pass unchecked.

Religion-based identity may not be exclusive to Islam qua religion, for one might argue likewise about Judaism or Tibetan Buddhism. However, given the fact that Islam is the second largest religion on earth, this tenacious, voluntary attachment demonstrated so pronouncedly by its adherents from diverse cultures and from different corners of the world is both solid and striking.[2] A person's voluntary self-description as "Muslim" thus becomes, to borrow from Bill Ashcroft et al., "a powerful identifier" that one chooses to adopt and "cannot be denied, rejected or taken away by others" (*Key Concepts* 80). Despite fierce schisms from within and ferocious assault from without, Islam, both as a faith and a civilization, has, in aggregate, acquired a global, cross-cultural reach that embraces diversities of languages, races, ethnicities, and regions. This dynamic adaptability has been an evolving process that continues till today, despite volatility and unforeseen challenges lurking at every turn along the path.

### "MUSLIM" OR "ISLAMIC"?

This book attempts to investigate the manifestations of identitarian Islam, not in its theological guise but in its literary embodiment by writers whose roots are situated in the culture and civilization of Islam. Significantly, a distinction needs to be made at the outset between the terms *Muslim* and *Islamic*. This distinction is critical for understanding the word *Muslim* in the book's title. *Muslim* is derived from the Arabic word that denotes the *person* who espouses the religion of Islam or is shaped by its cultural impact, irrespective of being secular, agnostic, or practicing believer. The term *Islamic* emphasizes the *faith* of Islam. It denotes thoughts, rituals, activities, and institutions specifically proclaimed and sanctioned by Islam or directly associated with its theological traditions. Such a crucial distinction is often missed or ignored, particularly in mediocre writing, sensational reporting, or calumnious descriptions.

However, there are illuminating and thought-provoking exceptions. In *The Venture of Islam: Conscience and History in a World Civilization*, Marshall G. S. Hodgson makes a notable distinction between the two adjectives *Islamic* and *Islamicate*, a term of his own invention "with a double adjectival ending on the analogy of 'Italianate'" (59). For him, the first adjective "must be restricted to 'of or pertaining to' Islam *in the proper, the religious sense*," while the second adjective "would refer not directly to the religion, Islam, itself, but to the social and cultural complex historically associated with Islam and the Muslims, both among Muslims themselves and even when found among non-Muslims" (59). While Hodgson's enunciation of *Islamic* is quite lucid, the coinage *Islamicate* sounds unwieldy and pretentious. Also, because *Islamicate* is concocted from a European lexical root, it becomes etymologically compromised and rendered unsuitably alien to the cultural context of Islam. On the other hand, Mohammed Arkoun, in his otherwise thought-provoking article, "Artistic Creativity in Islamic Contexts," fails to capture the nuanced distinctions between the two adjectives "Islamic" and "Moslem" [*sic*], since, to him, both are derived from the same root; he considers both to be misapplied "in these times of generalized semantic confusion" (65). He blames this erroneous overuse of these two adjectives not only on the "Islamist movement" to validate its claims and serve its political agenda, but also on

> Westerners [who] have constructed a simplistic mental category which lets them group under the generic name of Islam all cultural works offered for their intellectual consumption or aesthetic contemplation, rather than making an attempt at critical discernment, as is done for all works concerning Christianity and the secular national territories in Europe. (65)

To redress this misuse, Arkoun tries to show "the theoretical and practical advantages of substituting the term *Islamic contexts* for the misleading adjective 'Islamic' not only as applied to artistic creativity, but also used in regard to literature, philosophy, science, and even the law which supposedly derives from sacred texts" (65–66). Notwithstanding Arkoun's valuable points, I opt to avoid the adjective *Islamic* in relevance to the current literary context of this book and settle for the simple adjective *Muslim*. The latter choice allows for the *specificity* of the individual writer's conception, vision, and rendition of the culture of Islam. This foregrounding of the individuality of representation immunizes against the reductionist equation of the whole culture of Islam with what one author produces in a single work of literature. No author, no matter how talented or committed, can ever claim to speak for a culture in its comprehensive entirety. What we see in any work of literature is one individual's view at a specific site and juncture of history.

Accordingly, for the flexible purpose of our discussion here, the term *Muslim narratives* suggests the works produced by the person who believes firmly in the faith of Islam; and/or, via an inclusivist extension, by the person who voluntarily and knowingly refers to herself, for whatever motives, as a "Muslim" when given a selection of identitarian choices; and/or, by yet another generous extension, by the *person* who is rooted formatively and emotionally in the culture and civilization of Islam. It is in the latter sense that I can justify, perhaps to the consternation or surprise of many readers, the inclusion of Salman Rushdie's *The Satanic Verses* in this discussion. Simply put, I am using the term *Muslim* in the widest sense.[3]

## LANGUAGE POLITICS

Muslim narratives in English have thus evolved into a solid and significant segment of any debate that involves the culture and civilization of Islam. Gone are the days when the representation in English of Muslims and their cultures was dominated by others—whoever they may be, and whatever sympathies they manifest: from William Beckford to Walter Scott, from Richard Burton to E. M. Forster, from T. E. Lawrence to V. S. Naipaul. Since any narrative reflects, mediates, and even reshapes the ethos of the culture from which it emanates, Muslim narratives in English then represent remarkable achievements of self-actualizing, identity-defining processes. Whatever their political, religious, or aesthetic leanings, these Muslims producing narratives in English affirm, with varying degrees, their affiliation with Islam as a source of spiritual and/or aesthetic inspiration.

Muslim narratives in English prove that the English language, despite all its colonial evocations and its atavistically anti-Muslim connotations, can be utilized as a sophisticated Muslim currency of credible communication. Words such as *fatwa, hajj, hijab, halal, inshallah, imam, intifadha, jihad, mecca, shari'a,* and *ummah* have already established themselves in contemporary parlance, notwithstanding the sensational stereotypes associated with each of them. Indeed, one can say that Muslim authors of narratives in English, each in her or his own fashion, have functionally muslimized the language without seeking sanction from any authority, be it literary, religious, or institutional. Moreover, in specific cases, English has become an expedient medium that empowers the Muslim writers to convey myriad hazardous, subversive schemes that otherwise are not possible in the first language. Certainly, English, as "*the* world language" (Said, "Figures" 3), is too vital a means for many Muslims to be shunned or demeaned: millions of Muslim immigrants in English-speaking countries rely on it out of the necessity of daily life; others utilize it as a valued channel of artistic and intellectual expression; and still others use it as a vehicle to articulate and celebrate the values, visions, and histories of Islam through the mass media, including the Internet. As the unnamed narrator of Tayeb Salih's Arabic novel *Season of Migration to the North* puts it, "we'll speak their language without either a sense of guilt or a sense of gratitude" (49–50). In effect what we are witnessing here is a process, unplanned but inevitable, of the muslimization of the English language: English is in the process of being transformed from an Islamophobic to an Islamophile language.

In 1982, the late Palestinian-American academic, Isma'il Rajai al-Faruqi, published a timely monograph, *Towards Islamic English*, in which he understandably, if vociferously, complained about the distortions in the translations and transliterations of important Islamic names and concepts, especially the venerated names and descriptions associated with Allah and the Prophet. He considered this malpractice to be "an intellectual and spiritual disaster of the highest magnitude ... [which] carries a universal injustice against the human spirit" (8). To remedy this situation, al-Faruqi compiled about sixty pages of key Islamic names, terms, and idioms and gave his "correct" translations and transliterations to them. The idea behind this effort is to advise Muslims and non-Muslims alike to follow these versions. Al-Faruqi's valiant effort here is part of his wider project to "Islamize" knowledge, which, as I understand it, suggests that there should be an Islamic perspective to the pursuit and practice of all areas of scientific and intellectual endeavor, to be bound and guided by the edicts of Islam and its ethical sanctions. While one can see the relevance and ambition of such a project, one can immediately realize that such boundaries would be too hard and oppressive to maintain, with the scientific and intellectual grounds constantly shifting. More germane to the discussion here, his notion of the "Islamization" of the English language is quite different from the already-existing phenomenon of muslimized English. "Islamization" demands disciplining, theological agency, or guardian institutions à *L'Acamdémie française* or the Arabic language academies in some Arab countries, Egypt in particular. Even if we assume the validity of these august bureaucracies, such a structured, systematized scheme requires vigilance and resources that may be infeasible and futile. On the other hand, the muslimization of the English language is a spontaneous, structureless cultural process that evolves as more and more Muslims use English as their first or second language in important daily interactions with others in a variety of social, commercial, and intellectual contexts.

More importantly, the concept of "Islamization" of a language constitutes a distinctly external strategy. It constantly manifests characteristics of alienness because it is imported or imposed from without. On the other hand, the muslimization of English, as a daily practice and not a mere concept, is already in progress, operating *within* the purviews of, to borrow Umberto Eco's phrase, "language as a social treasury" (67). Functioning actively and almost imperceptibly throughout social, intellectual, and political conventions, as well as other points of human and media contacts, Muslim-friendly English cannot by now be stigmatized as alien, even though its most striking linguistic morphologies are rooted in non-Western sources. Herein a civilizational confluence takes shape. As Frantz Fanon observes in *Black Skin, White Mask,* "to speak means to be in a position to use a certain syntax, to grasp the morphology of this or that language, but it means above all to assume a culture, to support the weight of a civilization" (17–18). Now a reality, muslimized English, or "english" as Ashcroft et al. would suggest (*Empire* 38), is an inevitably evolving process of grafting and hybridization, engaged in continual, cross-cultural negotiations among multiple constituent languages of diverse constructions and enunciations. In this context, Salman Rushdie's works, especially his pre-fatwa ones, serve as a good illustration. In an astute observation, Barbara D. Metcalf argues that

> [w]hatever Muslims may think of him, Salman Rushdie, perhaps more than any other of the creative bicultural writers in English today, has laid an exuberant, euphoric claim to English as his own, mixing in Hindu-Urdu terms and references with no apology or explanation, punning across languages as those who hear English from the distance of bilingualism most successfully do. (xvi)

If the English language is now in the process of being muslimized, it goes without saying that the dynamics also works in the other direction. Muslim languages too are being infiltrated by a variety of English terms, idioms, and expressions. It is quite a natural process of cultures interfacing. However, many Muslims resist it as an "intrusion," as if it can be really stopped, and a denigration of Muslim languages, especially Arabic, which, as the language of revelation in the Qur'an, holds a venerated status. At a 1996 conference, "English and Islam: Creative Encounters," organized by the International Islamic University in the Malaysian capital Kuala Lumpur, I vividly recall hearing an eloquent speaker argue that English being "Islamized" was fine with him so long as Muslims were vigilant that Islam itself was not being "Anglicized." The fault in this valiant argument is that it fragments an organic, indivisible process, and assumes that cultural fluxes and confluences can be made to order. On the other hand, such a position does not show much "faith" in the resilience of the religion to preserve its spiritual cohesion while it opens up to new, inevitable and irreversible, encounters. Islam has been through such a hybridization process several times in past centuries and has enriched and been enriched by other languages and civilizations, the most striking example of which would probably be the Persian language and culture and how they now fit elegantly within the world of Islam.

In his influential book, *Decolonizing the Mind: The Politics of Language in African Literature,* Ngugi wa Thiong'o raises several challenging questions: "Why, we may ask, should an African writer, or any writer, become so obsessed by taking from

his mother-tongue to enrich other languages? Why should he see it as his particular mission? . . . And why not create literary monuments in our own languages?"
(8). Ngugi's argument here comes with a background of hurt and humiliation ex-
ercised, in multifarious forms, by brutal colonial administrations against practically
all the colonized languages and cultures. To use the Pentagon's version of
newspeak during the 1991 Gulf War, the English language has served as an "asset"
and "ordinance" in the colonial arsenal, witness Thomas Babington Macaulay's
supremacist educational scheme in India to form "a class of persons, Indian in
blood and colour, but English in taste, in opinion, in morals, and in intellect"
(249). Resentment and resistance toward those racist policies are natural and legitimate reactions. However, in our modern, mobile world, colonialism, given its
supple opportunistic dynamics, has altered its stripes and taken to subtlety and
subterfuge. The neocolonial powers see no profit in pursuing the now discredited language policies such as the ones espoused by Macaulay in India, or practiced by Christian missionaries in schools in Africa and among the natives of
North America: they realize that it is a losing battle on that front. To maintain
their exploitative, hegemonic grip, neocolonialism is now using the deceptive language of globalization and the idiom of commodified culture. Neocolonialism
has shifted and skillfully redrawn the battle lines. Accordingly, the culture of resistance too must adjust to these realities: what was appropriate and valid a century
ago may not fit anymore. The English language, once an instrument of cultural
hegemony, has now undergone, to borrow two key terms from Ashcroft et al.,
processes of "abrogation" and "appropriation" (38). Writers from the ex-colonies
of the British Empire, including the Muslim writers discussed in this book, have,
persistently and through various means, exposed, cleansed, and refashioned the
English language to fit their own agendas. In his pithy foreword to *Kanthapura*, the
Indian novelist Raja Rao lucidly articulates the challenges of refashioning English
as an "alien" language to express the feelings of characters from Indian villages:

> One has to convey the various shades and omissions of a certain thought-
> movement that looks maltreated in an alien language. I use the word "alien",
> yet English is not really an alien language to us. It is the language of our intel-
> lectual make-up—like Sanskrit or Persian was before—but not of our emo-
> tional make-up. We are all instinctively bilingual, many of us writing in our
> own language and in English. We cannot write like the English. We should not.
> We cannot write only as Indians. We have grown to look at the large world as
> part of us. Our method of expression therefore has to be a dialect which will
> some day prove to be as distinctive and colourful as the Irish or the American.
> Time alone will justify it. (n. pag.)

Of course, this complex, often paradoxical, process ultimately leads to the acqui-
sition of the English language, or any other for that matter, as a useful tool of

one's own. The Somali novelist Nuruddin Farah takes a pragmatic, utilitarian approach when he chooses to write in any of the European languages, be it English or Italian:"Languages are like knives . . . ; you use them; if you don't sharpen them often enough, they get rusty, and like blunt instruments, they don't serve you well" (Jussawalla and Dasenbrock 47).

Moreover, using the English language as a tool of literary expression is not meant to denigrate the mother-language or lead to its *appauvrissement*. These are two separate processes. In fact, if Afro-Asian writers "enrich" the English language by producing works in it, can the enrichment be one-sided? Couldn't one argue that the mother-languages too become enriched, by being spurred into creativity? It should be axiomatic that as one language fertilizes another, the fertilizer itself becomes fertilized. Cross-pollination and creative cultural encounters operate in multiple directions.

Herein then lies the happy irony of Muslim writers "appropriating" a language with a perceived hostile history toward Islam and turning it into a medium of conveying inclusivist ethos, enriching understanding, and establishing bridges. An instrument for demystifying and de-alienating Islam and Muslims, muslimized English, like African or Indian English, becomes a site of encounter for cultures and peoples on equal terms, by peaceful means, and through intelligent—at times humorous, at others touchingly humane—discourses whose modes and modalities shift from antagonism to understanding, from exclusion to integration, from contest to compromise, and, more importantly, from resistance to reconciliation. Now with a corpus of literary works in English of their own, Muslims cannot be excluded anymore from the cultural arena; they are active participants themselves in the literary endeavor. Literature in English is indeed evolving toward *a great tradition* that makes its claim to "greatness," however we may define this slippery term, through embracing a diverse range of discourses, ethnicities, nationalities, and class/gender/race affiliations. With the collapse of colonialism, at least in its blatant conquestory form, the combat for national rights and cultural identity has taken new and complex forms, whereby the boundaries have become blurred. The English language, which has been an "asset" of colonial superiority, can now be claimed as a medium of inclusion and compromise in the neo/postcolonial era. Of course this does not mean that key issues of global, hegemonic politics have been solved or are about to be solved equitably, but at least an erstwhile "ordinance" of enmity has been "neutralized." "Converting" the English language from "foe" to "friend" is no mean achievement.

It would be naive to assume for a moment that metamorphosing the English language from a symbol of superiority and status to a shared asset to be cleverly used as a medium of thought, expression, and communication would defuse all conflicts and restore justice to the East–West, love–hate crosscurrents. Anyone who reads Samuel Huntington's controversial piece about what he terms the "clash of civilizations" with his sweeping, suspect contention that "Islam has bloody borders" (35) realizes that the conflict mentality is still alive, if only enfeebled, stoked by fanatics and ideologues on both sides of the divide. Nevertheless, the muslimization of the English language would add a fascinating dimension to the debate, making it more complex and multidimensional. It points toward the shift in the form and idiom of the encounter. In the realpolitik of this world, culture and other superstructural components of the Marxist paradigm are shaped and defined by the strategic *agents* of a system, that conceal dominant, exploitative agendas. The muslimization of the English language has merely "neutralized" one out of numerous other assets operating for the highly efficient, dominant system.

## PEDAGOGY

Muslim fiction in English emerged confidently with Ahmed Ali's landmark work *Twilight in Delhi* and is now an established literary tradition, a recognized and respected one at that, popularly and academically. One could point out several prominent works: in 1981, Salman Rushdie's novel *Midnight's Children* received the Booker Prize; in 1994, M. G. Vassanji's novel *The Book of Secrets* received the prestigious Giller Award in Canada; and in 1995, Bangladeshi-Australian Adib Khan's novel *Seasonal Adjustments* received the Commonwealth First-Novel Prize, with the awarding committee praising it for "provid[ing] a Muslim voice to Australia's multicultural literature" (*Chimo* 40). Moreover, both Abdulrazak Gurnah's *Paradise* and Ahdaf Soueif's *The Map of Love* were shortlisted for the Booker in 1994 and 1999, respectively. Whatever our critical, religious, or ideological responses may be to these works, the corpus of Muslim-English narratives is, and should be, a fascinating source for investigation and appreciation, thus creating the impetus for producing this book. These writers have taken up a daunting linguistic, aesthetic, and intellectual challenge and have given voice, with varying degrees of clarity and commitment, to the erstwhile unrepresented, underrepresented, or misrepresented Muslims. More significantly, their writings subvert the binary paradigms of self/other, us/them, East/West toward a mature inclusivist ethos of both/and, without indulging in reductionist platitudes and without altogether eliding or erasing the distinctive composite components of the hybridized Muslim-English text.

Like any minority discourse, Muslim narratives in English have initially been relegated to the margin of the so-called canon in English studies. As an instance, Ahmed Ali's *Twilight in Delhi* almost did not make it to print in 1940, for complex political and historical reasons, which I discuss in chapter 1. However, the situation changed since Rushdie's *Midnight's Children* won the Booker Prize in 1981. Other names such as Nuruddin Farah, Ismith Khan, and Zulfikar Ghose were making inroads into the syllabi of different university courses dealing with what used to be called "Commonwealth literature." Happily, the concept of the canon has been challenged and has now been irreversibly altered and expanded, thanks to the efforts of fair-minded, forward-looking critics, academics, and advocates of literatures of lesser diffusions. While this entire debate was progressing (or raging on) in Western academe, English departments in several, if not all, Muslim countries seemed oblivious or unaware of such radical developments. As they cope with very limited resources and face crippling bureaucratic hurdles hampering their efforts to keep abreast of current debates in the discipline, many of these institutions seem stuck in a time warp. It is therefore incumbent upon all the Muslim universities in South Asia, the Middle East, and North and sub-Saharan Africa to adopt in their curricula the works of these Muslim writers, not only to link their students to a current literary phenomenon that would articulate their feelings and their pride in their culture but also to celebrate the excellence of these Muslim writers and give them a boost by disseminating their works among students who would be most enthused to respond to them. If many instructors in various North American colleges and universities can easily—and within current curricular rubrics—adopt and teach these Muslim writers, then it should be paramount to introduce them into their proper Muslim setting as well. Of course, the suggestion here is not that we should ignore other Anglo-American literary figures, both classical and contemporary, but we need to open space for M. G. Vassanji, Ahdaf Soueif, Adib Khan, and Nuruddin Farah, as well as other "postcolonial" figures such as Wilson Harris, Ngugi wa Thiong'o, Anita Desai, and Toni Morrison. One other point: the works of these Muslim writers are relevant not only in the area of English studies but also in interdisciplinary studies linking literature with other adjacent disciplines: cultural studies, comparative religion, social anthropology, and political science.

## TOWARD MUSLIM FEMINISM

The writings of Attia Hosain, Zainab Alkali, Mena Abdullah, Fatima Mernissi, and Ahdaf Soueif prove that Muslim women can speak for themselves eloquently and assertively in their own distinctive voices. Their pride in the culture of Islam and their rejection of both patriarchical practices and Western hegemonistic feminisms render their discourses complex and challenging. The maturity and sophistication of Muslim women's writing are a definitive answer to the biased stereotypical images that we continually come across about the backwardness and enslavement of Muslim women. Some of these claims do regrettably have bases of truth in them: sadly in many regions and situations, Muslim women are marginalized, abused, and even brutalized—with the nightmarish aberration of

the Taliban regime in Afghanistan being one outrageous example. Many traditional customs shackle women's aspirations to assert themselves, fulfill their potential, and express their creativity. Patriarchy, as ever and everywhere, is
entrenched and holds all reigns of power and privilege. Its discourse is self-
serving, arrogant, and oppressive. In the face of this situation many modern
women activists turn to Islam as the definitive recourse: "They root themselves
in the territory of Islam to demand authority to speak out against those who are
trying to exalt them as symbols but to exclude them as persons" (Cooke xxv).
Women's activism, at times supported by progressive and enlightened men,
evolved over the years but especially in the 1980s toward a trend or movement
that some arguably call Muslim or Islamic feminism, which as Margot Badran
defines it "is a feminist discourse and practice articulated within an Islamic paradigm. Islamic feminism, which derives its understanding and mandate from the
Qur'an, seeks rights and justice for women, and for men, in the totality of their
existence" (1). However many Muslim women activists are not quite comfort-
able with the label "feminism" because of the baggage of its Western cultural as-
sociations: "Some reject the term 'feminist' to describe what they are doing.
Some act as feminists even if they do not use the term. A few are happy to call
themselves feminists" (Cooke viii). Under whatever banner they operate, Muslim women activists or feminists see the causes and cures for their situation to be
too complex to be reductively rendered by ideological firebrands not well informed of the social, historical, and cultural contexts involved. Muslim women's
narratives in English prove that judgmental, mediatized sensationalism is quintessentially unfair or unfounded. Solutions to gender conflicts within Muslim
societies can only be grounded in the *specificity* of locale and accordingly negotiated while avoiding abstract, universalist formulae, since each culture and community has to arrive at them separately.

## THROUGH THEORY AND BEYOND THE "POSTS"

While Muslim narratives, especially in the early stages, emphasized their Muslim affiliation, one can witness in contemporary Muslim narratives other "competing" factors that claim the attention and inspiration of the writer. This
situation is created by the twentieth-century phenomena of immigration and
exile, where one is bound to come into contact with other literary and cultural
traditions. This is not necessarily negative or threatening. Indeed, someone like
Rushdie celebrates it in an exuberant metaphor when he refers to himself as "a
bastard child of history" (*Imaginary Homelands* 394).

The contact with others is inescapable, indeed welcome, leading to a confluence of creative energy that can challenge, enhance, or enrich Muslim affiliation. However, one needs to be aware of the delicate *équilibre instable* of such a

phenomenon. As cultures interface, new paradigms emerge and new challenges arise, whereby values become destabilized and competing claims from diverse constituencies cause confusion.

This brings us to a very thorny issue regarding Western academic fascination with theory as an instrument of investigative knowledge and radical thinking. At times, this fascination metamorphoses into an obsession with the trope *theory*. Warranted or not, this term pops up in almost any discipline, all in order to appear trendy and fashionable. This, of course, diminishes its effectiveness. However, on a more engaging and productive level, there are impressive theoretical undertakings involving three major spheres of investigation, all with an eerie prefix of "post": poststructuralism, postmodernism, and postcolonialism.[4] These three systems of intellectual production have radically transformed the way we read texts and have shaped the discourse with which we discuss them. The fields of critical and intellectual inquiry have been profoundly energized and rendered more challenging to anyone undertaking serious explorations in those three fields. More significantly, these three "posts," with varying degrees of intensity and refinement, have infiltrated Western academe, interrogating and defying its foundational assumptions. The cozy, staid status quo is no longer tenable. The ontology of the literary endeavor has been challenged, radicalized, and reshaped as have the boundaries and definitions of *genres, canons*, and *great traditions*. The positive impact of these activist, energetic trends that stir Anglo-American academe—its politics as well as the discourses emanating from it—expands the horizons of textuality to include literatures and arts of the marginalized Other, by actively seeking out and celebrating minority discourses and the "literatures of lesser diffusion," by rectifying key operational concepts such as "humanity," "humanities," and "civilizations," and by giving them informed and inclusivist dimensions so as to go beyond the confines of the Euro-American, Judeo-Christian orbit.

However, this eager urge toward theory, salutary in its intent, has devolved into a slippery self-referential mode of discourse that has, at times, degenerated into onanistic, obscurantist *jeu de mots*. It has also led to vaulting over literary texts in favor of never-ending arcane discourses, to be followed by a set of arcane counterdiscourses, to be followed, yet again, by another set of equally futile discourses couched in recondite idioms; regrettably, all these cerebrally intensive yet arid activities fail to engage meaningfully with the literary texts aching for attention and to offer cogent critical responses that could enrich the creative process and benefit students and serious readers of literature. Is it any wonder, then, to see theory's sphere of influence be so narrow as to retreat within the walls of academe. As Said argues, "Post-structuralists and post-modernists . . . , with few exceptions, [have] lapsed into a sullen technological narcissism" ("My Encounter"). Likewise, Aijaz Ahmad, writing from a fixed Marxist firmament, critiques succinctly the sweeping urge to embrace theory by viewing it as a suspect endeavor to "displace an activist culture with a textual culture, to combat the more uncompromising critiques of existing cultures of the literary profession with a new mystique of leftish professionalism" (1). What is missing in this bizarre, thorny affair is a discourse of lucidity and humanity. Poststructuralist and postmodernist critiques, often though not always, seem to relish in an exercise of obfuscation to the detriment of concrete, meaningful values. As one can happily dispense with facile, reductionist exposés, one can as well ignore pretentious, jargonistic cant.

As for postcolonialists, they too are hounded but from different directions. Perhaps the most colorful instance of provocative critique of them is delivered by Kwame Anthony Appiah, who borrows an evocative idiom from the world of commerce and refers to postcolonialists as a "comprador intelligentsia,"

> a relatively small, Western-style, Western-trained, group of writers and thinkers who mediate the trade in cultural commodities of world capitalism at the periphery. In the West they are known through the Africa they offer; their compatriots know them both through the West they present to Africa and through an Africa they have invented for the world, for each other, and for Africa. (149)

Likewise, Paul Tiyambe Zeleza considers postcolonial theory as "an insatiable discourse that indiscriminately appropriates the literatures of the oppressed but speaks in the calcified and contemptuous language of inscrutable scholastic power" (19) as well as in "convoluted, constipated jargon" circulating through "incestuous intertextual conversations among the anointed few" (20). Zeleza concludes his sustained severe critique by raising some legitimate points:

> A postcoloniality that inferiorizes and ghettoizes the literatures of Asia, Africa, the Caribbean, and other parts of the third world, and of minority populations in Western countries, is an accomplice of imperialist ideology. Any theorization of these literatures unconnected to the critical discourses of the literary communities concerned only ends up reproducing the colonialist epistemology it seeks to deconstruct. (29)

Another aspect, subtle but discursively serious, involves the dearth of useful "postcolonial" theoretical material germane to the issue of religion or the sacred as a key conceptual category, as compared to the valorized ones of race, class, gender, nation, migration, and hybridity. Significant contestatory sites these may be, the reality of the neocolonial condition involves obvious *additional* categories or discourses that could theorize social and political conflicts among and between numerous religious forces—be they Hindu, Jewish, Christian, Muslim, or Sikh. At times but not always, die-hard, extremist proponents of these faiths spearhead these conflicts through inciting violence and waging organized, armed campaigns.

While postcolonialism involves numerous heterogeneous discourses, making it impossible to view the field as uniform, there is a discernible common denominator that indicates a resistance to engage with religion as a key category pertinent to the debate about contemporary neocolonial reality. Such an inattentive or deliberate marginalization of religion as a force or factor with its own complex dynamics, if my observation is right, reflects privileging a secular, Euro-American stance that *seems* to shape the parameters of postcolonial discourses. This skewed point of reference stems from the hegemony of the Euro-American academy with its efficiency, superior resources, and pervasive means of dissemination. The result is a dissonance between postcolonial discourses and anticolonial praxes, between the polished halls of academe and the desolation of slums, refugee camps, torture chambers, and combat trenches.

This discursive lacuna in postcolonial theory becomes especially pronounced in the case of Islam, a religion that has a distinctive history of resisting and fiercely fighting colonial hegemony. It is odd that "postcolonial theory" cannot offer insights about the activism of Islam, despite the fact that one of its seminal texts, Edward Said's *Orientalism*, that "open[ed] up the fields of postcolonial studies" (Kennedy 16), is prompted and permeated by a challenge to the colonial representations of Islam as biased constructions whose corrosive corollaries are discernible today in multiple insidious fashions across diverse domains of power. It also strikes me as quite odd that Islam with a militant anticolonial heritage is often neglected or glossed over even in supposedly comprehensive studies of colonialism and the resistances to it. For instance, Robert Young's *Postcolonialism: An Historic Introduction*, a work described by Homi Bhabha on its back cover as "truly insightful . . . intricate and exhaustive," a work devoted to chronicling and theorizing the anticolonial genealogy and link it with the current "postcolonial" debate, mentions Islam only occasionally, as in the segments dealing with the Algerian liberation war, but not as a religion with its own terms of reference but under the rubric "Islamic nationalism" (173). In other words, Young subsumes religion under the category of nation. Compare Robert Young's position with Frantz Fanon's observation in *The Wretched of the Earth* that colonialism not only oppresses people in the present but also "distorts" and "disfigures" (169) their past and thus "the struggle for national liberty [in Algeria] has been accompanied by a cultural phenomenon known by the name of the awakening of Islam" (171).

One unfortunate consequence to the marginalization of religion in the postcolonial debate is that the discursive fields of contestation have become dominated by either medievalist religious fanatics or smart establishment figures who theorize about such counterfeit currencies as "the clash of civilizations" or "the end of history." The endowment of these suspect theories with prophetic potencies and the elevation of their originators to canonical stature make it the more urgent to engage in these issues rather than letting the field be dominated by binarism and reductive oppositional polarities. The middle terrain could have been occupied by postcolonial theory. It could have assumed preemptive agency on behalf of people of goodwill and in the name of fair play and just peace, especially when the battle is unequal between the dispossessed and the hegemonic powers. The need is acute for a rigorous interrogation of the layers of power, normative values, and retrograde fanaticism.

What emerges from the midst of this tremulous debate is the need for the decolonization and dehegemonization of the theoretical enterprise. It needs to be transformed from a predominantly Euro-American asset of discourse into, to borrow a metaphor from Gilles Deleuze, a handy "toolbox" out of which one *selects* items and concepts to be deployed in the service of artists, authors, and intellectuals operating in neocolonial conditions. When at least fifty percent of the people of the so-called developing countries, a significant segment of which being Muslim, are illiterate, and when these same people suffer from a bundle of other social, political, and ecomonic problems, over-indulgence in theory divorced from the brutal reality of their harsh conditions becomes a perversion. The luxury of sophisticated obscurantism yields no meaningful benefits to the cultural lives of societies far removed from the privileged, affluent contexts in which those theoretical speculations have been produced.

All said, one should nevertheless refrain from rejecting these abstract speculations out of hand. They merit engagement and exploration, while eschewing unquestioning adulation or obsequiousness. The theoretical speculations of the three grand "posts" of the twentieth century still retain their potency as we proceed through the twenty-first, but the approach now is to be selective, dialogical, critical, and cautious in the granting of any degree of validation.

ONE

# Ahmed Ali and the Emergence of
# Muslim Fiction in English

<hr />

A single shelf of a good European library was worth the whole native literature of India and Arabia.

Thomas Babington Macaulay

Where the empire went, the cannon and the Canon went too.

—Robert Scholes

WITH THE 1940 PUBLICATION OF AHMED ALI'S NOVEL *TWILIGHT IN Delhi*, literary history was being made. It was the first novel written by a Muslim ever to be published in English, thereby projecting the perspective of a colonized culture and civilization that had hitherto been denied the opportunity to speak for itself. Before publishing his novel in English, Ali was already an established writer in Urdu; however, he might have been prompted to write in English because prominent works had already been published in English by two well-known Indian writers who were Ali's contemporaries. Mulk Raj Anand's *Untouchable* appeared in 1935 and *Coolie* appeared in 1936; and Raja Rao, already an established writer of stories in Kannada, brought out in 1938 his first novel *Kanthapura*, articulating in the foreword what has become in essence a motto for many non-English writers who appropriate English as a medium of their self-expression: "to convey in a language that is not one's own the spirit that is one's own" (n. pag.). Of course, this phenomenon of belated self-representation in texts written in European languages has become too familiar a situation that applies not only to Ali's Indian Muslims but also to practically almost all colonized, "third worldists." Indeed, the first publication of the novel in war-preoccupied Britain has a fascinating story of its own. After Ali had finished writing the novel, he traveled to London—a taxing trip and a costly undertaking for an Indian in the late 1930s—to have the manuscript printed. However, because Ali's narrative recalls highly pronounced scenes of the 1857 revolt (referred to in colonial officialese as the "Mutiny") of the Muslims of old Delhi against the British occupation of India, the printer found the book too politically subversive to be in circulation. Had it not been for the intercession of E. M. Forster with the censor and had it not been for Virginia Woolf's readiness to publish the novel in her Hogarth Press, *Twilight in Delhi* might have never seen the light of day (Anderson 439–40).

Apart from being a forerunner in an emerging (now established) literary tradition of Muslim fiction in English, the novel handles its specific historical material on two levels. First, it depicts the life of a middle-class Muslim family in Delhi during the first two decades of the twentieth century. Through this family, Ali projects the political ethos of Indian Muslims in periods when Britain was still firmly clutching its crown jewel. In his introduction to the novel's second edition, Ali, who is "a Muslim fourth to the Indian big three of the 1930s—Rao, Narayan and Anand" (King 244), articulates his authorial intention:

> My purpose was to depict a phase of our national life and the decay of a whole culture, a particular mode of thought and living, now dead and gone already right before our eyes. Seldom is one allowed to see a pageant of History whirl past and partake in it too. (*Twilight* vii)

Toward such an end, Ali's complex strategy led him to "juxtapose and correlate a detailed and variegated external reality with the passionate dreams and delusions experienced by his characters . . . [and] to overarch both fragmentary worlds, external and internal, with the author's unifying voice of symbolic insight" (Stilz 380). Second, while blending the private with the public, the familial with the communal, the novel interlinks the present with the past. More specifically, the reader senses the deliberateness of these historical flashbacks when the family's wedding ceremony coincides with the Raj's Durbar, celebrating the 1911 coronation of George V, which in turn evokes in the mind of the protagonist, Mir Nihal, graphic memories of the British ruthlessly quelling the 1857 revolt. From Mir Nihal's perspective, being as it is the novel's privileged voice, the gaudy celebration of a British monarch in Delhi has turned the city "which was once the greatest in Hindustan" [the Urdu name for India] into "an exhibition ground" (138):

> Here it was in this very Delhi, Mir Nihal thought, that kings once rode past, Indian kings, his kings, kings who have left a great and glorious name behind. But the Farangis came from across the seven seas, and gradually established their rule. By egging on Indian chiefs to fight each other and by giving

them secret and open aid they won concessions for themselves; and established their "empire." . . .

   The procession passed, one long unending line of generals and governors, the Tommies and the native chiefs with their retinues and soldiery, like a slow unending line of ants. In the background were the guns booming, threatening the subdued people of Hindustan. Right on the road, lining it on either side, and in the procession were English soldiers, to show, as it seemed to Mir Nihal, that Delhi has been conquered with the force of arms, and at the point of guns will she be retained. (149)

Interlocking the political with the religious, the narrative details the celebration of the British and their lackeys as they pass by the main mosque, Jama Masjid, center and symbol of the anti-colonialist resistance:

The procession passed by the Jama Masjid whose facade had been vulgarly decorated with a garland of golden writing containing slavish greetings from the Indian Mussalmans to the English King, displaying the treachery of the priestly class to their people and Islam. (150)

   Interestingly, the idiosyncratic narrator of Ahmed Ali's third novel, *Of Rats and Diplomats* (1985), refers to the same historical incident by stating satirically that "the British [were] celebrating the death of an Edwardian king by holding a grand Durbar on the ashes of Mughal pride in ravished Delhi" (5). The historiographical rendition of selective events recuperated from collective memory injects the narrative in *Twilight in Delhi* with an emotionally charged rhetoric. The specificity of the locale, the Jama Masjid, provides an emblematic focus that integrates nationalism with religion, anti-British sentiments with Islam:

It was this very mosque, Mir Nihal remembered with blood in his eyes, which the English had insisted on demolishing or turning into a church during 1857. . . . Sir Thomas Metcalf with his army had taken his stand by the Esplanade Road, and was contemplating the destruction of Jama Masjid. The Mussalmans came to know of this fact, and they talked of making an attack on Metcalf; but they had no guns with them, only swords. One man got up and standing on the pulpit shamed the people, saying that they would all die one day, but it was better to die like men, fighting for their country and Islam. (150–51)

This religious, anticolonialist fervor continues to the early days of the independence drive when Gandhi's non-cooperation movement evolves. On hearing about the death of a Muslim youth who had been killed while attending the movement's meeting, Habibuddin, Mir Nihal's perceptive and favorite son, declares, "The English frankly say that they fear no one but Muslims in India and that if they crush the Mussalmans they shall rule with a care-free heart" (262). This statement is validated by numerous letters and documents published by British officials in India. For instance, William Howard Russell wrote in the *Times* in early 1858 that

> the Mahomedan [*sic*] element in India is that which causes us most trouble and provokes the largest share of our hostility. . . . Our antagonism to the followers of Mahomed is far stronger than that we bear to the worshippers of Shiva and Vishnu. They are unquestionably more dangerous to our rule. . . . If we could eradicate the traditions and destroy the temples of Mahomad [*sic*] by one vigorous effort, it would indeed be well for the Christian faith and for the British rule. (qtd. in Khairi 28–29)

Because the Muslims were the dominant force behind the revolt of 1857, the British, who called it "a Muhammadan rebellion" and "a handiwork of the Muslims" (qtd. in Khairi 26), singled them out as their most mortal enemy from among the population of India. Thousands of them were massacred or "were blown to bits from the mouths of cannon. Still thousands of others were, after a trial under Martial law lasting a few minutes at the most, found guilty and sent to their death" (Khairi 27). W. W. Hunter, a British civil servant, stated in 1868: "After the Mutiny, the British turned upon the Mussalmans as their real enemies so that failure of the revolt was much more disastrous to them than the Hindus" (qtd. in Akbar 32). In his autobiography, Jawaharlal Nehru, the first prime minister of India, also affirms this British policy of anti-Muslim discrimination: "After 1857 the heavy hand of the British fell more on the Muslims than on the Hindus. They considered the Muslims more aggressive and militant than the Hindus, possessing memories of recent rule in India and therefore more dangerous" (460).

The thrust of Ahmed Ali's thematics in this novel is to suggest passionately, prophetically, but always lyrically, that India's Muslims are falling on perilous times as they face the British occupation, conveying through the novel's title a dejected premonition of the subsequent fragmentation of Muslims in the subcontinent. The novel thus functions through nostalgia for the glorious era of the Mughals and prophecy about the pending collapse of the Muslim power and glory in India, with the ruins of Delhi becoming "symbolic of the ruin of Islam" (King 244). Interestingly, in Anita Desai's novel *Clear Light of Day*, whose title and setting evoke Ali's novel, similar, yet syncretically contexted, sentiments are expressed about Old Delhi's decline in postindependence India: Bim, the novel's privileged voice, bemoans the fate of Delhi:

> Old Delhi does not change. It only decays. My students tell me it is a great cemetery, every house a tomb. Nothing but sleeping graves . . . here nothing

happens at all. Whatever happened, happened [a] long time ago—in the time of the Tughlaqs, the Khiljis, the Sultanate, the Moghuls—that lot. (5)

The dual agents of nostalgia and prophecy become further pronounced in Ali's second novel, *Ocean of Night* (1964), where he dramatizes the process of degeneration of the Muslim nobility of Lucknow toward its self-inflicted doom. The amorality and recklessness of Nawab Chhakkan, a descendant of an old Taluqdar (landowning) family that collaborated with the British during the 1857 uprising to be rewarded with feudal privileges, foreshadows the disintegration of a community when it loses the sense of its destiny. The Nawab's drunkenness and debauchery cause his ruin, leading to his demise by a murder–suicide. As one of the novel's minor characters, the Marxist Siddiqi, puts it to a friend, "We as a nation are suffering from nostalgia. Go back to the past is your constant cry. But how can you go back to the past? Which past? I tell you you can't" (54). The argument here is that no nation, community, family, or individual can overcome current misery through recalling past glory. As with the doomed fate of Delhi in *Twilight in Delhi*, the prophesied decline of Lucknow in *Ocean of Night* symbolizes the fragmentation of the Muslim community in India. While *Ocean of Night* succeeds in evoking an ambience of decay and decline, it lacks the focus and lyrical vibrancy of *Twilight in Delhi*. Its effectiveness is also tarnished by the preaching, essayistic quality of its narrator. (Indeed, one glimpses such a tendency in Ali's earlier novel too, but it is kept relatively restrained.) Moreover, the swift, synoptic shifts of discourse and the occasional racy reversals of the characters' mood and actions "mak[e] the narrative disjointed" (Raizada 19) and undermine the novel's dramatic impact. These limitations could prompt one to consider *Ocean of Night* "more of a phantasy [*sic*] than a novel" (Raizada 22) and to evaluate Ali as a "one-novel novelist" (Trivedi 43). However, one could appreciate Ali's strategy here as being based on storytelling techniques derived from the oral Indian/Muslim tradition, whereby an intrusive, often digressive, teller plays such a dominant role that it licenses him or her to impede or redirect the narrative flow by recurrently reciting nostalgic poetry, culled from collective memory, and injecting it (as Ali often does) into the narrative. Being a powerfully effective mode of emotional and cultural expression, poetry operates as an apt emblematic commentary on character and action, and because of its *ancienneté* in Eastern societies, it serves as a literary linkage with a nostalgic past and a repository of its civilizational glory.

While a gap of a quarter of a century separated the publication of Ali's first two novels, his third, *Of Rats and Diplomats* (1985), appeared after a gap of almost another quarter of a century. While the first two novels aim at representing decay and decline within an Indian context, the third expands the perspective toward universal levels of signification. Instead of foregrounding nostalgia and prophecy, the narrative deploys farce and satire as condemning tools of a reality that has metamorphosed so corruptly that it is fatally and fatalistically beyond redemption. With an acerbic style that recalls at once Jonathan Swift's and Franz Kafka's, the novel is an allegory of the hypocrisy and moral degradation of life in the twentieth century: the narrative reveals the vulgar machinations of diplomacy, skillfully operating with a veneer of politesse and suavity. Through the antics of a quirky, profligate, emblematically named narrator, Ambassador Sourirada Soutanna, recently assigned to Ratisan, we are introduced to the steamy, gossipy, intrigue-filled world of "well-dressed men with no brains" (1). With conflicts and wars in the background, post-Hitler humanity seems to have learned little from the cruel carnage of an earth "all cluttered up with broken cars, tangled tanks and crashed planes, brainless skulls and tattooed limbs" (1). Unabated, the preparations for other wars continue, toward which the conspiratorial duplicity of "dunces and diplomats" who "show off . . . opulence and behave with superiority" (72) becomes instrumental. In fact, diplomacy in the novel functions, predictably and calculatingly, as simply a continuation of war through other means. While war kills openly, diplomacy corrupts surreptitiously. Being himself an experienced diplomat, Ali suggests that diplomacy is a world where there is no honor in agreements, no trust in relationships, and no loyalty in friendships. Savagery in the past was at least brazen and unpretentious; in modern times, it has become insidiously camouflaged, rendering itself more confusing and lethal.

*Twilight in Delhi* was so exclusively focused on the Muslim community that one notices the almost total absence of Hindus in the crowd of one hundred or so named characters in a novel set in the capital of India, even though "within the walled city as well as in the wider municipal area, Hindus had been throughout more numerous since before the Mutiny" (Trivedi 65). Moreover, the female characters seem passive and their role secondary, notwithstanding a subtle authorial respect for their perspective and sympathy for their marginalized status, as, for instance, shown in the depiction of the pathetic, forced marriage of Mehroo, Mir Nihal's daughter, to a man she does not love (193–95). We should, accordingly, discern the Delhi of the title to be the male Muslim Delhi of the Mughals. These limitations appear strikingly odd in a novel that many critics considered to be of "epic structure" (Niven 5), "composed in open form" (Raizada 11), and concerned with "presenting through concrete and evocative little details the very texture of a way of life" (Sharkar 75), thereby becoming "very likely the most indigenous and home-spun of all Indo-Anglian novels" (Trivedi 70).

This selective focus is replaced by a more inclusivist viewpoint in *Ocean of Night*, where we encounter several non-Muslim characters, albeit secondary, taking part in the action. Moreover, since the events here occur in the decade preceding India's independence, a faint background exists of concern with prevailing national issues in Indian politics, such as the policies of the Congress Party (53–54) and the Shi'a-Sunni riots in Lucknow during Muharram (139); there is also a passing reference to Hitler marching into Czechoslovakia prior to the Second World War (139), and the Marxist Siddiqi even quotes Lenin to debunk the Gandhian concept of nonviolence (55). Equally significant is the dominant role given to Huma, the sympathetic courtesan who functions as the novel's heroine. The recurrent projection of her perspective and the foregrounding of her capacity for warmth, courage, and genuine generosity—as with her noble act of returning the Nawab's expensive gifts to his aggrieved widow—make her, in essence, the novel's moral signifier. All these features indicate a more open perspective, a definite shift in Ali's sociohistorical stance from what we observed in *Twilight in Delhi*. In *Of Rats and Diplomats*, the narrative moves toward global issues of international politics through the deployment of the all-embracing agency of allegory. When proceeding sequentially from one novel to the other, one can thus see the progressive expansion of the narrative optic. Nevertheless, the satirical style in *Of Rats and Diplomats*, half-farcical, half-macabre, represents such a radical departure that "hardly anything in Ali's earlier longer fiction (excepting some of his Urdu short stories) could have suggested the development of his present style" which takes "Ali's fiction into the postcolonial era and into a postcolonial mode . . . a step away and more than a step forward from what he has done before" (Hashmi 150).

More importantly, the three novels by Ali are permeated by a certain view of history that is quintessentially Sophoclean: tragic and fatalistic. On the one hand, individuals and communities bear a clear responsibility for their own decline. Their lack of profound understanding of themselves and their surroundings, their inalertness to sociohistorical transformations, and their imperviousness to an ever-changing reality all contribute to their self-induced malaise. In *Twilight in Delhi*, the self-indulgence of Asghar, Mir Nihal's younger son, who seems "unconcerned whether the country lived or died" (259), leads to the misery of his emotional life. In *Ocean of Night*, Kabir, Huma's potential alternative lover after the Nawab abandons her for a more sensual courtesan, fails to appreciate and respond to her genuine affection, leading to his ultimate defeat and despair; and the Nawab's collapse is clearly caused by his own moral and financial recklessness. On the other hand, the characters' fates seem metaphysically and strategically circumscribed by conditions beyond their choice or control, such as minority status, colonial constriction, historical process, and cosmic destiny. The fatalistic motto is articulated toward the end of *Twilight in Delhi*: "Who can meddle in the affairs of God?" (287). The agonies of Mir Nihal's final days are described within a similar context of predestination, whereby "life remained over which men had no command and must go on . . . at the mercy of Time and Fate" (288). Despairing over the doomed decline of Delhi, the narrator describes the irreversible transformations underway:

> The old culture, which had been preserved within the walls of the ancient town, was in danger of annihilation. Her language, on which Delhi had prided herself, would lose its beauty and uniqueness of idiom. She would be the city of the dead, inhabited by people who would have no love for her nor any

association with her history and ancient splendour. But who could cry against
the ravages of Time which has destroyed Nineveh and Babylon, Carthage as
well as Rome? (206)

In *Of Rats and Diplomats*, Ambassador Soutanna concludes the novel with a reflective remark on the relentless cycles of metamorphoses in which "mankind has
been *caught . . . completely*" [emphasis added]: "whether renewal or decay, the wheel
of law will not cease so long as the earth survives and the skies endure. . . ." (154).

Astutely observant and prescient, Ali captures a crucial phase in Indian history and, drawing on his intimate knowledge of the Muslim community, he projects his vision to posterity with fidelity, lucidity, and elegance. His first two
novels recreate a memorable civilizational ambience through evoking fascinating, though fast-fading, images of Delhi and Lucknow. E. M. Forster graciously
connected Ali's magnum opus with his own, stating in a note to *A Passage to
India* that "the civilization, or blend of civilizations, which produced Aziz has
been movingly evoked by the novelist Ahmed Ali in 'Twilight in Delhi'" (368).
Now a landmark in Indian and Muslim literary tradition, *Twilight in Delhi* initiated an exciting path leading to works by several other writers in English who
derive their inspirational and narrative material from cultures and civilizations
rooted in Islam. Of course within this exciting literary phenomenon, the name
of Salman Rushdie comes first to one's mind, not only because of the sad saga
surrounding *The Satanic Verses*, but also because in a certain curious sense Ali's
*Twilight in Delhi* anticipates Rushdie's *Midnight's Children*. The four decades that
separate the two texts have witnessed considerable qualitative progress in the
works of Muslim writers in English. The remarkable critical and popular success
of *Midnight's Children* signifies a strategic shift in the paradigms of marginality
and canonicity. Specifically, not only is Rushdie's work more prominent and recognizable—for myriad reasons beyond the current concern of this analysis—but
is also radically different technically and thematically. While Ali portrays lyrically
and nostalgically a world that is traditional and static, Rushdie sees reality as a
flux phenomenon, changing or yet to be born. As Rushdie steers away from
strict sectarian focus, he ambitiously embraces the multifarious world of the subcontinent, with creeds, conflicts, and contradictions rolled together. This is
achieved through an impressive array of interlocking, self-procreating episodes
operating on fictional and metafictional levels. As Rushdie's Saleem Sinai rhetorically wonders, "Is this an Indian disease, this urge to encapsulate the whole of
reality? Worse: am I indeed infected, too?" (75). While in *Twilight in Delhi* a
"major flaw is the near total absence of irony and humour as operative principles" (Sharkar 80), in all of Rushdie's oeuvre a playful, parodic mode prevails,
"pitting levity against gravity" (*Satanic Verses* 3). However, despite obvious strategic and discursive differences between Ali's and Rushdie's novels, the two writers share an acute sense of historical destiny whereby an individual's fate is

inextricably intertwined with that of the community's: Saleem Sinai declares, "[T]hanks to the occult tyrannies of those blandly saluting clocks I had been mysteriously handcuffed to history, my destinies indissolubly chained to those of my country. For the next three decades, there was to be no escape" (9).

If Ali's *Twilight in Delhi* has evolved into "both a classic and a legend" (Anderson 440), it has achieved such an impressive status deservedly. Indeed, its significance to the Muslim literary tradition in English is as pioneeringly pivotal as Chinua Achebe's *Things Fall Apart* is to African literature in English. H. H. Anniah Gowda argues in a cogent comparative analysis of the two writers that

> both these novelists handle societies whose *milieu* was fast disappearing under the impact of the British rule.... *Twilight in Delhi* and *Things Fall Apart* derive their strength from the quality of their authors' perception of the social forces at work in ancient, proud but flexible civilizations and from their admirable knowledge of human psychology shown in the development of their central characters. (53)

Like Achebe's attachment to the Igbo culture of Nigeria, Ali's allegiance to the Muslim civilization of India is committed but never uncritical. His fiction exposes the marginalization of women, condemns the vulgarity of manipulative politicians, and reveals the banality and lethargy of reactionaries who cling to outmoded values of clan, class, or quasi-caste distinction and fail to respond to the challenges of change and social transformation. Ali does not hesitate to show the venality of the parasitic "priestly class" that collaborates with the colonizers and resists progressive evolution. He thus succeeds in merging "the office of psalmist with the function of a national bard, to associate a religious wisdom with an historic vision" (Niven 3). Proud of his Islamic heritage and affiliation, Ali represents Islam not as a set of strict theological dogmas but as a dynamic and legitimate source of his characters' spiritual, emotional, and ethnic identity—an identity that refuses and resists the colonial domination of the "Farangis" over India. In this sense, Ali's "twice born fiction," to use Meenakshi Mukherjee's term for the dual parentage of the Indo-Anglian novel, is at once self-representative and self-critical. It also projects a subversive, revisionary view of history that debunks for the reader in English the official colonial description of events in the empire. (Ironically, the initial apprehension of the British censors concerning the "subversiveness" of *Twilight in Delhi* may thus be justified.) Put in a historical perspective, Ali has broken new ground by launching an altogether fascinating literary tradition of Muslim writing in English, thereby giving the erstwhile inaudible, if not also invisible, subjects a voice to project the other side of the story and to prove that spunky "subalterns" can speak for themselves.

TWO

# Voices of Their Own:
# Pioneering Muslim Women Writers

How did the tradition succeed in transforming the Muslim woman into that submissive marginal creature who buries herself and only goes out into the world huddled in her veil? Why does the Muslim man need such a mutilated companion?

—Fatima Mernissi

DESPITE THE STEREOTYPICAL IMAGE OF MUSLIM WOMEN BEING servile and secluded, most of the early Muslim narratives in English were produced by women. The six women writers dealt with in this chapter are pioneers in conveying the specificity of their experiences as women and as Muslims in a language that is alien to their culture. The foreignness of the medium made them sensitive to the image they were projecting of their culture to the outside world. Many must have been aware of the limitations of such a medium but also of its advantages too. Attia Hosain puts it quite candidly: "I regret that I do not write in the language of my own people. . . . It prevents me from having any contacts with them, but when I write in English, in this there is also its own advantages; I can tell others about my own people. We are displaced writers and do not forget about our own national routes [sic]. We carry in our soul a deep anguish" (qtd. in Kalinnikova 167). These women writers question, subvert, or challenge the social dogmas of their time and environment regarding the status of women, a status that has been circumscribed by male power, yet they are keen to express, each in her own way, their loyalty and affiliation with the culture of Islam. While they mildly or strongly oppose patriarchal appropriation of Islamic precepts to marginalize and subject women, they appear keen to call for a woman-friendly reading of Islam. The debate that these pioneering women have initiated and dramatized is current and relevant. Muslim women continue to contribute their fair share to the literary heritage of Islam.

### ROKEYA SAKHAWAT HOSSAIN

While Muslim fiction in English assumed prominence with the publication of Ahmed Ali's 1940 nostalgic novel *Twilight in Delhi*, it was not the first work of fiction written in English by a Muslim: the pioneering honor goes to a Bengali woman, Rokeya Sakhawat Hossain (1880–1932), who published in 1905 a short story, "Sultana's Dream." In this "witty utopian fantasy" (Tharu and Lalita 340) through which the courageous author "ridicules Indian stereotypes and customs" (Jahan 4), the author reverses the gender roles and cleverly argues how our world would be a more peaceful and better place to live in if only women were to become the power wielders and men were secluded, shut indoors, doing household chores. Because war-inclined men are confined in Hossain's utopian land, peace prevails: "You need not be afraid of coming across a man here. This is Ladyland, free from sin and harm. Virtue herself reigns here" (8). For women, all the adversities and afflictions in their real lives are eliminated in this utopian world: no child marriages because women are not allowed to marry before the age of twenty-one; no denial of education because they need to fulfill their potentials through going to school and university; and, most importantly, women are not secluded. This situation contrasts what the female dreamer recalls about women's depressing reality: "We have no hand or voice in the management of our social affairs. In India, man is lord and master. He has taken to himself all powers and privileges and shut up the women in the zenana [women's secluded area in the house]" (9). According to Roushan Jahan, "Sultana's Dream" represents "one of the earliest 'self-consciously feminist' utopian stories written in English by a woman" and its author "is the first and foremost feminist of Bengali Muslim Society"; she immediately justifies her usage of the term *feminist* by stating that "one hesitates to use a term that is not context-free, and *feminism* does mean different things to different people, yet it is the term that automatically occurs to many who read Rokeya's work now" (1). Pursuing a similar line of discourse, Inderpal Grewal, in her comment on the story's first sentence where the playful narrator claims to be "thinking lazily on the condition of Indian womanhood" (7), astutely observes that Hossain foregrounds "the essence of being a woman, that being a woman is seen as an ontological state common to female persons across class, caste, and religion, but also in a political sense, as a position within society that is structurally open to oppression" (243). To give her story a nondenominational significance, Rokeya Hossain makes Ladyland's religion universal: "Our religion is based on Love and Truth. It is our religious duty to love one another and to be absolutely truthful" (16).

Essentially an essayist who wrote mainly in Bangla, Rokeya Hossain was motivated to write this short piece of narrative "partly to demonstrate her proficiency in English to her non-Bengali husband, who encouraged her to read and write English, and who was her immediate and appreciative audience" and partly "to test her ability in literary forms other than essays" (Jahan 1–2). In any case, Rokeya Hossain's utopian story represents a pioneering landmark in Muslim narrative in English. Had this social activist devoted, or been allowed, more time, what other fictional works in English could she have produced that emulated the originality and subtle humor of "Sultana's Dream"?

## IQBALUNNISA HUSSAIN

In 1944, four years after the publication in England of Ahmed Ali's landmark novel *Twilight in Delhi*, Iqbalunnisa Hussain published in India the first novel written by a Muslim woman, *Purdah and Polygamy: Life in an Indian Muslim Household.* As the title suggests, the novel tends to have a mimetic, sociological orientation. This impression is confirmed in the foreword by C. R. Reddy, the then vice-chancellor of Andhra University, who refers to Iqbalunnisa Hussain as "the Jane Austen of India," when he describes her female characters as "true to life, simple, natural, unsophisticated, intimate" (1); he also quotes a faculty member from his university's English department who "wrote after reading the book at [Reddy's] instance—'In this book, almost for the first time, *true* Purdah life is depicted with *utter* realism'" (4; emphases added). While we are not offered any details about the novel's background or the author's biography, except for a fleeting remark in Reddy's patronizing foreword claiming that he "had helped in her educational career" (1), the novel certainly represents a remarkable achievement for its stamina and domestic detail. This 310-page, episodic novel depicts the drama of three generations of an upper-class Muslim family in the late 1930s. It operates through reporting, mimesis, irony, and occasional didacticism, but primarily through an amazing narrative energy that projects minute details of household life within the confines of the women's quarters. The novel represents the practice of polygamy, whereby financially able men are allowed to marry up to four wives, as a fact of life in the specific privileged milieu depicted, with its rationale and fair application cautiously questioned. The protagonist, Kabeer—metonymically named, meaning "grand"— heads a household of four wives, censoriously watched over by his cantankerous widow of a mother whose machinations over her daughters-in-law never ceases until the end of the novel when Kabeer dies. Puzzlingly, the novel avoids making any political statement about the resistance of Indians to British colonialism in the turbulent time preceding the partition/independence of the country. In fact, the British characters are depicted with sympathy and sensitivity, due perhaps to the author's focus on the wealthy elite of Indian society who relished cozy contacts with the British establishment. This stance gives the discourse a conservative, apolitical, almost collaborationist, slant. In this respect, it is instructive to contrast the politics and praxis surrounding the works of Ahmed Ali and Iqbalunnisa Hussain. The fact that Ahmed Ali had to (and could) travel by sea during the Second World War to London, the empire's megalopolis, where he succeeded in getting his novel printed while Iqbalunnisa Hussain published hers at home in then colonized India, can signify many things depending on one's perspective. Gender politics being one such perspective, it is evident here that the Muslim male enjoyed more space and mobility than his female counterpart. On the other hand, while Ali's text suffered initial banning by the censor in Britain because of its angry, anticolonialist discourse, Iqbalunnisa Hussain's must have been regarded by the authorities as a safe text to circulate, since it projected a restrained view of purdah politics and depicted a harmonious relationship between its British and Indian characters.

It is equally instructive to compare Iqbalunnisa Hussain's novel with Rokeya Hossain's Bangla work, entitled *Avarodhbasini* (The Secluded Ones) about life in purdah. In *Avarodhbasini*, Rokeya Hossain chronicles, through forty-seven brief episodes, many harrowing and a few humourous incidents that illustrate the absurdity of imposing strict and total seclusion on women: it is revealed here that women are denied the right to be educated and are prohibited from stepping outside their homes; they are also prohibited from having contact not only with any nonclose family male member, but also with other women who are not of the same religion and social class. Rokeya Hossain observes that the higher the social status, the stricter and more oppressive was the observance of purdah, since strict adherence to purdah was seen as a status symbol. *Avarodhbasini* concludes with Rokeya Hossain's cry of agony on behalf of women prisoners of purdah:

"Oh, why did I come to this miserable world,
Why was I born in a purdah country!" (81)

Rokeya Hossain's *Avarodhbasini* is a piece of protest writing derived from actual events that shows the cruelty of child marriages, the absurdity of purdah practices, and the injustice of denying women their right to education. While Rokeya Hossain resorts to writing nonfictional narrative in Bangla to polemicize the issue of women and to reach her audience directly, Iqbalunnisa Hussain opts for fiction in English to deal with the same issue; obviously the latter's choice makes the novelist removed (indeed twice removed) from her Indian readers. While Rokeya Hossain's strategy could be direct and combative, Iqbalunnisa Hussain's is mild and subtle, resorting often to irony. The opening of the novel's fifth chapter recalls the opening of Jane Austen's *Pride and Prejudice*:

It is a well-known fact that man is superior to women in every respect. He is a representative of God on earth and being born with His light in him deserves the respect and obedience that he demands. He is not expected to show his gratitude or even a kind word of appreciation to a woman: it is his birthright to get everything from her. . . . A woman as a wife should be subservient in everything to man's comfort and exist for him and for him alone. She should have no particular liking to anything. Her work should as a matter of course begin and end with him. (49)

Occasionally, the novel foregrounds the same issue in a direct contestational tone, voiced, interestingly enough, by a male character:

Man being both the legislator and executor has brought in laws to suit his interests. He has monopolised freedom and luxury. A woman has no right to question even when she is wronged. She must retaliate now. No one will blame her. Her cause is right and just. (114)

While irony enlivens the narrative and makes its discourse more effective, the novel's conclusion dissipates the effectiveness of the message. The narrative, linear and mildly didactic as it is, just ends and the rhythmless tempo comes to a sudden summary closure, as if its stamina has been unceremoniously depleted. Nevertheless, read symbolically, the narrative begins with the patriarch's death and symmetrically concludes with the death of his heir, Kabeer. Women may fall sick but seem to survive the men, who despite their privileges and powers, appear to be rather prisoners of their desires or their preassigned social roles. Marriage in such a context becomes a transaction to be negotiated and manipulated. The wife becomes the husband's "property" (62) as discardable as "a dropped tear" (173), a status that certainly creates and codifies abuse. As the narrative exposes—through skillful and subtle use of subversive irony—the absurdities, contradictions, and cruelties of the twin practices of purdah and polygamy, the significance of this novel resides in its raising questions, tentative and mild, rather than projecting a lucid and definitive discourse.

## ATTIA HOSAIN

After *Purdah and Polygamy*, the Indian writer Attia Hosain published, in 1953, a collection of socially conscious, mimetic stories, *Phoenix Fled*, followed in 1961 by an impressive novel, *Sunlight on a Broken Column*. Mulk Raj Anand, in his avuncular introduction to the novel, describes it as "one of the most sensitive novels in Indian English writing" whereby the author combines "a poignant, tragic narrative with an undercurrent of stoic calm" (xi). Through the maturing sensibility of its sympathetic heroine-narrator, Laila, the novel registers the transformation in the life of a wealthy Muslim Taluqdar family during the critical period of the preindependence/partition of the subcontinent. Privileged yet sympathetic to the poor, confined by purdah yet seeking

freedom through education and a few daring acts, proud of her Islamic identity yet opting not for Pakistan (the Land of the Pure) but for secular India,
Laila comprehends and contextualizes these paradoxes in her life. Courageously and convincingly, Laila transcends a confining environment that puts a
premium on duty rather than feeling, on family solidarity rather than honesty,
and on clan and class interest rather than anticolonialist aspirations. Attia Hosain uses precise, lyrical language to convey the feelings of her spirited heroine,
whose cross-section of friends transcends class and communal connections:
specifically, Laila's affectionate sympathies with her feisty Hindu Aya, Nandi, is
one of the novel's engaging segments. While Attia Hosain who "knew Mohammed Ali Jinnah, but disagreed with him over the question of a separate
homeland for Muslims" (Bhuchar 44) and while her two works are subsumed
by a secular and progressive vision, she expresses a deep affection for her Islamic heritage when compared with European values: as Anita Desai aptly
observes in her introduction to *Phoenix Fled*,

> "Westernization" is seen as destructive of the old, traditional culture. The latter
> may be full of cruelties and injustices, but it is a pattern of life known and un-
> derstood, therefore more acceptable and more fitting than an alien culture that
> has been neither fully understood nor assimilated. Attia Hosain's work is by no
> means an unreserved paean of praise for the old culture but is certainly full of
> an inherited, instinctive love for it. (xx–xxi)

Unlike Rokeya Sakhawat Hossain's and Iqbalunissa Hussain's characters
that never leave purdah life except in a dream or through surreptitious acts,
Attia Hosain's heroine Laila becomes purdah-free. This coincides with the anti-
British nationalist struggle: there is a synchronicity between Laila's awareness
of her circumscribed position as a woman and her clear commitment for a free,
secular India.

The novel's lucid anticolonial tone recalls Ahmed Ali's in *Twilight in Delhi*
and points to several intertextual links between the works of these two authors.
Both Ali and Hosain have been prompted to produce their works in English, instead of Urdu—the language that both loved and wrote their earlier works in—
in order to project Muslim sentiments to the outside world, at the dear expense
of being severed from most of their Indian audience. In his introduction to the
1994 edition of *Twilight in Delhi*, Ahmed Ali explains why he had taken the trouble of going to London to have his novel published there and why he chose
English as his medium instead of Urdu:

> The cause [of India's freedom from colonialism] deserved a world-wide audi-
> ence. If presented in Urdu, it would die down within a narrow belt rimmed by
> Northwest India. There were many instances to show that British injustices in

India were dismissed as local matters. But if a case were brought to London, the home government became involved, which depended on public good faith and was answerable to King and Parliament. (xvi)

Ahmed Ali's and Attia Hosain's novels invoke nostalgically the bygone days of Muslim glory and splendor: the regal elegance of the Mughal court in Delhi and the refined sensuality, artistry and poetry of the Kingdom of Oudh in Lucknow. That lively radiant past makes the decaying present painful to contemplate. Like Mir Nihal's Delhi, Laila's ancestral home "Ashiana" is undergoing its own private dying "twilight" in postpartition India; in fact, the decaying ancestral home depicted in Attia Hosain's novel becomes an evocative microcosm for dying Muslim Delhi in Ali's novel: both settings fall victim to the vagaries of history, symbolize disfranchisement, and foreshadow the precarious future reserved for the Muslims of India. Mushtari Bai, the charming courtesan that appeared in *Twilight in Delhi*, reappears in Attia Hosain's novel as a pathetic pauper well beyond her prime. Reflecting the fate of Mir Nihal's Delhi and Laila's Ashiana, Mushtari Bai gives a human face to a dying erotic past that coexisted within a puritanical Muslim milieu. Nothing escapes decay; no one escapes the ravages of time. And the titles of the three novels foretell the intertextual link between Ahmed Ali's *Twilight in Delhi* and *Ocean of Night* and Attia Hosain's *Sunlight on a Broken Column*. The latter title, borrowed from T. S. Eliot's *The Hollow Men*, deploys light imagery that evokes the titles of Ali's two works: light "broken" or dimmed in "twilight" to be drowned in an "ocean of night." With death as a motif, the vision permeating Ali's and Hosain's works is quintessentially tragic yet not macabre; doomed by destiny or fate (Kismet) yet precipitated by misguided human will; permeated with sadness yet redeemed by compassion, loyalty, and love.

With the partition looming, the Muslims in Attia Hosain's novel faced two agonizing choices: either abandon all their properties and memories and depart for newly established Pakistan, or stay in independent India as a beleaguered minority threatened by massacre. The following fiery, yet emblematic, conversation between Laila and her alter ego of a cousin, Zahra, who opted for Pakistan, illustrates painful internecine debate that raged through many Muslim families: Laila begins by challenging Zahra about the carnage Muslim families faced during the partition:

> "Where were all their leaders? Safely across the border. The only people left to save them were those very Hindus against whom they had ranted. Do you know what 'responsibility' and 'duty' meant? To stop the murderous mob at any cost, even if it meant shooting people of their own religion."
>
> Zahra replied with equal anger, "What is so extraordinary about that? Do you think we did not have the same sense of duty on our side? Do you think the same things did not happen there? You are prejudiced."

Her words defeated me. They showed me that all avenues of understanding between us were closed. I had appeared to her prejudiced, taking sides, when I so passionately believed in friendship and tolerance.

But we made up, Zahra and I, as we had always done; there was so much we had in common, so much to remember. (304–05)

Untill today the debate is not settled about the rationale for the creation of a truncated Pakistan in 1947, which had been a dear dream to millions of Muslims in India, and which was so sinisterly mangled by the last viceroy Mountbatten's administration. Thanks to arrogant British colonial mapping, a practice that they had so cynically and self-servingly pursued likewise in Africa and the Middle East, the borders were drawn hurriedly and arbitrarily—mainly to the detriment of the Muslims, especially with the partitioning of the provinces of Bengal and Punjab. Most brazenly, the departing British colonialists maneuvered to leave scenic Kashmir, "80 percent Muslim, ruled by a Hindu prince, bordering both Pakistan and India, the source of important rivers" (Gandhi 181), as part of India, thus constituting a perennial bone of bloody conflict between the two countries. Maulana Abul Kalam Azad, a prominent Muslim leader of the Congress Party who opposed the partition and later became the minister of education in India, argued that

[t]he basis of partition was enmity between Hindus and Muslims. The creation of Pakistan gave it a permanent constitutional form and made it much more difficult of solution [sic]. The most regrettable feature of this situation is that the sub-continent of India is divided into two States which look at one another with hatred and fear. (247)

The Muslims who were left in India and the Hindus who were left in Pakistan faced an orgy of slaughter. Given the price paid for the partition—being between one to two millions killed from among Hindus, Muslims, and Sikhs, as well as the massive material damage—and given that until today the future of the Muslims living in India looks unsettled, some say bleak, one wonders by hindsight whether the partition of the subcontinent was a wise path to pursue. As one of history's ironies, there are now more Muslims living in India than there are in Pakistan.

## MENA ABDULLAH

Attia Hosain's positive pride in her Islamic heritage is echoed in Mena Abdullah's collection of twelve stories, *The Time of the Peacock* (written in collaboration with Ray Mathew). These simple, sequential, yet subtle and interlocked stories project the perspectives of Indian Muslims who originally arrived in rural Australia in the second half of the nineteenth century; their initial employment was to train camels across the wilderness, settling afterward as farmers. During the odious era of "The White Australia Policy," these Indian Muslims were curiously referred to as "Afghans" stereotyping "all who wore turbans, exotic attire and shared the Moslem [sic] faith, quite irrespective of their diverse linguistic and cultural backgrounds" (MacDermott 203).

Abdullah's narrative is given focus by the maturing voice of its sensitive, observant young narrator, Nimmi, whose endearing energy and imagination propel action and provoke reflection. Significantly, Nimmi, curious and inquisitive, affirms precisely and distinctly her ethnicity: "I, young as I was, could see the whole of my life as strange—a dark girl in a white man's country, a Punjabi Muslim in a Christian land" (21). This stark statement lends credence to the notion that one's ethnicity does not refer "to a thing in itself but a relationship . . . typically based on *contrast*" (Sollors 288), highlighted here by color, gender, regional/national origin, and religion, with the latter receiving an accentuated emphasis in the collection as a whole.

Throughout the stories, the contrast manifests itself in terms of "us" and "them," and in terms of what is judged to be properly Muslim as distinct from what is perceived to be typically Australian. In order to preserve their cultural values and practices, Australia's Indian Muslims resort to the defensive attitude of constructing family-centred cocoons, whereby they inhabit an approximation of life in India, sheltering themselves from occasional acts of racism. To overcome their alienation, they develop a special affiliation with the landscape by inventing a semblance of India. Nimmi's mother creates a garden of Indian flowers as "her own little walled-in country" (2). This symbolic attachment to the new/old land is enhanced by a corresponding intimacy with the animals that are given dignified Indian names or referred to in familial or endearing terms: the eagle is a "High Maharajah" (53); the vixen is Kumari, a princess; Shah-Jehan, the peacock, is Nimmi's "little brother" (7); the imaginary, wise tiger is "Grandfather Tiger"; and the little bird "Russilla" is "a friend, from heaven" (13). Marginalized as they are, the Indian Muslims find the animals friendlier and the landscape more hospitable than some of the Australians who call them "Niggers" (in "Because of the Russilla") and mock their dress and food (in "Grandfather Tiger").

Parallel to these occasional instances of racism, the narrative, significantly, highlights acts of affection and solidarity on the part of other Australians who befriend the Indians, respect their religion, and make them feel "like relations" (19). Interestingly, in "The Singing Man" the narrative commingles the Indians' nostalgia for their Kashmir or Punjab with the yearnings of the wandering Irish accountant, Paddy-the-Drunk, singing and pining for the green meadows of Ireland. Likewise, the counterpoising of the narrative about the Australian "brushranger" Thunderbolt with that of the Punjabi "dacoit" Malik Khan (through the technique of story-within-story in "The Outlaw") signals similarities in honorable codes of conduct among people of all races, even among those who are compelled to resort to the extremes of violence.

More important, the narrative foregrounds the diversity in the response of the Indian Muslims to their "foreignness" in Australia, problematizing in the process the lack of uniformity in the manner of affirming their ethnicity. In one story, "The Child That Wins," we witness a range of attitudes with regard to what must have been an unusual event then: an Indian Muslim marrying an Australian woman. The groom's father, supported by Nimmi's favorite, the comic-relief-figure, Uncle Seyid, opposes it. The father worries (perhaps too presciently) that children of cross-cultural marriages "belong nowhere" (74), neither Muslims, Indians, nor Australians; the well-meaning traditionalist Uncle Seyid believes that a Muslim should marry only someone from his faith because "your own is your own" (74) and "what was right was right forever, and that what was Muslim was always right" (73). On the other hand, Nimmi's parents, whose own marriage symbolizes a striking, syncretic marriage of a Muslim to a Brahmina, give a cautious, tacit endorsement to the marriage. Their attitude reflects a certain sophisticated, reconciliatory idealism rooted in Nimmi's mother's vague principle that "people are people" and in Nimmi's father's genial declaration that "[i]f you stay anywhere long enough . . . people get used to you. They take you in to their houses and their ways" (74). Alternatively, the marriage itself signifies a readiness for organic integration justified by both genuine bonding and pragmatism. The conflict is resolved cleverly through converging these diverse streams with the birth of a baby, heralding hope and harmony.

"The Child That Wins" underscores the necessity to change and adapt to the realities and exigencies of immigration. While the discourse reveals an obvious pride in the characters' sense of their ethnicity and empathy for their angst over losing it in an alien, at times hostile, culture, a centrifugal tendency emerges among them pointing toward merging with the new culture without necessarily deracinating themselves. This issue becomes critical when the education of children—the new generation of Australian-born Muslims—is concerned. In "The Babu from Bengal" the foresighted Wali Husson urges his friends to send their children to Australian schools to learn and to integrate into their new society, so as to spare the parents the exploitation of the Babu, a half-literate conniving clerk:

> The white people send their children to school. We send ours to work in the paddocks. The white children are learning to choose. Ours are learning to be farmers, peasants, people the Babu can use to make money from. This is because their fathers are stubborn and dislike change. (89)

What is being articulated here is not merely a strategy for survival, but a genuine willingness to meet the Other and to emulate attitudes that the Muslims can comprehend and relate to, such as the pursuit of learning. Throughout, the narrative endorses the spirit of change by foregrounding compromise and acceptance of their new identity as Australians while cherishing their Indian heritage: the triple sets of binary oppositions along the axes of time, space, and ethnic barriers (then/now, there/here, and us/them) are thus deftly defused and reconciled through such statements as "The old ways were good, but the new ways are better" (104). Similarly, in the story "High Maharajah," the reconstructing of a damaged kite from Indian bamboo reed and Australian paper (potent symbols for cultural roots and acquired identity), making the hybridized "Australian kite sing" (57), signals the evolvement of a new composite personality, expressing "a distinctively Asian-Australian sensibility that is part of Australia's history" (Gooneratine 118). The ethos of tolerance and compassion are culminated in the last story "A Long Way." Evoking in the reader's mind John Bunyan's *Pilgrim's Progress*, the story operates allegorically through the metaphor of an arduous journey undertaken by a Pakistani mother determined to send a jumper she has made for a son who studies in Australia; as she tries to arrive in Karachi on time to hand deliver it to a friend departing for Australia, this Muslim mother meets believers from other religions (Hindus, Dalits, and a Christian priest) who all show her affection and admiration. Like a carefully conceived allegory, the story, and with it the whole collection, concludes almost didactically by building up toward the book's central statement that appears in the last page: "the world is all our people" (112); this all-embracing insight confirms Nimmi's innocently pastoral vision of a child articulated in the book's first sentence "the world was our farm and we were all loved" (1).

Thus, the discourse of *The Time of the Peacock* functions, to extend Edward Said's musical metaphor, "contrapuntally" (*Culture* 18); it suggests, perhaps a little idyllically, that compromise is quite possible when exercising flexibility and foresight. Significantly, one can see that all the concessions are one-sided: the minority has to be accommodative of the majority. Deflecting confrontational conditions, the ambience of universal détente that permeates *The Time of the Peacock* makes it, as one Australian reviewer for the *Bulletin* aptly suggests, "that kind of book: to be passed on within a family, with love" (qtd. in Gooneratine 115). The book's fascinating thematics, accordingly, progresses from the "dissociative sense" (Sollors 288), which emphasizes ethnic distinctiveness being jealously guarded in a daunting environment of immigration/exile, toward an integrative ethos that celebrates a caring, compassionate humanity: as Rashida, Nimmi's sister and one of the book's privileged voices, insightfully declares, "In all things beautiful Allah smiles" (27).

## FARHANA SHEIKH

Those "things beautiful" are surely hard to locate in Farhana Sheikh's *The Red Box*, which depicts the double victimization of Pakistani women in Britain through racism and exploitation as cheap manual laborers, often by wealthy Pakistanis. The damage caused by this double transgression is paralleled by that of their double migration: first from India to Pakistan at the partition of the subcontinent and then from Pakistan to Britain due to economic necessities. More important, the preferential status given to boys over girls in Pakistani families further traumatizes the women: male family members show no qualms about exploiting tradition and/or religion to manipulate or abuse sisters, wives, or lovers; as Alamgir Hashmi observes in his review of the novel, "Pakistani society is seen as a failure of the hopes of 1947, and as a dead-end particularly for women" (145).

Deploying a tape recorder as a plot device and a signifying register of an evolving discourse, Sheikh relies heavily on interviewing techniques and on minute dialogue/polylogue transcription to depict the relationship between the three main female characters: the interviewer is Raisa who prepares for a graduate thesis on race and education and meets at regular intervals with two young high school students: Nasreen and Tahira. Initially, this interviewer–interviewee relationship seems tiresome and asymmetrical: the interviewer—an attractive, educated, seemingly successful professional from a well-off family—is privileged in posing all the questions to the two young interviewees, who reveal their intimate views and feelings about diversely complex topics such as sexuality, gender roles within immigrant Pakistani families in Britain, racism at school, and, significantly, the degree of their religious commitment as immigrants in a non-Muslim society. The asymmetry is skillfully redressed in the novel's penultimate and longest chapter that takes the form of a letter sent from Raisa to Nasreen and Tahira: in this confessional epistle, Raisa reveals that the semblance of success and security of the privileged professional hides considerable pain and puzzlement that are just as trying as those faced by Nasreen and Tahira. The novel concludes conceptually, yet not quite organically, pointing to a mature readiness to accept challenges and comprehend injustices such as racism and sexism. Rather than being fully developed constructs, these three characters are initially introduced as voices codified schematically as in a morality play; however, the narrative gently assumes a progressive complexity leading to the development of defined mental images about each of the three characters. More importantly, to these female characters, the term *Muslim* represents the primary identity signifier, ahead of class, gender, or nationalism. Moreover, Islam provides them with moral models for personal and social behavior to which they willingly adhere (19). While the three main female characters describe themselves as Muslims— in fact so unambiguously that they interchangeably use the words *Muslim* and

*Pakistani*—each perceives the terms in her own way: Nasreen, literally and conservatively; Tahira, liberally, even rebelliously; Raisa, being the novel's mature voice, reverentially and understandingly. Religion to these female characters is no mere abstraction, but a concrete set of mores they espouse despite the inhospitable environment in which immigrants have to survive. However, their declared embrace of Islam as a mode of living as well as a faith consequently singles them out as the Other and may relegate them to the margins of an intolerant dominant culture. Nevertheless, one leaves the novel with a distinct sense that these women, with Raisa being a model, can assert themselves and surmount difficulties by sheer integrity, determination, and hard work.

The writings of Rokeya Sakhawat Hossain, Iqbalunnisa Hussain, Attia Hosain, Mena Abdullah, and Farhana Sheikh demonstrate that for these five women writers, whose roots are firmly linked to the Indian subcontinent, Islam, whether in the domain of ethics or aesthetics, represents a preoccupying fascination and a telling leitmotif. As Sara Suleri, born in Pakistan and now an established American scholar, has eloquently put it, "it is difficult to renounce the elegance of Islam" (193). One is often struck by the ardor of the affection shown by the Muslims of the subcontinent toward their religion. Of course, there are complex cultural and historical reasons for such a manifestation of affiliation. However, when one moves from the subcontinent toward the Middle East and Africa, one witnesses in general a less vehement declaration of faith with just as equal commitment to it (except, of course, for the Taliban-like extremists who have a power drama of their own to stage). Perhaps African and Middle Eastern writers feel "so securely ... Muslim" that they do "not need to make an issue of it" (Said, "Anglo-Arab" 19).


## ZAYNAB ALKALI

The two novels by the Nigerian Zaynab Alkali, *The Stillborn* (1984) and *The Virtuous Woman* (1986), reveal a dispassionate affiliation with an Islamic heritage that is accepted as an integral part of Africa's cultural identity. One of Nigeria's celebrated writers and certainly the first woman novelist to emerge from its Muslim North, Alkali skillfully blends Islamic references, idioms, and metaphors with those derived from ancestral African religion and Christianity, reflecting a symbiotic, if at times discriminatory, cohabitation of the three cultures. In this context, Alkali's fiction astutely illustrates what the elder in Ali Mazrui's novel of ideas, *The Trial of Christopher Okigbo*, has pronounced about Nigeria's "eternal tripartite tension": "Islam, Euro-Christianity, and indigenous tradition struggled to forge a single nation. Nigeria was Africa in embryo" (139). Alkali's two novels dramatize the maturing, confidence-building experiences of young heroines who enjoy subliminal, empowering relationships with wise, dignified grandfathers who have mystical links with ancestral spirituality. Moreover, Alkali's works highlight the role of education as not only a tool for liberating women from exploitation and marginalization but for transforming them and endowing them with roles of power previously reserved for men only: at the conclusion of *The Stillborn*, the confident, rejuvenated, economically independent heroine, Li, is addressed respectfully by her older sister, Awa: "you are the man of the house now" (101). Not only do Alkali's novels show her heroines' developing self-confidence, but also their deep attachment to the spontaneity and vitality of village life in contrast to the shabbiness, pretentiousness, and brutality of city life: as the disillusioned Li declares, the city "destroys dreams" (94). However, each novel suggests that the heroine's allegorical journey to the city has to be undertaken as a rite of passage.

While Alkali's heroine at the conclusion of *The Stillborn* develops a feisty, assertive sense of overcoming a father's mad obsession with discipline and a husband's emotional manipulation and abandonment, she quite gratuitously surrenders her hard-earned privileges by agreeing to go back to the now crippled, vulnerable husband, residing in the city. Li's lame justification *seems* to be based on the concept of family unity and her child's assumed need for a father. Such a sudden and unconvincing twist defeats the novel's heroic thrust and amounts to "throwing sand into the feminist *gari*" (Ogunyemi 63). Alkali's deliberate ideological deflation is rooted in her view of herself as a Muslim woman and her "allergy" to a label such as feminism. She explains her circumspect stance lucidly, yet polemically:

> I advocate togetherness, coexistence, because I believe by our very natures we are created to be together, and coexisting is not the same as being equal. The question of equality is irrelevant. There are more than enough roles in life to accommodate us all. I always draw the analogy of the heart and the brain. How can these two strive to function the same way when even by their very natures they are made differently? A woman can never be anything else but a woman. Her role in life is as important as that of the man, but not the same. ("Important" 1256)

## CONCLUSION

Since each of the six writers discussed in this chapter reflects her own perspective and priorities shaped by a distinctive cultural and aesthetic formation, one naturally cannot expect a unitary discourse emanating from all of them, especially as they traverse four continents and span a period of more than three-quarters of a century. However, one can develop certain conceptual points of convergence among them. While these writers speak with assertive, affirmative voices about the confinement, marginalization, and even abuse of Muslim women, their discourse tends to be conciliatory not confrontational, paradoxical not absolutist, polemical not totalizing. Significantly, the works of these women writers reveal an unequivocal sense of pride in their Islamic culture, while at the same time condemning and combating the abusive excesses of patriarchy when it appropriates and exploits the religious argument to preserve its own spiritual and material hegemony. The discourse of the Muslim women writers strives, with varying degrees of militancy, for an agenda that is quite distinct from Euro-American feminism(s), however we may perceive it/them to be; some may even avoid the term *feminism* altogether, while others opt for a "womanism that is not at all a replica of Western feminisms" (Ghazoul).

More importantly, the mere fact that these women writers produce their narratives in English may cause involuntary self-censorship to avoid projecting unflattering images about their own culture to a mostly alien audience liable to misconstrue or be unaware of the context of their narrative discourse; thus they spare themselves the syndrome of "the privileged native informants of liberal third worldist feminism" (256) that Gayatri Chakravorty Spivak identifies in Bharati Mukherjee's heroines.

Moreover, their writing represents not only a fascinating phenomenon of articulating feelings and perspectives of their own through adopting a medium and a language that were not theirs, but a promise to perhaps extend and expand the scope of their focus beyond mainly urban, middle-class concerns (the exception here is Zaynab Alkali). We may even see a more militant and confrontational response to the discourse produced by male-made theocracies, as we currently see in some Muslim women's narratives in French and in Arabic.

THREE

# Dissecting Dictators:
# Nuruddin Farah's *Close Sesame*

How dare you enslave the people, born free when their mothers gave birth to
them.

        —'Umar ibn al-Khattab (Second Righteous Khaleefa)

DEEPLY ROOTED AS THE DOMINANT FAITH AND CULTURE IN SOMALIA,
Islam provides the context within which Nuruddin Farah's fiction operates its
two motifs: the marginalization of women in a tribalistic, patriarchical society,
and the terror inflicted by the brutal dictatorship of the now-defunct dictator
Ziiyad Bare, sometimes referred to in the novels as the "Generalismo." The skillful and subtle intermeshing of these two motifs underpin the vitality and density
of Farah's narratives. Like the self-exiled James Joyce, Farah spent most of his
adult life in exile, particularly in other parts of Africa, yet all his eight novels to
date are set in Somalia, hence the inescapable encounter with the ubiquitous Islamic traditions and rituals practiced in one form or another. However, there is a
diversity of opinions about Farah's depiction of Islam in these novels. Norman
Cary argues that "the attitudes of Farah's characters toward religion range from
naïve acceptance to hypocritical cynicism to Western-style skepticism" (115).
More ominously, Alamin Mazrui, in his discussion of Farah's sixth novel, *Maps*,
evokes Salman Rushdie's parodic portrayal of Islam in *The Satanic Verses* and associates it with Farah's "debasing the religion and its Book" (216); for Mazrui,
Farah's "metaphoric and symbolic strategies" and "his satirical projection of Islam
. . . [have] clearly taken the path of a cultural apostate" (217). On the other hand,
Barbara Turfan takes a discriminating approach by highlighting a valid distinction
between the condemnation of the abuses perpetrated in the name of Islam and
of the faith itself: she argues that Farah's "attitude toward Islam is by no means

hostile. Rather, it is the distortion of Islam by its practitioners and by those who seek to use it to their own advantage that provokes his criticism" (177). While one may agree that Farah's portrayal of Islam does not *seem* to be entirely positive, one nevertheless needs to nuance the judgment and particularize it to specific novels or to specific characters within each novel. Also one needs to be prudent not to identify a hypocritical character's exploitation of Islam as either a stain on the entire religion or as the author's definitive attitude toward a religion that holds such a central role in the life of his people. More importantly, one could argue that Farah's attitude toward Islam undergoes a tentative qualitative shift from a rejectionist and predominantly negative stance to a more reflective and respectful, if distant and disengaged, appreciation of it as being essentially benign and tolerant, though maybe not progressive enough to match the challenges of modernity. Farah's initial negativity toward Islam is perhaps partly due to his conception of it as an essentially alien, Middle Eastern religion, not a homegrown African product. Such a stance echoes the attitude of the Senegalese novelist and cineast Sembène Ousmane, who regards Islam as a non-African, imperialist faith, similar to the Christianity that the European colonialists tried to impose on Africa later (Cham 181). Alamin Mazrui debunks such a conception of Islam: he argues forcefully that Islam is not only a living component of Africa's cultural texture but also a mark of ethnic definition to many Africans:

> There are certain societies in Africa in which Islam as a cultural expression is virtually an indispensable attribute of their ethnic identity. The Hausa of West Africa and the Swahili of East Africa are cases in point. It is perhaps possible to have a Hausa or Swahili person who is not a Muslim in religious faith, but it is far less conceivable to have a Hausa/Swahili individual who is not Islamic in cultural practice. (206)

No work reflects the evolution in Farah's depiction of Islam better than his 1983 novel, *Close Sesame*, which together with *Sweet and Sour Milk* (1979) and *Sardines* (1981) forms a trilogy titled *Variations on the Theme of an African Dictatorship*. Unlike the major characters of Farah's four preceding novels with strong, struggling women or young, articulate men, Deeriye, the hero of *Close Sesame*, is a devout septuagenarian Muslim man who has once been active in the struggle against the Italian occupation of Somaliland. For his integrity and dedication to his nationalist ideals, Deeriye has paid the heavy price of spending many years in prison away from his beloved wife and children. Now in the autumn of his life, Deeriye lives with his highly educated son, Jewish-American daughter-in-law, and grandson. Foregrounding the empathy between Deeriye and his daughter-in-law is a signifier of enlightened Muslims' receptivity toward interfaith, cross-cultural harmony as well as their respect for women, "always a touchstone for enlightenment in Farah" (Adam 208). Apart from sporadic asthmatic attacks

that make him unconscious, Deeriye's preoccupations involve a yearning to capture visions of his deceased wife, Nadiifa (literary, meaning "clean" in Arabic and
by connotation "pure" or "pious"), through recurrent, inspirational dreams, and
a worry about his son's participation in an underground revolutionary cell bent
on the perilous task of combating the ruthless regime.

Farah's portrayal of Deeriye is strikingly precise and vivid. The depiction of
the pious Deeriye contrasts Farah's treatment of two elderly characters from earlier works. Farah's first novel, *From a Crooked Rib*, opens with an unpleasant reference to the heroine Ebla's unnamed grandfather: "He could only curse. That
was all he could do" (3). Farah's satire of the grandfather is quite poignant, aimed
at exposing his false piety:

> The old man counted the beads of his rosary. There were ninety-nine of them,
> which represented the names of God. He was totally emaciated. His colleagues
> in this world had reported back to God a long time ago. (4).

In *Sweet and Sour Milk*, Keynaan, the polygamist patriarch and the collaborationist with the dictatorial regime that murdered his son Soyaan, gloats to his
second son, Loyaan, about how pervasive his paternal power is:

> I am the father. It is my prerogative to give life and death as I find fit. I've cho-
> sen to breathe life into Soyaan. And remember one thing, Loyaan: if I decide
> this minute to cut you in two, I can. The law of this land invests in men of my
> age the power. I am the Grand Patriarch. (95)

Equally telling, Keynaan, who beats his wives and children, couches his innate
misogyny in Islamic terms when he tells Loyaan that "women are for sleeping
with, for giving birth to and bringing up children; they are not good for anything else. . . . They are not to be trusted with secrets. They can serve the purposes Allah created them for originally, and no more" (84). Such a mentality, not
uncommon among some retrograde Muslim men, becomes a fertile ground for
the emergence of ruthless dictatorships oppressing entire nations. This correlation between tyranny and patriarchy is articulated in Wilhelm Reich's epigraph:
"[i]n the figure of the father the authoritarian state has its representative in every
family, so that the family becomes its most important instrument of power" (97).
In a strikingly refreshing foil to Keynaan, Deeriye loves his dead wife, remains
loyal to her memory, and shows affectionate respect toward his daughter and
daughter-in-law. Thus, through the portrayal of Deeriye, Farah deflates the
stereotypical image of the opportunistic, cynical patriarch that his own fiction
has previously created.

For Deeriye, Islam *is* his identity; his role model is the Somali religious-
nationalist hero Sayyid Muhammad Abdulle Hassan, referred to reverentially as

the "Sayyid" (a title confined in the Muslim Middle East only to a descendant of the Prophet). Moreover, Islam, for Deeriye, is the source of his strength, stability, and inner peace. By contrast, Kochin, the anxiety-ridden hero of Farah's second novel, *A Naked Needle*, that recalls Stephen Dedalus of Joyce's *A Portrait of the Artist as a Young Man*, describes himself thus, "I am Muslim, surely, although I don't practice it" (102); however, this claim seems merely nominal for this alienated, Italian-educated character detached from his milieu. Deeriye fits functionally within the Somali tribal society, even though he is not tribalistic, either in mentality or in behavior. While he adheres to the tribal code of honor, solidarity, and protection of sanctuary seekers, he transcends clannish concerns and engages in the costly and hazardous anticolonial struggle. Moreover, in his dignified old age, he eschews clannish conflicts and self-seeking opportunism to ingratiate himself with the General's murderous, neocolonial regime. As well, during his long years of political incarceration, Deeriye is a beneficiary of clan solidarity that supports his family during his absence. While languishing in jail, Deeriye is comforted by the thought that his affable brother-in-law would take care of his wife and children. This familial cohesion is partly tribal, partly religious; to put it differently, the solidarity is tribal but rooted in the Islamic call to be the keeper of one's siblings. Muslims extend this principle of familial solidarity to neighbors. In Deeriye's eyes, good neighborliness is a cardinal concept for the devout: "A neighbour, according to Islamic thought, is one's closest and therefore first protector. God is our neighbour. A wife is a man's neighbour. The husband, the wife's" (57).

As in Ngugi's fiction, most of Farah's characters are emblematic ideological constructs, refined to reflect dialectical, binary polarities in which the middle terrain is not sufficiently populated or adequately nuanced. However, the narrative does possess cardinal merits of depth, psychological intensity, and symbolic symmetry, enhanced by a "rigorous exactitude in language" (Ewen 192). Farah's work has often been *explicated* within quasi-Marxist or feminist contexts, even though some may perceive a contradiction in being a feminist and a Muslim male writer. However, if one looks carefully, one can discern that the foundational frame of Farah's ethics is hinged on Islam. He condemns the corrupt politics of the cynical, self-serving exploitation of the name of Islam so as to manipulate the masses while maintaining a stifling grip over them. A regime that claims to be based on "Marxist-Leninist Islam" is being obscenely manipulative in its adoption of labels. The reference to the General's ninety-nine names and to the slogan that there is "no General but the General" is a perverted plagiarization of the Qur'anic reference to Allah's ninety-nine names and to the Muslim declaration of faith that "there is no deity but Allah." Emblematically, in *Close Sesame*, the members of the underground cell, including Deeriye's son, all have Qur'anic names of angels: Mursal, Mukhtar, Mahad, and Jibriil. These four toil haplessly toward restoring social and political justice, guided, at least metonymically speaking, by the spirit of Islam.

Significantly, Mursal, who has written a Ph.D. dissertation on the political relevance of the Qur'an in an Islamic state, discusses with his father the totalitarian regime's lack of legitimacy by referring to specific figures in the early period of Islamic history when schism and turmoil reigned between the idealistic, yet outnumbered, adherents of the faith led by the figure of Imam 'Ali, the Prophet's cousin and the fourth Islamic Khaleefa, and the wily, opportunistic figure of Mu'awiya, the governor of al-Sham (Syria). The conflict was neatly concluded with the assassination of the brave and pious 'Ali, while performing his prayer, and by Mu'awiya (spelled Mucaawiya in the novel) declaring himself a Khaleefa, and later illegally appointing his inept son Yazeed as a successor. According to the great Muslim philosopher, Ibn Rushd (1126–98), Mu'awiya was the first person to corrupt the principles of Islam by establishing, in the name of Islam, the first dynastic system of governance in Muslim history: that "dynasty became notorious for running the Empire for its own benefit as though it were its personal fief" and its tyrannical practices were "more characteristic of the pagan age than of Islam" (Glassé 408). Describing Mu'awiya's sly style whereby "religion was sidetracked and political considerations given preference in affairs of the state" (64), Rafiq Zakaria argues that as "a master tactician, he used every device at his disposal: some of his enemies were cowed by threats, others by war, and the rest by tact and diplomacy. There was no election, no selection, no nomination: his was plain and simple usurpation of power by force" (62). Mu'awiya thus set the precedent that became the norm to be followed by a series of ruling families in the entire Muslim world until today, including, ironically, some "hereditary" republican states. The name of Mu'awiya's son, Yazeed, is associated with the most shocking event in Islamic history. At the battle of Karbala (680 CE), his troops massacred all the male descendants of the Prophet, except for a sick boy; more gruesomely, they slew and decapitated al-Hussein, the Prophet's beloved grandson, and triumphantly carried his head on a spear into Yazeed's court. That massacre of the Prophet's family, beleaguered and grossly outnumbered by Yazeed's troops, led to the grand schism in Islam between the majority Sunnis and the minority Shi'a. The Shi'a and some Sunnis regard Mu'awiya and his dynasty as usurpers of power from its legitimate claimants, that is, the Prophet's descendants, and regard Yazeed as one of the most odious figures in early Islamic history.[1] Farah cleverly exploits the name of Yazeed ("Yaziid" in Farah's spelling) for its anagrammatical connection with the name of Ziiyad Bare, the Somali dictator. This becomes apparent in the following conversation between Mursal and Deeriye:

> "Just two points. Tell me, Father, with what do you associate the names of Mucaawiya and Yaziid?"
> "That is point one?"
> "Point one. Yaziid and Mucaawiya," he repeated and wouldn't continue until Deeriye answered.

"The first with usurpation of the Caliphate, according to some Islamic historians anyway, I mean according to the Shicayte [*sic*] interpretation of the events as we know them; the second with tyranny, Yaziid that is."

*"Yaziid: you can say that name again!"*

There was a brief silence in which both said the name "Yaziid" softly, with Deeriye looking alarmed when he got the meaning, the historical connection, which any Somali would get from a play on the name. (13)

The subtle discourse here signifies that a tyranny that usurps power, terrorizes the citizenry, and violates human rights can in no way be called Islamic because it violates social Islam's twin concepts of *'Adl* (justice) and *Rahma* (compassion), with the latter taking precedence when the situation merits. One of the established traditions in Islamic governance is that when *'Adl* prevails in society, fear of the ruler disappears among the citizenry because the ruler is guided by principles regulating the behavior of the ruler and the ruled and the code of conduct between them. Both the ruler and ruled are watched over and ultimately judged by Allah and open criticism of the ruler is not only tolerated but encouraged. In such a theoretical context the *Amir* (leader or ruler) is not only a self-sacrificing servant of the community, but also a role model for integrity, discipline, and generosity. For believers across the Muslim world, the Prophet's practices and authenticated statements during his tenure as the leader of the nascent Islamic Ummah represent the foundational criteria for just governance. Despite his status as both the spiritual and political leader of the Ummah, the Prophet used to consult with his followers, especially in situations of crisis, soliciting and encouraging people to come forward with ideas. A shining example of this consultative approach is the crucial decision that he took to adopt the sage advice of Salman the Persian—one of his pious companions, parodied by Rushdie in his *The Satanic Verses*—to dig a deep trench around the vulnerable southeastern part of Medina to protect the city from the invading army of Quraysh in the battle of the Trench (627 CE); the plan was a stunning success and Medina and its outnumbered Muslim defenders were saved. Not only is the ruler enjoined in the Qur'an to conduct régular *Shura* (consultation) with the people in matters of collective concern, but the ruler is also obliged to act humanely and transparently. In contrast to this paradigm of governance, the General's regime, with its elaborate security services, embodies efficient state brutality. Fear dominates all layers of society to the degree that even friends and relatives could be suspects of betrayal or spying: to the reader, the fear is so effectively palpable throughout Farah's *Trilogy* that "one feels relieved to have got out of the book[s] safely" (Ewen 202). In this "republic of fear," the General brooks not the slightest criticism and is in no mood for transparency:

The masses must be kept guessing. The masses are inferior, they cannot in any case understand how a government functions, they cannot appreciate this or that. No one is sure what will happen; no one is certain who will come knocking on your door; no one must be in a position to know in advance what will take place. (*Sardines* 140)

Cruel and corrupt, tyranny is then an anathema to Islam. Moreover, the energy associated with Islam's emergence swept aside, in theory at least and at the initial stages, clannish concerns, and any distinction among the community of believers that is based on race, tribe, or class. Fidelity in faith and in deed was the cardinal criterion. The regime that Farah condemns in his fiction unscrupulously tramples over every edict of good governance in Islam, yet it does not hesitate, when expedient, to wrap itself in a veneer of Islamic slogans to the farcical mongrelization of Islam and Marxism-Leninism. This grotesquerie is magnified through a motif of madness. Throughout the novel, madness, "a discourse . . . without grammar" (206), is a signifier with multiple layers of derangement. First, the system itself is mad, causing total destruction of the country and ruling over a people that hates its cruelty and obsession with surveillance. Second, the Sayyid, Deeriye's idol, has been described by the British as "the Mad Mullah" (30) to taint his reputation. Third, the regime's efficient system of terror pushes the most educated and conscientious members of society into madness. This is illustrated in Khaliif's case, a former civil servant terrorized by the security forces to madness; ironically, his madness shields him from persecution and turns his uninhibited voice into a symbol for the raging conscience of the people silenced by an unscrupulous dictatorship. More importantly, the madness motif is also illustrated in the resort of the four members of the underground cell to hazardous acts, rendering them, in effect, mad. As Deeriye's daughter, Zeinab, puts it, "We're witnessing a world gone mad" (110). In other words, madness becomes a metaphor for the degeneration not only of the government system from being dutifully just and compassionate to being cruel and corrupt, but also for the degeneration of the country's best minds toward risky, futile acts of desperation.

It is perhaps within the context of desperation, though not necessarily madness, that one can give a possible explanation of Deeriye's final act of defiance to the regime in his attempt to assassinate the general. This futile act seems "out of character" for Deeriye, represented throughout as devout and contemplative. Theoretically, assassination in Islam is not allowed because it involves treachery and taking an unfair advantage of a foe. However, the late Iraqi writer, Hadi al-'Alawi, an exiled Marxist, wrote a book, titled *al-Ightiyal al-Siyasi fil Islam* (Political Assassination in Islam), arguing against the grain of the majority of Muslim historians that in some exceptional cases the Prophet condoned the assassination of a select few of his influential enemies who were otherwise reluctant to fight in open combat (15–37). Besides, two of the four Rashidi Khaleefas (that is, the righteous four who led the Muslim community following the Prophet's death) were assassinated: the second, 'Umar ibn al-Khattab, and the fourth, Imam 'Ali. More importantly, Mu'awiya, founder of the Ummayad dynasty, himself a survivor of an assassination attempt, is known to have used poisoned dishes of honey as a way of eliminating his enemies and rivals: it is rumored that he has once claimed that "Allah has soldiers made of honey" (al-'Alawi 67). While Farah craftily shrouds Deeriye's resolution to "meet" the General with numerous ciphers, one can see that there is an evolution in the position of the pious Deeriye, whereby he shifts from being a passive, if conscious, political witness in his old age to an activist and a practitioner of *lex talionis*, responding to the murder of his son, Mursal, by the General's secret security. His attempt to assassinate the General fails when his gun gets, significantly enough, entangled with his prayer beads. Norman Cary reads Deeriye's daring move as a "quixotic gesture which costs him his life but does not seem to weaken the regime" (119). On the other hand, Derek Wright gives a faithfully polyvalent reading of Farah's text:

> While in one version, the rosary impedes the weapon, in the other version it has *become* the weapon. The prayer beads replace the gun, which plays no part in the event. In one version, Deeriye fails to shoot the General in any sense; in the alternative version he shoots the tyrant down—not with gun-fire, but with the holy purifying fire of Islam, the idealistic religious ardour of the zealot. (29)

Deeriye's shift from passivity to activism is obviously spurred by numerous motives. As a devout Muslim, he is first urged by a sense of justice. The Prophet has urged the believers not to remain indifferent to evil: "When you see an evil act" he enjoined the faithful, "you have to redress it with your hand; if you could not, then with your tongue; if you could not, then condemn it in your heart and that is the minimum manifestation of faith." Within the context of this edict, one can see that Deeriye is pursuing the first category of action prescribed; he takes the matter into his own hands; his unsuccessful attempt on the life of the General becomes an act of justice rather than revenge. Obviously, Deeriye, certainly not a delusionary Don Quixote, is perceptive enough to know that the pursuit of justice in this case is a perilous exercise and that the outcome would be "'either of the twin blessings' of which the Prophet spoke: *victory or martyrdom*" (143). In his religion-steeped imagination, martyrdom reaps him an additional promised reward: a reunion with Nadiifa, beckoning to him as the "houri" assigned to him "*on earth as well as in paradise*" (198). Accordingly, the novel's political discourse, as Derek Wright perceptively argues, is resolved by "the sacrificial logic of martyrdom and the eschatological life of the soul" in which "death . . . is envisaged as triumph not defeat; as an access to power, not loss of it" (29).

With the collapse of Ziiyad Bare's regime, his fleeing the country, and his ignominious death in exile, and with the dictatorship causing the country to degenerate into an insufferable clannish chaos, one might be tempted to regard Farah's work, especially his politically specific first *Trilogy*, as being dated. Such a proposition would be valid if Farah's work were functional propaganda pieces. Given the complex patterning of the narratives and the psychological layers depicted in them, Farah's works are obviously bent on exposing a state of affairs that is not confined only to Somalia but disastrously prevalent in Muslim countries, especially in the Middle East. There is no shortage of despots and tyrants whose mocking brutalities and lethal practices still operate so efficiently that their iron-fist rules surpass Kafkaesque and Orwellian dystopias in the depth and dimension of their horror. Like the works of Nadine Gordimer exposing apartheid's grotesquerie, Farah's play a variation that could be easily applied to many other self-proclaimed generals: Somalia is but one gulag out of many that distressingly extend so wide afield. Moreover, Farah's novels point to a visionary insight that despotism of any ideological or theological guise is an aberration carrying the seeds of its own demise. Such narratives have an enduring quality.

While Farah's writings reveal keen concerns with African issues, he sees himself as having more in common with writers of Islamic heritage such as Tayeb Salih, Tahar Ben Jelloun, and Salman Rushdie rather than with other African authors of Christian background such as Chinua Achebe, Wole Soyinka, and Ayi Kwei Armah: "They quote from the Bible consciously. I don't" (qtd. in Jussawalla and Dasenbrock 50). Needless to say, Farah is just as engaged as these writers are with matters of race, the ravages of European colonialism of Africa, and the consequent deformities of neocolonialism, leading to the emergence of local despots. However, he nuances the particularity of his own artistic identity by highlighting the fact that he has "been brought up in the narrative richness of *The Thousand and One Nights*" (qtd. in Jussawalla and Dasenbrock 50): as an illustration, one can see that the very title *Close Sesame* is derived from one of the Shahrazadic tales. He adds that his fiction is "metaphor-based, leitmotiv-based [*sic*] writing, which is also Islamic, because Islam is a very symbol-conscious culture" (Jussawalla and Dasenbrock 51). While these statements suggest Farah's de facto cultural identification with Islam, he is not uncritical when it comes to the treatment of women. In response to a clichéd question put to him that "there is something about Islam that is distinctly anti-women," he retorts, "[n]ot more than other faiths. For Islam, Christianity, and Judaism, the book religions,[2] as we call them, take the same sort of hostile, male-oriented position vis-à-vis women" (qtd. in Jussawalla and Dasenbrock 56). This statement is double-barreled in its being a defence and a critique of Islam: he rejects labeling Islam *alone* as being misogynistic, while he acknowledges the hostility toward women that is often committed in the name of Islam. Significantly, Farah's stance here echoes a similar position taken by a Muslim feminist, Rana Kabbani, who argues that "Islam is regularly singled out as the religion which subordinates women. In reality all three monotheistic religions, Judaism and Christianity as well as Islam, are equally dominated by male establishments. All must be condemned on this score or none" (15). Indeed, Farah's novels resonate with an engaging sympathy with the aspirations, frustrations, and agonies of his female characters. His condemnation of female genital mutilation alone—a non-Islamic practice that takes place among Muslim, Christian, and animist communities in Africa, yet is erroneously associated with the name of Islam—is one of the distinguishing features of his narratives. Moreover, he also condemns other egregious practices such as polygamy, denying women access to education, and the whole patriarchal, clannish attitude that victimizes women.

Despite Farah's nuanced, reverential stance toward Islam, his depiction of Deeriye's genuine faith is conveyed through a sober tone in this novel that is the favorite of its author, who thinks it will outlive all his other works (Pajalich 69). The affection that Deeriye shows toward the three women in his life (his wife, daughter, and daughter-in-law) demonstrates that one can be a devout Muslim male *and* respectful of women. Similarly, Deeriye would see no contradiction in "being a Sayyidist, a Somali nationalist, and a Pan-Africanist all at the same time" (201). Likewise, Deeriye sees no contradiction in fighting both colonial occupation of his country and neocolonial tyranny inflicted on it. Functioning as the Jamesian "central intelligence," Deeriye articulates one of the novel's sharpest statements: "We Africans did not struggle against the white colonialists only to be colonized yet again by black nincompoops" (84). Accordingly, in *Close Sesame*, elegantly defined by Maggi Philips as a "mosque of word" that is "deeply theological and structurally unified" (193), Nuruddin Farah succeeds in presenting Islam as a metaphor for resistance to both colonial and neocolonial tyrannies and in reverentially depicting it as a potent factor that permeates the national animus for justice and self-assertion.

FOUR

# The Qur'anic Paradigm and the Renarration
# of Empire: Abdulrazak Gurnah's *Paradise*

My ink is black; do not ask me to paint a rainbow.
                    —Muhammad Sa'eed al-Sagar, exiled Iraqi poet

IT IS A WELL-KNOWN FACT THAT ALL MUSLIMS CONSIDER THE QUR'AN
the primordial source for spiritual, social, and legal reference. The hold that this
holy text has maintained over the lives and imaginations of the believers has
been solid and pervasive for over fourteen centuries in large segments of the
world. No sign of erosion of its centrality has emerged; on the contrary, its
agency is spreading to new regions such as Europe, North and South America,
and Australasia. Even non-Muslim intellectuals are becoming increasingly cog-
nizant of its vitality as an authoritative text of profound impact on contemporary
reality. For instance, in *The Western Canon*, Harold Bloom refers to the Qur'an,
which he includes in his list of seminal works for "the theocratic age," as "the
crucial work" and warns that "ignorance of the Koran is foolish and increasingly
dangerous"; it is significant not only "for its aesthetic and spiritual power" but
also "the influence it will have upon *all our future*" (497; emphasis added). However, few non-Muslims are aware of the Qur'an's narrative content: the Qur'an
tells of the exemplary stories of many prophets and messengers who preceded
the Prophet Muhammad, and hence have been embraced by Muslims as part of
the holy Muslim family of Allah's chosen few. (A prophet [*Nabi*] is someone to
whom Allah has been revealed without being called on to propagate the vision,
while a messenger [*Rasul*] is instructed to go a step further by declaring the faith
and delivering the message; hence, every messenger is a prophet but not vice
versa.) The intent here is to link Prophet Muhammad (being the final messenger) with the chain of Middle Eastern prophets, to celebrate their monotheistic

55

declarations, and advance the concluding message through the definitive discourse and narrative of the Qur'an and the Prophet's tradition (his practices and pronouncements). One can thus see that the Qur'anic narratives serve both theological and strategic purposes by positioning Islam firmly and unequivocally as a monotheistic faith whose primary proclamation is "There is no god but Allah and Muhammad is His Messenger."

It is instructive to observe here that the Qur'an contains no detailed narrative involving the Prophet's life. In fact, the name Muhammad is mentioned in the Qur'an only 4 times, while, for instance, Isa (Jesus) is mentioned 25 times, Ibrahim (Abraham) is mentioned 69 times, and Musa (Moses) is mentioned 136 times.[1] Since the Prophet himself used to cite and refer to these Qur'anic narratives, they have become entrenched and enshrined in Muslim collective memory as a valuable inspirational treasury. Anyone who reads Naguib Mahfouz's ingenious, allegorical novel *Children of the Alley* immediately recognizes how Mahfouz's masterpiece creatively adheres to the Qur'anic paradigm and respectfully reconstructs the monotheistic version of creation, expulsion from Eden, and then the appearance of the three monotheistic messengers, to conclude with the alley's experience with a new "messenger," symbolizing science/knowledge.[2] Mahfouz succeeds in maintaining the narrative in harmonious integrity on both allegorical and realistic levels. The alley represents old Cairo not only with its bustle and ambience of crowded daily life, but also as a microcosm for the world. On a minor scale and of less cosmic signification, Abdulrazak Gurnah's narrative strategy in *Paradise* is to adopt specific features of a single Qur'anic narrative, derived from "Surat Yusuf" (chapter 12), and reconstruct it in an East African setting during the early years of the twentieth century.

By recalling a narrative rooted in the Qur'an, and before that in Genesis, the novel foregrounds, through this layered palimpsestic project, two holy texts, as if to rekindle an Abrahamic linkage ravished into amnesia by contemporary cultural confusion or interreligious hostility.[3] Moreover, Gurnah deploys a Foucauldian formula of a double-layered power drama: a private tier involving a trio (Yusuf, Uncle Aziz, and his wife, Zulekha), and a grand one concerned with British–German rivalry to dominate and exploit Africa in spite of the natives' resistance.

Gurnah is one of the least recognized "postcolonial" novelists: after six novels ranging from the promising to the elegantly accomplished, no serious in-depth analysis has been published about his work thus far, except for the occasional review. Even after the shortlisting of *Paradise* for the 1994 Booker Prize, the critical oversight persisted, a curious phenomenon indeed that tells more about the temperament and politics of scholarship than about works that deserve highlighting. At any rate, *Paradise* is not only Gurnah's most skillfully engaging work, but also his most discursive evocation of Islamic motifs, adapted and situated to cross-border African loci in the period preceding the

First World War. As a coming-of-age novel, *Paradise* traces the rites of passage of the handsome hero, Yusuf, from a twelve-year-old boyhood shackled into servitude as a *rehani* (a human pawn) in exchange for his father's debts, to the troubled paralysis of youth heading toward indentured military service in a European war in Africa.

While the focus of the novel is projected on Yusuf's sense of evolving identity within his circumscribed world and limited choices as a young *rehani*, the novel situates Yusuf's fate within a context of conflict involving Africans, Arabs, Indians, and Europeans. In this respect, Gurnah covers the same terrain that M. G. Vassanji has charted in his two novels *The Gunny Sack* (1989) and *The Book of Secrets* (1994). Vassanji presents the events from the perspective of the Isma'ili Muslims who have moved from India to Eastern Africa to work as traders and low-ranking functionaries in German and British colonial administrations. Vassanji (himself an Isma'ili) treats the collaborationist Asians with sensitivity and subtlety. Gurnah, on the other hand, presents the events from the perspective of the Swahilis and Arabs. There are hints to the Arabs' role in the slave trade, yet the Zanzabari Arabs (Gurnah's ethnic affiliation) are treated with a similar degree of sensitivity to that of Vassanji's Isma'ilis, referred to fictionally as Shamsis. Both writers, however, reserve their overt criticism for the Europeans, with Gurnah being the severer critic of the two. While Vassanji refers, not without irony and humor, to the severity and harshness of the Germans' punishment, especially their notorious "khamsa ishrin" (twenty-five lashes) as seen in *The Gunny Sack* (14), Gurnah highlights in numerous incidents their arrogance: "They [the Europeans] had no eyes for anyone, and strode about with a look of loathing" (69). The Europeans' superior attitude is illustrated in the scene where the German administrator renders his prompt, rough justice in the conflict between Uncle Aziz and Chatu, the African chieftain; he disregards the Africans surrounding him, ignoring their look as he chooses to wash himself in front of them: "At last the European came out of his tent, his face red and creased with sleep. He washed himself thoroughly as if he was on his own and not surrounded by hundreds of people" (170). Significantly, all the Africans, in their multiplicity and diversity, realize that the Europeans have power, political and military, and that they are in Africa to loot and ravish the land:

> The traders spoke of the Europeans with amazement, awed by their ferocity and ruthlessness. They take the best land without paying a bead, force the people to work for them by one trick or another, eat anything and everything however tough or putrid. Their appetite has no limit or decency, like a plague of locusts. (72)

In one of the central statements uttered by the hermitlike Hussein, the novel's prophetic and moral voice, he observes astutely:

> I fear for the times ahead of us. . . . Everything is in turmoil. These Europeans are very determined, and as they fight over the prosperity of the earth they will crush all of us. You'd be a fool to think they're here to do anything that is good. It isn't trade they're after, but the land itself. And everything in it . . . us. (86)

Hussein's foresight specifies that the damage will not only be economic and political but cultural as well; he perceptively predicts that Eurocentric historiography shall be inculcated into the minds of Africa's future generations:

> We'll lose everything, including the way we live . . . and these young people will lose even more. One day they will make them spit on all that we know, and will make them recite their laws and their story of the world as if it were the holy word. When they come to write about us, what will they say? That we made slaves. (87)

Part of the ease with which the Europeans take over the country is the mythology that develops around them. Even a sadististic sexist like Mohammed Abdalla, Uncle Aziz's henchman, is scared of them:

> We are told they can eat metal and have powers over the land, but I can't believe this. If they can eat metal, why shouldn't they be able to eat us and the whole of the earth? Their ships have sailed beyond all known seas, and are sometimes the size of a small town. . . . I saw one in Mombasa some years ago. Who taught them to do these things? Their houses, I hear, are built with marble floors that shine and gleam so softly that a man is tempted to pull his cloth up a few inches lest it should get wet. Yet they look like skinless reptiles and have golden hair, like women or a very bad joke. (120)

As Uncle Aziz's journey to the interior fails, there is a pervading sense of resignation among the Africans and the Arabs that "the Europeans and the Indians will take everything now" (176), and the conclusion of the novel confirms that the victors are the Germans and the English as well as their collaborationist Indian traders. Yusuf's joining the German recruits makes the defeat total and turns the idyllic dream of paradise into the excremental squalor and a looming lethal chaos in which Africa becomes a war zone for an intra-European war. In an ironic twist to the Qur'anic heroic tale of Yusuf breaking free from his slavery, leading Egypt out of its famine, and reuniting with his beloved parents, Gurnah's Yusuf squanders his maturing strength by exchanging one form of slavery for another (a less honorable one at that), and thus the signal of his total surrender.

While the novel's palimpsestic enterprise evolves from the Qur'anic paradigm, *Paradise* interlinks schematically with two other novels set in Africa: Joseph Conrad's *Heart of Darkness* and Tayeb Salih's *Season of Migration to the*

*North.* These three novels are patterned on a narrative trajectory focused on deciphering an enigmatic, enchanting figure that assumes an all-embracing spell over the follower. Similar to the unfolding of Marlow's fascination with Kurtz, "the nightmare of [his] own choice" (121) in *Heart*, and the unnamed narrator's consuming curiosity about Mustafa Sa'eed in *Season*, the process of enchantment to be followed by demystification in *Paradise* is indexed to a physical journey: through rites of passage, an exploration of inner self evolves, leading toward fresh insights of universal implications. For obvious technical reasons, the narrative voice in *Paradise* is not granted to Yusuf's inexperienced, semiliterate perspective, yet is kept very close to his fledgling perceptions. Thus, instead of getting the mature, secure feelings of a surviving narrator as in *Heart* and *Season*, who tells the tale with the encapsulated wisdom of hindsight and "after the fact," we gain in Gurnah's novel the immediacy of action, propelled toward an abrupt, open-ended closure. While Conrad's and Salih's novels conclude on a sly note of hopeful, if dejected, affirmation of life's complex values, Gurnah's comfortless closure, clinching Europe's total terror over Africa, leaves the reader "with smarting eyes" (246).

While the Europeans totally dominate at the continental level, Uncle Aziz dominates at the interpersonal level. As Hamid, his minor trade partner, says, "His name suits him perfectly" (70). The word *Aziz* appears in the Qur'an with two meanings: "al-'Aziz" is one of Allah's ninety-nine names meaning "the Exalted" or "the Almighty". It also appears in "Surat Yusuf" as the name of Pharaoh's prominent courtier (the Potiphar) who buys the young prophet Yusuf as a slave and brings him to his wife—whose name, according to Muslim tradition, is Zulekha:

> And the man in Egypt who bought him said to his wife, "Treat him honourably. He may prove useful to us or we may adopt him as a son." (Ayah 22)

In either sense of the word, al-'Aziz is associated in the Qur'an with power; as a potential adoptive father, it also suggests the power of the patriarch. Moreover, in the novel, except for Yusuf, all those who deal with Uncle Aziz address him or refer to him as "Seyyid" (master), including his young second wife Amina (229). Needless to say that the choice of the name Aziz together with the two other names in the triumvirate (Yusuf and Zulekha) is intended to prompt an immediate evocation of the Qur'anic source. This Oedipal triangle, that predates Oedipus, is shaped and maintained by a power dynamic of Uncle Aziz's engineering.

At once kind and cruel, generous and exploitative, sympathetic and sinister, Uncle Aziz is the novel's complex construction and most remarkable achievement. Couched in ambivalence, he represents the quintessential Foucauldian power figure. Enigmatic with a charisma, he is often described in conflicting appellations as "a champion merchant" (186) or a "champion cut-throat" (20). He may be a "crook" (88) who takes young *rehanis* from his debtors and unconscionably exploits them as slaves, yet he charms them by his elegant poise and relaxed smile. He may be the "son of a devil . . . possessed by the daughter of Iblis [Satan]" (202), yet when the tribal sultan (chief) Chatu, an African Kurtz and a greedy hoarder of ivory, waxes merciful, after looting Uncle Aziz's merchandise and killing some of his men, Uncle Aziz retorts bravely and emphatically with the cardinal Islamic concept that "Mercy belongs to God" (162). His concern with the religious rituals seems genuine: he observes his prayers, reads "Surat Ya Sin" (chapter 36, which Muslims consider to be the heart of the Qur'an) during the burial of his dead men. Like a devout nonalcoholic Muslim, he refuses, at his peril, to drink beer, and when the African sultan asks him mockingly, "What kind of cruel god is it which doesn't allow men to drink beer?" He courageously replies, "A demanding but just God" (140). A consummate professional trader, he treats the men he hires correctly and looks after them when sick; Yusuf even sees tears in his eyes when Chatu's men severely beat Mohammed Abdalla.

This ambiguity toward Uncle Aziz is effectively conveyed through young Yusuf's spontaneous awareness of the wily merchant's "strong and unusual odour, a mixture of hide and perfume, and gums and spices, and another less definable smell which made Yusuf think of danger" (3); like animals who use scent to sense predators, Yusuf's sense of smell here is instinctual and psychologically compelling. Reserved and aloof as he is, he nevertheless shows his warmest affection, as much as he can demonstrate it, to Yusuf; as Mohammed Abdalla tells Yusuf, "He has a place in his heart for you. . . . Do you know why he feels kindly to you? Because you are quiet and steadfast, and at night you whimper at visions none of us can see. Perhaps he thinks you're blessed" (173). Uncle Aziz often casts a protective mentor's eye toward Yusuf and encourages him admiringly by marveling, "How you have grown on this journey" (174). However, because he keeps Yusuf as a *rehani*, one is justified in being suspicious of such a praise; one senses that Uncle Aziz cherishes Yusuf in the manner of a businessman who prizes a precious possession that proved to be a successful investment.

Obviously, the references to Yusuf's steadfastness, quietness, and having dreams in the novel recalls Yusuf's Qur'anic namesake, albeit in a holy context: the Qur'an emphasizes prophet Yusuf's steadfastness in his faith, his resistance to temptation, his lovingly gentle manners, and his ability to interpret dreams, an ability that symbolizes Allah's reward for his virtues. The novel foregrounds reductively all these qualities as well as the element of male beauty in a subtle, evocative gesture of acknowledgment of the Qur'anic source. Accordingly, one can argue that the Qur'anic narrative functions as a flexible frame of reference reworked so as to suit contemporary discourse. This palimpsestic project, however, cannot be accessible to the non-Muslim reader who may not be aware of the Qur'anic context, but that is a calculated authorial risk worth taking. Moreover, in a certain sense, Yusuf can be seen as an emblem for the lone, innocent, visionary, or the exiled intellectual, or the marginalized "third worldist" cut off from his roots and left vulnerably rudderless in a confused, confusing universe where greed and lethal conflicts reign. It is an unprincipled world where the rules of the game are blurred and the demarcation lines are constantly shifting according to the dictates of the power wielders, both local and global. Symbolically, competing tribal and colonial powers dictate the route of Uncle Aziz's trading caravan, expediently charted to avoid contacting them. Yusuf's confusion about his kinship with his Uncle Aziz only exacerbates his anguished quest for identity and, conversely, makes him more insistent on calling him "Uncle" instead of "Seyyid," which is everyone's term of subserviently addressing Aziz. In such a controlled context, Yusuf's consciousness is shaped and indexed by his awareness of power. Power also circumscribes his sexual awakening, another signifier of maturity. Uncle Aziz not only wields wealth and power but also seems to enjoy sexual privileges; he alone has two wives, while his closest aides are left languishing in privation. The men relieve their urges in predictably less satisfactory ways: Yusuf through furtive touches or masturbation; Khalil through an old woman, Ma Ajouza, in exchange for money; and the brutal Mohammed Abdalla through forcefully sodomizing the men under his charge.

The old Ma Ajouza's playful sexual overtures to Yusuf foreshadow the latter's more serious advances to Amina, Uncle Aziz's second wife. While the Qur'an portrays Yusuf's manly beauty as a reflection of his purity and inner beauty, the novel foregrounds Yusuf's beauty as a sexual asset that endears him not only to women, young and old alike, but also to the men on the journey who anticipate wrongly that he might fall prey to Mohammed Abdalla's sodomistic snare. While Yusuf physically and sexually survives the perilous journey, his awareness of his sexuality develops to such a degree that he is ready to take initiatives on his own, such as proposing to Amina to elope with him.

Abdullah Yusuf Ali, the prominent Qur'anic translator and commentator, ventures a fascinatingly fanciful speculation about al-'Aziz and his marital life. Citing the *Encyclopaedia Britannica*, he argues that the highest court officials in ancient Egypt were eunuchs and that the terms *court officer* and *eunuch* were "practically synonymous":

> The 'Aziz, we may assume, was a eunuch and childless. His wife, whom our tradition calls Zulaikha, was nominally his wife. She was a virgin. Our poetical tradition says that she was a princess from the West who saw [Yusuf] in a dream first and fell in love with him. (556 n. 1659)

This suggestion of sexual impotence provides a subtle motivation for al-'Aziz's "wife" to pursue sexual fulfillment in the predestined figure of her dreams, Yusuf. Likewise, the novel's childless Aziz strikes the reader as being asexual, in spite of his having two wives. Aziz, powerful and patrician, covers up his implied impotence and compensates for it by a consuming passion for trade and travel that keeps him away from his walled-in wives for lengthy periods of time. Correspondingly, Yusuf's emerging sexuality signifies his transition into manhood and a growing awareness of the circumscription of his freedom. Yusuf's overture of love to Amina signals a thirst for freedom and a rare attempt at warmth and intimacy.

Despite flashes of warmth and spells of affection, Gurnah's world is quintessentially loveless and tragic: the harshness of the experiences undergone allows little room for hope or humor. It is a vision of a sinister reality in which values are twisted cynically and systematically in both private and global spheres. Overtures toward love and beauty, communion with nature, and access to the potential world of dreams are either aborted or twisted into sordidly violent nightmares of vulgarity, exploitation, and cruelty.[4] While the Qur'an holds hope and promise of paradise for the virtuous, such a possibility does not exist in the concrete reality of Gurnah's Africa, where fear and power prevail over the pursuit of love and freedom. In such sordid situations, decency becomes a lonely, wretched enterprise whereby silence or departure (or both as the novel's conclusion indicates) becomes the inevitable course of conduct. Hope, here, is a dear commodity: paradise, the Qur'anic promise of bliss and beauty, is hard to envision, especially in the light of Amina's perceptive pronouncement, "If there is Hell on earth, then it is here" (229).

Yusuf's last gesture, joining voluntarily a European army to go to war, is not a private act of courage but a senseless exercise of futility that engenders collective consequences. Depressingly, it is an abandonment of his two closest friends, Khalil and Amina, to their fate under Uncle Aziz's firm, if gentle, tyranny. Thus, Yusuf's dominant instinct is embodied, finally and ironically, in survival not solidarity, flight not fight, change of masters not challenge to oppression. The conclusion carries a fatal note of despair rather than a triumphant affirmation of the individual's sense of destiny. This is indeed an ironic reversal of the Qur'anic Yusuf whose crowning achievement of grace, intelligence, and wisdom becomes "an instrument of the providence of God" and an "exemplar of the conjoining of prophecy and power" (Cragg 171, 172); Gurnah's Yusuf devolves into a nihilistic signifier or, at best, an ambiguous denial of the possibility of salvation amid an ambience of fear, squalor, and waste. As Jacqline Bardolph observes, "the bitter taste at the end of the novel gives an ambivalent meaning to the title: precolonial Africa was and was not a paradise. The novel recreates [sic] a bygone era which has its romance but does not sentimentalize the past" (78).

With an analeptic trajectory toward the early twentieth century, the novel thus presents a countercolonial retrospective in the luminous tradition of "postcolonial"/"third worldist" texts such as Achebe's *Things Fall Apart* and Ngugi's *A Grain of Wheat*, except that the colonial power condemned here is European in general and, as one critic argues justifiably, that the novel "is clearly not a liberationist text," and that "the novelist's construction of the African response to colonisation as essentially receptive puts him at odds with other East African writers, most notably the Kenyan dissident, Ngugi wa Thiong'o, whose later fiction, in particular, celebrates the continuity and strength of African resistance" (Schwerdt 92). While Gurnah's discourse intimates the futility of resistance and befogs the prospective of freedom, its sheer exposure of the efficient ruthlessness of European colonialism makes its critique forceful and effective to the degree that it reveals the ravishes without being bound to offer an alternative vision: this strategy is marked by the absence of an enabling exit agenda. Likewise, while Gurnah's narrative is firmly anchored in the Qur'anic paradigm, its vision is radically different. In Surat Yusuf, Ayahs (verses) 2 and 3, the Qur'an introduces the narrative as "ahsanal qissas" (one of the most beautiful of stories), "la'alakum ta'qiluun" (so as you [believers] may acquire wisdom). The wisdom derived is that when foresight, fortitude, and forgiveness are gracefully and steadfastly maintained, paradise is reachable. Gurnah deliberately twists the message: paradise is not possible because purity and beauty cannot survive in a world corrupted by greed and dominated by the cold calculations of power figures of the like of Uncle Aziz and his operative, Mohammed Abdalla, that "hard-hearted twister of souls without wisdom and mercy" (34). Thus, "when the ceremony of innocence is drowned," hope becomes rare. Uncle Aziz's garden, which in Yusuf's imagination is evocative of the Qur'anic *Jannah* (garden-paradise), is nothing but a mirage. Prophet Yusuf's Qur'anic dreams and his gifts for interpreting them are Allah's rewards for his purity and piety, endowing him with wisdom and enabling him to ascend to political power. In the novel, the dreams are conversely metamorphosed into squalid nightmares about which Yusuf is derided by a sexist, foul-mouthed figure like Mohammed Abdalla (whose name recalls the Prophet's in a puzzling parody of the Prophet's qualities of grace, courage, and compassion), or at best to be teased about, as when Amina punningly banters him, "I could tell you were a dreamer. . . . When I watched you in the garden I imagined you were a dreamer" (229). The relationship between Amina and Yusuf, which holds promise and potential, has to be aborted to serve the novel's nihilistic agenda. (Indeed, Yusuf sexually consummates none of his relationships with any of the women he comes close to in the novel.) In the same vein, the novel's two positive voices, Hussein and Hamdani, are convulsed and contained into the irrelevance of an angry hermit and a semisilent singer, respectively. Moreover, the novel contains, in its carnivalesque polyphony, the strident counter-Qur'anic voice of the Sikh mechanic Kalasinga—a fascinating fictional construct that recalls the fleeting figure of the harlequinlike Russian in Conrad's *Heart of Darkness*—who proclaims, "I'll be in paradise screwing everything in sight, Allah-Wallah, while your desert God is torturing you for all your sins. . . . To that God of yours almost everything is sinful" (102).

Gurnah thus decontextualizes the Qur'anic paradigm from its Islamic cele-brational source and uses it for a secular political message. Islamic aesthetics has always maintained a linkage between art (such as arabesque, calligraphy, music, and literature) and spirituality. Gurnah cannot subscribe to such a linkage be-cause his discourse seems to suggest that man neither deserves paradise nor har-bors the hope of making it possible, at least not yet.[5] While Gurnah does succeed in producing an engaging multilayered narrative, his complex paradoxical dis-course at once blunts and enhances its anticolonial ardor. The novel's final im-pact, while diverging from the hopeful inspirational aesthetics of the Qur'anic source, devolves, especially in its dim, scatological closure, toward defeat and de-spair; the novel's dark, if enchanting, irony signals here that only Kurtzian hor-ror reigns in the Euro-colonized paradise of Africa.

# FIVE

# Exilic Contexts, Ambivalent Affiliations:
# M. G. Vassanji and Adib Khan

That who lost gold, may find replacements in the gold market
That who lost a beloved, maybe within a year will forget
But that who lost a homeland, where would he find it?

—popular Iraqi song

ONE OF THE MOST CRUCIAL QUESTIONS MUSLIM WRITERS IN English face today involves the demanding identitarian affiliations that manifest themselves at emotional, cultural, linguistic, or political levels. This challenging situation has been precipitated by the global phenomena of immigration and exile, by-products of European imperialism and its aftermath. According to Miriam Cooke, Muslims "can think transnationally while retaining deep connections with a specific place, whether it be of birth, of choice, or of compulsion" because Muslims' identity is "geographically flexible" and "oscillates between diaspora and origin" (xxii). Neither static nor uniform, the diasporic/exilic context encompasses both a state of mind and a condition of reality: migration, double, and even triple migration. Indeed, as the Canadian writer M. G. Vassanji observes, "We live in an age where [sic] exile is becoming the normal state" (qtd. in Kanaganayakam 132). Specifically, as Muslims move from South Asia, the Middle East, and Africa to English-speaking societies such as Britain, North America, or Australia, their adoption of English as a medium of livelihood and survival becomes obligatory. Previously, as colonized subjects in their country of origin, many of them might have had an option because their erstwhile encounter with English had been regulated by the degree of their contact with British colonial administration and, for a minority of collaborators, by the scope of their interest in aligning themselves with the colonial enterprise.

65

For the majority of the colonized population, they could always fall back on their native culture and its institutions as a resistance shield against colonial culture. For instance, the Qur'anic schools in Algeria were strikingly successful sites of preserving Arab-Islamic culture against decades of colonial Frenchification policy. Faced with a situation of exile, the writer's sensibility is naturally challenged by a multiplicity of affiliations that avail or impose themselves. Writers as diametrically diverse as V. S. Naipaul and Salman Rushdie acutely probe, negotiate, and represent varied degrees of ambivalence toward these multiple affiliations within contexts of shifting values and constant flux. The ensuing discursive formations, often hybridized, are illuminated by an awareness that exile is, in essence, a destabilizing situation of being at the interstices of borders and cultures, an awareness that confronts the writer with the polemics of ethnicity, historicity, and politics, on the one hand, and textuality and narrative strategy on the other. Anyone who studies the narratives in English by Muslims who write in an exilic environment, such as Farhana Sheikh, Ahdaf Soueif, M. G. Vassanji, and Adib Khan would notice a profound preoccupation with liminality and shifting boundaries, articulating in the process a complex phenomenon that I wish to call "ambivalent affiliations": it is a situation whereby multiple factors and bonds, often conflicting, lay claim to the individual's identitarian sensibility, yet none of which is quite fulfilling by itself.

## M. G. VASSANJI

The differentiating marker of M. G. Vassanji's work from that of other Canadian writers is its vibrant, affectionate depiction of the double migration of his South Asian characters. These, mainly Indian Muslims of the esoteric Isma'ili (referred to fictionally as the Shamsi) sect,[1] make their first voyage to East Africa in the late nineteenth century as part of the labor mobility within the British Empire, working as semiskilled laborers, small traders, and junior colonial functionaries. As such, they are installed as a buffer zone between the indigenous Africans and the colonial administration. The second voyage begins in the 1960s and 1970s from postindependence Africa toward Europe and North America. As Vassanji's narrative indicates, this second wave of migration by his characters is prompted by racial tension (between native Africans and those of South Asian ancestry) and socioeconomic changes as the now mostly South Asian comprador class finds its privileges radically curtailed or threatened with the rise of African nationalism.

This saga of global uprootedness and unstable migration is dramatized in Vassanji's first four works of fiction: three novels, *The Gunny Sack* (1989), *No New Land* (1991), and *The Book of Secrets* (1994), and a collection of sixteen stories, *Uhuru Street* (1992). Significantly, these four works are interlinked by cross-references to episodes, events, and characters that appear in more than one work, as if suggesting that such is the impact of certain images and experiences residing in private or collective memory that they have the power to emerge and reemerge indefinitely.

*THE GUNNY SACK AND UHURU STREET*

The instigating narrative impulse for *The Gunny Sack* is a gunny sack bequeathed to the narrator by his feisty grandaunt Ji-Bai; the sack crowdedly contains an infinite number of stories, chronicling the private and communal histories of four generations of an Indian family that immigrated to East Africa. The narrator Salim gives focus, drama, and diversity of tone to this otherwise seemingly random recuperation of *temps perdu.* Salim evokes his namesakes in V. S. Naipual's *A Bend in the River* and Salman Rushdie's *Midnight's Children.* More importantly, Vassanji affirms that his choice of the name was prompted by its inclusive ambiguity:

> . . . my initial reason was to choose a name which was deliberately ambiguous, one which could be both Indian and African, and thus describes my narrator. And Salim lends itself to such a duality; as does Juma, the surname. I knew that both Rushdie and Naipaul had a Salim but that did not bother me. I was doing something different. (qtd. in Kanaganayakam 128)

That Salim interfaces his Proustian recollections with the sack's stories about his family's and community's collective histories, not all of which are pleasant or dignified, illustrates the casting of the narrator's lot with the fate of his ethnic group. This strategy represents one of the common features of "third world"/"postcolonial" narratives, whereby characterization signifies not an exercise of isolation but a deliberate endeavor at contextualizing an individual's destiny within that of a family's, an ethnic community's, or a nation's.

The narrator's effortlessly astute blending of the private and the public is enhanced by his self-conscious attempts (verging occasionally on the metafictional) to present an elliptical, unofficial, unorthodox history through mingling modes and moods, introducing realistic details of high drama to be closed off fancifully and anticlimactically, and interjecting fictional fabrications with historical facts and figures. Breaking away from conventional models of nineteenth-century English novels, the narrative begins not from the beginning, as the narrator's English schoolteacher Miss Penny Mrs. Gaunt would probably exhort him to do, but from the end; instead of introducing a hero or a major character, the iconoclastic narrator introduces a sack:

> Memory, Ji-Bai would say, is this old sack here, this poor dear that nobody has any use for any more. Stroking the sagging brown shape with affection she

would drag it closer, to sit at her feet like a favourite child. In would plunge her hand through the gaping hole of a mouth, and she would rummage inside. Now you feel this thing here, you fondle that one, you bring out this naughty little nut and everything else in it rearranges itself. Out would come from the dusty depths some knick-knack of yesteryear: a bead necklace shorn of its polish; a rolled-up torn photograph; a cowrie shell; a brass incense holder; a Swahili cap so softened by age that it folded neatly into a small square; a broken rosary tied up crudely to save the remaining beads; a bloodstained muslin shirt; a little book. (3)

Appositely nicknamed Sheru, after the resourceful heroine of *Alf Layla wa Layla* (The Thousand and One Nights), the sack assumes henceforth a centrality parallel to that of Shahrazad:

Now Ji-Bai's bones clatter in my sack.

It sits beside me, seductive companion, a Shehrazade postponing her eventual demise, spinning out yarns, telling tales that have no beginning or end, keeping me awake night after night, imprisoned in this basement to which I thought I had escaped.

(There should be no misunderstanding. This drab gunny is no more Shehrazade than I am Prince Shehriyar. She is more your home-grown type, a local version, good at heart but devoid of grace—yet irresistible—whom I name this instant Shehrbanoo, Shehru for short. Shehrbanoo, Shehrazade, how close in sound, yet worlds apart.) (5–6)

Anthropomorphizing the sack is certainly no innocent or minor register; it represents an affirmation, an umbilical linkage to the narrative tradition of Islam, with which the narrator feels aesthetically and emotionally at home. However, for Vassanji's characters, as with Rushdie's, Islam, while a source of self-definition, is more of an ethnocultural qualification than a theological weltanschauung.

Since the gunny sack configures emblematically as the embodiment of the community's collective memory, one needs to investigate the criteria whereby the narrator chooses and displays the historical data. As the new historicists would affirm, the study of history is a process: selective and fictive. A narrativized history such as *The Gunny Sack* is no exception. For instance, although the narrative depicts the harshness of German colonization of East Africa (especially its cruel, humiliating system of whipping: the notorious *khamsa ishrin*)[2] there are scant references to the atrocities of British colonial rule. Ngugi's *A Grain of Wheat* readily comes to mind as a clear contrast to Vassanji's depiction of the same period. Of course, history is in the eye of the beholder or projector; we do not have one history but histories, which are products of perspectives. This conscious, selective amnesia/recall process becomes further evident in the narrator's preoccupation with the corruption and inefficiencies of postindependence institutions, on the one hand, and the racial conflict between native Africans and Asian-Africans on the other.[3] For instance, in *The Gunny Sack*, we encounter graphic details about the cruelty and carnage of the racially motivated coup in Zanzibar in 1964, an event that struck terror into the heart of the narrator's community; these scenes anticipate Adib Khan's depiction in *Seasonal Adjustments* of the chilling massacres committed by the Pakistani army in Bangladesh in 1971. What Vassanji's novel does not say about British colonialism is more important than what it says: there is an ellipsis, a subtext that needs to be probed. One can interpret Vassanji's "glossing over" the oppression of the British period as an indication that a significant segment of the South Asian community in Africa was enjoying a relatively convenient modus vivendi with the colonial authorities. Appropriately, this lacuna is filled in Vassanji's third novel, *The Book of Secrets*. The collaborationist situation seems to have evolved as a result of the common colonial practice of "divide and rule," whereby a minority is given a semblance of privilege in discrimination against the subjected majority. Correspondingly, such a practice naturally finds a receptive response from a minority community keen on survival and security:

> Among the trading immigrant peoples, loyalty to a land or a government, always loudly professed, is a trait one can normally look for in vain. Governments may come and go, but the immigrants' only concern is the security of their families, their trade and savings. Deviants to this code come to be regarded and dismissed as not altogether sound of mind. (*Gunny Sack* 52)

Such an attitude was bound to create resentment among African natives because they saw betrayal and opportunism on the part of the South Asian immigrants. As well, the immigrants, whether tradesmen or colonial functionaries, were seen as accomplices to British colonialism, in whose vested interest the South Asian immigrants were lured toward Africa. While the sea contacts between India and East Africa dates back deep in history, British imperialism gave them "impetus":

> ...when the need arose, Britain turned to the subcontinent, bringing over hundreds of people as plantation workers, railway builders, clerks, customs officials, policemen, and soldiers. In the latter categories Asians were thus placed in a position of authority, by a foreign power, over the indigenous majority. Caught between the ruling whites and the black Africans, the Asians stayed together, forming communities which, although the years passed, did not integrate and thus did not lose their *distinctive identity*. (Sarvan 512)

Consequently, a stark cleavage is created between the native Africans and the Asian-Africans, leading to an understandable resentment on the part of the first group, who may regard the second as an "exploiter class, a dukawallah, mere agents of the British, these oily slimy cowardly Asians" (*Gunny Sack* 228). Indeed, this racial conflict becomes a major motif in *The Gunny Sack* and in several stories in *Uhuru Street,* specifically in "Breaking Loose," "What Good Times We Had," "Ebrahim and the Businessmen," and "Refugee." The Asian community's implication with the colonial establishment (albeit at a subservient or, at best, junior level) and its real or perceived unwillingness to integrate with the indigenous Africans became the two condemning counts struck against it. Balancing off the seemingly privileged perspective accorded the Asian community, the narrative presents the alternative point of view through Amina, the militant Africanist with whom Salim falls in love. The following dialogue cogently illustrates the issue:

> "Why do you call me 'Indian'? I too am an African. I was born here. My father was born here—even my grandfather!"
>
> "And then? Beyond that? What did they come to do, these ancestors of yours? Can you tell me? Perhaps you don't know. Perhaps you conveniently forgot—they financed the slave trade!"
>
> "Not all of them—"
>
> "Enough of them!"
>
> . . . And what of *your* Swahili ancestors, Amina? If mine financed the slave trade, yours ran it. It was your people who took guns and whips and burnt villages in the interior, who brought back boys and girls in chains to Bagamoyo. Not all, you too will say. . . . (211)

Moreover, Amina articulates her resentment against white supremacist humiliation of Africans:

> Do you know what it was like to be an African in colonial times, Indian? It was to be told that no matter what you achieved, you were ultimately a servant. Miss Logan our headmistress once took me aside and told me, "Amina, my ayah has gone away, could you help me for a few hours today?" My ayah has gone away. . . . After all this, what of self respect? How many years before we regain it? I look at an Indian or a European, and I wonder, "What *really* does he think of me?" How can one *not* be militant? (211)

The Salim-Amina relationship assumes a symbolic, ideological signification, yet the fact that it goes nowhere indicates the difficulty of integrating the two communities. However, in the conclusion of the short story "Breaking Loose" the possibility for "trying to break away from tribalism" (*Uhuru Street* 90) appears more promising. Earlier in the story the heroine, Yasmin, is chided by her mother for befriending an African: "With an Asian man, even if he's evil, you know what to expect. But with *him?*" (87). Significantly, Yasmin resists her mother's edicts; her epiphany comes about through an educated awareness of the inevitability of change:

> The world seemed a smaller place when she went back to the University. Smaller but exciting; teeming with people struggling, fighting, loving: surviving. And she was one of those people. People, bound by their own histories and traditions, seemed to her like puppets tied to strings: but then a new mutant broke loose, an event occurred, and lives changed, the world changed. She was, she decided, a new mutant. (88)

Although the narrative in *The Gunny Sack* and *Uhuru Street* is predominantly focused on the South Asians and their construction of a self-defensive cocoon in Africa, the narrator assumes a degree of ironic distance in this complex, politically charged discourse. What ultimately emerges is a discernible sense of ambivalence, whereby loyalty, commitment, or affiliation is mutant not fixed, interim not everlasting, relative not absolute.

## NO NEW LAND

This condition of ambivalent affiliation is replicated in *No New Land,* where the Asian-African immigrants in Canada are shown negotiating the sense and status of their belonging to yet another continent, country, and culture to which they once more had to immigrate. Referring to his own status as an "immigrant" writer in Canada, Vassanji states, "I have been called an Afro-Asian and I thought that that was rather apt, it describes my origin—but I am other things as well. Africa and India mean a lot to me. I am not an immigrant who believes that you leave everything behind. In the modern context, with what we know and observe of the whole world, that notion of immigration is simply weird" (qtd. Kanaganayakam 130). This statement serves as a useful index to explain many characters' dilemma in both *The Gunny Sack* and *No New Land* as they face the transience and flux of their exilic destiny. Unlike *The Gunny Sack,* in which "Vassanji combines an encyclopaedic memory with magisterial literary technique" (Birbalsingh 102), his second novel is concise, condensed, and "crystalline," to borrow an Iris Murdoch term; it is of a lesser scope and ambition, but nonetheless equally engaging and refined. In a certain sense, *No New Land* commences where *The Gunny Sack* closed off, despite the introduction of a fresh cast of characters.

The novel succeeds by projecting an image of a community beleaguered in yet another harsh, alien environment, if only superficially polite. It tells the experience of an Isma'ili Muslim family newly arrived in Canada from Dar es Salaam, Tanzania,[4] with the narrative primarily projecting the perspective of the father, Nurdin Lalani. *No New Land* opens with the startling revelation that Nurdin is charged with sexually assaulting a woman, when actually he has tried to offer her help on seeing her in distress. The tragicomic story of the Lalanis is complemented by the reflections and insights of their contemplative friend Nanji, who lives his own complex, private drama concerning frustrated love, intimidating racism, and an inordinate preoccupation with existentialist angst. Nanji's ruminations refine and elevate the discourse toward conceptual and abstract levels of expression; his sharply nuanced sensibilities speak for Nurdin's inarticulate bafflement with a new culture in which he is not sure how to fit. The narrative trajectory operates by correlating and blending these two segments, progressing toward its closure with the final arrival of a long-awaited avatar, appropriately named Missionary, who, in the manner of a deus ex machina, happily helps settle all outstanding scores.

Like its preceding novel, *No New Land* is permeated by a sharpened sense of history. The first chapter concludes with a crucial statement about the need to make peace with the past prior to proceeding ahead: "We are but creatures of our origins, and however stalwartly we march forward, paving new roads, seeking new worlds, the ghosts from our pasts stand not far behind and are not easily shaken off" (9). Missionary's function involves liberating Nurdin from the ghost of his autocratic father, inescapably "operat[ing] like fate" (20). This linkage between patriarchy and tyranny recalls one of the major motifs in Nuruddin Farah's novels, especially *Sweet and Sour Milk*; however, whereas Vassanji confines paternal autocracy within familial circles, Farah gives it a global, intensely political dimension. By the end of *No New Land*, deliverance is achieved:

> Missionary had exorcised the past, yet how firmly he had also entrenched it in their hearts. Before, the past tried to fix you from a distance, and you looked away; but Missionary had brought it across the chasm, vivid, devoid of mystery. Now it was all over you. And with this past before you, all around you, you take on the future more evenly matched. (207)

The interplay of the past with the present operates through eye imagery: while the stern look of the father pierces through the portrait in Nurdin's Toronto apartment, the CN Tower, "the concrete god who [doesn't] care" (176), "blinks unfailingly in the distance" (59). Missionary not only redeems the past but also anticlimactically demystifies the dominant symbol of the new:

> As he sat down on the sofa he called out playfully, "Eh, Nurdin. I see you've installed a goddess in your building, downstairs. Where is the god?"
> Nurdin, standing near the window, played along, gesturing at the Master in mock seriousness. "Come, Missionary, I will show you."
> The Master, with a smile and twinkle in his eye, got up and walked through the congregation and stood beside Nurdin. "There," said Nurdin,

pointing out the window into the distance. "There is our god. But he is a deep one. Mysterious."

The Master chuckled. "Ah, the CN Tower. I have been to the top of it, many years ago. Excellent restaurant." (186)

More important, *Missionary* settles, rather blithely and cavalierly, one of the key questions that runs through Vassanji's fiction: namely, when and where this flux of mutation is going to cease. Canada, despite all its imperfections, proffers the odyssey's conclusion: "He sat back with a satisfied sigh. Canada to him was a veritable Amarapur, the eternal city, the land of the west in quest of which his community had embarked some four hundred years ago. This was the final stop. He was very happy" (198).

However, this idyllic finale, filled with hope, harmony, and humor, does not conclusively clarify the central issue of affiliation to and with the new land. This indefiniteness, this ambivalence is understandable in the case of Vassanji's characters. The instability of double migration—hopping continents, trading cultures, and negotiating marginality—has prevented them from establishing roots. They have become, to use Rushdie's phrase, "bastard [children] of history" (*Imaginary Homelands* 394). It is not that the immigrant or the exile does not desire affiliation, but often he or she wishes it on convenient terms; and even then the sociopsychic situation is such that the belonging is not quite firm. Neither does such an equivocation represent arrogance or cowardice, but rather a forced phenomenon of human reality. Moreover, this condition of ambivalent affiliation is prompted and complicated by ugly racism.

Blatant or subtle, racism has been a dominant theme in the works of almost all Canadian writers of "third world" roots. Vassanji's characters—whether in Africa, Europe, or North America—are hounded and haunted by racism, real or perceived; it hinders their progress and cripples their emotional and intellectual growth, inciting them to give survival an exceptional priority in their lives. Although perpetual striving for survival in the hostile currents of mutation is not necessarily joyful, it can promise rewards and excitement for the feisty (like the showy lawyer Jamal in *No New Land*). Modest figures such as Nanji and especially Nurdin, "one of literature's 'small' men" (Blaise El), are not so self-assured, and they have to find shelter, comfort, and inspiration from within the collectivity.

This regress into the communal cocoon is an innate strategy for survival. Significantly, it affects the narrative trajectory in such a way that Vassanji presents—consistently and concurrently—bifocal images of private dramas within communal crises. In a provocative review of *No New Land*, Canadian novelist Neil Bissoondath observes a weakness in this blending process of the private and the public: he argues that Vassanji "often fails to present his background material with sufficient subtlety, so that community submerges character (i.e. the individual)" (44). He further elaborates on what he labels as Vassanji's "problem controlling his material," manifested in

> the background becoming the foreground for no apparent reason save author-ial self-indulgence and that headstrong urge to present community instead of letting community present itself. This problem with point of view is troubling, for the reader begins to question who is telling the story, Nurdin or this anony-mous *omniscient* voice. The result is an unfortunate distancing, causing the book to read like a tale observed rather than experienced, and diminishing its ur-gency. The sociological eye, interested but unimplicated, weighs rather too heavily on the narrative. (45)

This severe criticism, if germane, overstates its case. As narrative constructs, Vas-sanji's characters (especially the two protagonists, Nurdin and Nanji) project a vi-brancy and integrity, convincingly distinct from their context. Besides, Bissoondath does not take into consideration the validity of the author's keen concern for correlating character with community to the desirable degree of his imaginative option: "I wanted," Vassanji would retort, "to write a kind of people's history, but make it personal" (qtd. in Smith 29). For his intents and purposes, Vassanji succeeds in blending the private and the public, the local and the uni-versal, the serious and the ironic, thereby establishing himself as an accomplished Canadian writer of a distinct voice, vision, and technique. What we have here then is an exciting divergence of perspectives about authorial intention. Unlike Bissoondath, Vassanji gives an emphatic sociocultural role to the writer

> . . . as a preserver of the collective tradition, a folk historian and myth maker. He gives himself a history; he recreates the past, which exists only in memory and is otherwise obliterated, so fast has his world transformed. He emerges from the oral, preliterate, and unrecorded, to the literate. In many instances this reclamation of the past is the first serious act of writing. Having re-claimed it, having given himself a history, he liberates himself to write about the present. To borrow an image from physics, he creates a field space—of words, images and landscapes—in which to work with, and instal [*sic*] the present. ("Postcolonial" 63)

This is certainly a tough task and a tall order, but the sincerity of commitment is evident.

*THE BOOK OF SECRETS*

While memory is the narrative instigator in *The Gunny Sack*, a colonial text, a diary, is "the starting point for reclaiming history" (Kanaganayakam 133) in Vassanji's third novel *The Book of Secrets*. The diary, the titular book of secrets, is a clever interventionist instrument whereby Vassanji creates a colonial text then situates it within a context that foregrounds the limitations of the colonial perspective without necessarily condemning it outright. The driving impetus behind such a strategy is not only technical ingenuity, liminal insights, or polyphonic perspectives, but also a retaliatory discursive thrust that attempts setting the record straight. In almost every "postcolonial"/"third worldist" narrative, one can discern a political subtext that strives toward articulating a contradistinctive zeitgeist. There seems to be an urgency here to compensate for lost times, for denied opportunities, and for blank spaces in the narrative of empire that has erstwhile been occupied by what Michel Foucault calls *le discours dominant* produced by apologists of the colonial enterprise.

The novel is set in East Africa during three-quarters of a globally turbulent century of empire building and dismantling. The chronology commences in 1913 with the intrigues and machinations of two empires (the British in Kenya and the German in Tanganyika) determined to outmaneuver each other, thus extending their Great European war with all its carnage into other peoples' lands. Based on a Shahrazadic narrative pattern, this complex, layered novel opens with the narrator Pius Fernandes, a retired Goan schoolteacher of history in Tanzania, being entrusted in 1988 with a diary of an ex-colonial officer, Alfred Corbin, detailing his experiences as a newly appointed British administrator of a small town on the Kenya/Tanganyika border. This diary functions as a clever interlinking device, not only because it details what Corbin witnessed in 1913–14, but also because it connects with chains of events that span three generations and spread over three continents.

The novel's pivotal point is the enchanting, enigmatic figure of Mariamu. With a Swahili Muslim name that recalls the Virgin Mary, she is yet accused of being possessed by Shaitan (the Islamic equivalent of Satan); Corbin rescues her from harrowing exorcism and agrees to employ her temporarily as his housekeeper till she gets married to Pipa (meaning barrel), an ambitious shopkeeper. However, on her wedding night, Pipa accuses her of "impurity," of being deflowered by Corbin, leading to tantalizing suggestions throughout the novel that Mariamu's son, Ali, might be Corbin's, not Pipa's. Curiously, Mariamu's mysterious demise—gruesomely raped and murdered—endows her in Pipa's eyes with such spiritual powers that he erects for her in his shop an expiatory, syncretic shrine combining Hindu and Muslim symbols. Meanwhile, the abandoned child, Ali, is adopted by his Asian granduncle and African grandaunt. Growing into an attractive young man who impersonates in dress and manners the Isma'ili playboy Prince Aly Khan, Ali elopes with his Rita (à la actress Rita Hayworth) to England, where he becomes a successful international businessman. Significantly, Ali's mongrelized triple parentage, together with his subsequent triple marriages, symbolizes the three sources of cultural identity for the novel's Indian

Isma'ili community in East Asia (again, fictionally referred to here as Shamsis): Asia, through historical roots and religion; Africa, through settlement and trade; and Britain, through education and colonial affiliation.

This exciting, at times confusing, cultural hybridity emerges through the detailed drama of the community's triumphs and tragedies. The same community has been the resourceful inspiration of Vassanji's three earlier works of fiction. As there, the novel's political discourse is definitively, if imperceptibly, established. Unwanted and uninvited, the British–German war waged in Africa is not Africa's, but one more by-product of an arrogant imperial enterprise about which the Africans—despite the heavy sacrifices imposed on them—have no say. As an illustration of this coercive practice, Pipa, in an intriguing twist to the narrative, gets manipulated and forced into spying for both the British and the German intelligence services during the First World War. The reader feels the fear, suffering, and torture he undergoes while being coerced into a risky, cynical contract that he cannot comprehend.

The coercion is masterminded by a Captain Maynard, the ruthless secret service British officer who proudly code-names himself the Fisi (hyena). As the circumspect, historian-narrator Pius opines, Maynard "loved [Africa] and he hated it, above all he feared it for what it could do to him" (20). In a statement that recalls Kurtz's notorious motto in Joseph Conrad's *Heart of Darkness*, "Exterminate all the savages" (51), Maynard declares, "This is a savage country and could turn you into a savage. It is so easy to be overcome by its savagery, to lose one's veneer of Western civilization. This is what I have learned, what I dread most" (20). This one-dimensional Maynard exhibits no ambiguity in his perception and practices: he associates the white man with authority and order for which he needs to "show strength, fury" because, once again, "this is a savage country, it makes a savage out of you" (21). Through the Corbin/Maynard duality, the author aims at a subtle strategy to illustrate the complexity of the colonial claims: a sort of Apollonian/Dionysian pattern or a Dr. Jekyll/Mr. Hyde game. Thus, Vassanji highlights the humanity and civility of Alfred Corbin, a basically decent, if unimaginative individual who pursues a career in the colonial project for which Churchill has exhorted him to give "his whole life and soul" (13). Endowed with "a quiet, forceful diligence, a monastic rigour" (30), Corbin seems genuine enough in his belief that "the British empire, with its experience of ruling other lands and with its humane system, was the best nurturing ground for an emerging nation, for backward Africans and Orientals to enter the society of the civilized" (31). This all-familiar patronizing attitude is represented with milder irony than that of Chinua Achebe's compelling rendition of the district commissioner at the conclusion of *Things Fall Apart*, where the British officer callously ignores Okonkwo's corpse dangling from the tree, while he meditates on "the many years in which he had *toiled* to bring civilization to different parts of Africa" (147; emphasis added). In his brief for the imperial project, the retired Corbin claims years later, "We went with the best of intentions, to give our best" (329); however, he is also aware of Maynard's crucial role as the empire's iron arm: in a revealing entry in his diary, Corbin admits, "I cannot help thinking that if the blacks in my caravan decide to butcher me and my Indian, it would be Maynard or someone like him who would be sent to avenge us" (24).

The value of Corbin's diary resides not only in its revelation of the colonial mentality, in its careerist, correct, and seemingly benign attitude, but also as a narrative device to instigate and develop subsequent events while creating occasions for ironic readerly recognition of the rupture between appearance and essence, end and means, intention and results, claim and consequence.

Emblematically, the diary assumes a life of its own that is associated with the name (or spirit) of Mariamu. It was she who took or "stole" the diary together with the pen with which Corbin had been writing. This gesture on the part of the illiterate, silent subaltern represents a daring, subversive act that symbolically signifies a form of resistance, retrieval, and appropriation of the tools of the dominant discourse whose codes are to be deciphered a generation later. To the Africans, Corbin's diary is neither a private possession nor an ordinary item; the act of writing it becomes a mystifying metonymy for imperial power:

> They called it the book of our secrets, kitabu cha siri zetu. Of its writer they said: He steals our souls and locks them away; it is a magic bottle, this book, full of captured spirits; see how he keeps his eyes skinned, this mzungu, observing everything we do; look how meticulously this magician with the hat writes in it, attending to it more regularly than he does to nature, with more passion than he expends on a woman. He takes it with him into forest and on mountain, in war and in peace, hunting a lion or sitting in judgement, and when he sleeps he places one eye upon it, shuts the other. Yes, we should steal this book, if we could, take back our souls, our secrets from him. But the punishment for stealing such a book is harsh—ai!—we have seen it. (1)

As in *The Gunny Sack*, where "the wonder-filled" sack is anthropomorphized and nicknamed Sheru, the magic "bottle book" (2) here evokes once again *The Thousand and One Nights* and assumes mythological dimensions; as the historian-narrator states, "Because it has no end, this book, it injects us and carries us with it, and so it grows" (2). And grow it does beyond its time: it overreaches its epochal limits as it permeates the past, engulfs the present, and influences the future. Interestingly, the illiterate Pipa sees the diary as a posthumous repository of Mariamu's feelings with whom he tries to communicate in order to expiate his sense of guilt toward her as well as to extricate an answer about his agonizing question concerning whoever fathered Mariamu's son, Ali, nicknamed Aku:

So this was her gift to him; one which she, one day, some evening in better times, would have shown him had she lived? . . .

He was convinced the book contained the answer to his torment. What was the relationship between the ADC and his Mariamu? Was the boy, Aku, really his own? He could not read it, yet he would take this gift with him wherever he went. It was from her and she must be in it, described in it. The book contained her spirit. (172)

What evolves hereby is a parodic reinvention of the Holy Trinity: Pipa (the father), Ali (the son), and Mariamu (the holy spirit). Moreover, Pipa's Hindu–Muslim shrine for this English text to revere Mariamu evokes not only the scriptural, ecumenical dimensions of holy books prevalent in almost all religions, but also the complex cultural and political connections that evolve between the colonizer and the colonized, connections in which the Other is conceived (i.e., read) according to codes that fit the reader's perspective.

On the other hand, Pius, the novel's historian-narrator, initially sees the diary as "one forgotten fragment of an addendum to a well-documented history" (7). Realizing that the history of the empire is perhaps not that "well documented," he alters his view:

> Even before I began to pore over Corbin's entries which would subsequently so grip me, I could not help but feel that in some mysterious manner the book touched our lives; was *our* book. There was, I felt, much more there than the contents of its pages; there was the story of the book itself. Written here amongst us, later perhaps hidden, and now found among us, it must have left a long and secretive trail, a trail that if followed would reveal much about the lives and times it witnessed, and tell us why the diary finally surfaced where it did.
>
> I remember my moments of decision exactly—this book, this burden before me. It had, as I sat contemplating it, the aspect of a portal. (7–8)

Mariamu's appropriation of the diary thus establishes a lasting link between the colonized and the colonizer, a link from which there can be no "clean break" either political, historical, or cultural, even though this unstable link, as David Spurr argues, neither remains the same nor disappears altogether (6–7). Put differently, the act of colonization carries with it unforeseen consequences that go beyond the temporal and spatial dimensions of the act itself. If, as Thomas Richards asserts in *The Imperial Archive*, "an empire is by definition and default a nation in overreach" managing "the problems of control at a distance" (1), then naturally the act of forcing the empire to dismantle would carry consequences, moral as well as political, that pursue or haunt the colonizers in the metropolis— well beyond the site of colonial collapse or the moment of raising the flag of

independence—through diverse agencies of migration, political activism, destabilizing discourse, or revisionist historiography.

Apart from the diary and Mariamu, the novel's central construct of a historian-narrator, Pius Fernandes, lends focus and insight to the complex narrative
web of interlinked evocative events pointing in diverse directions. A Goan expatriate teaching history in Africa, Pius is conscious of his ambivalent affiliations; in
fact, few of the major characters in the novel have deep roots in Africa, if any:
most are either functionaries and officers of the colonial project or Indian mid-
dlemen and traders seeking a better life for themselves in the towns and villages
of East Africa. Recalling and reconstructing past events, retrieving and reading
earlier texts, Pius, with his "postcolonial" sensibility, is able to perceive his root-
lessness and reconcile himself with its reality, which for him and for the novel's
Shamsi community, is both liberating and tragic. A de facto custodian of confi-
dences and consciences, Pius offers his sage, if cautious, political commentary.
While he exposes the cruel practices of the colonial past, he occasionally veers
into critiquing Africa's neocolonial condition, before checking himself. He
hence describes the country on the brink of its independence, "preparing to
transmute . . . [and] bubbling with excitement":

> There was hope in the air, and a cheery confidence, symbolized in the
> promise of a torch of freedom to be mounted on the summit of Kilimanjaro
> for all to see, across the continent and beyond. If in later years bush-shirted
> demagogues waylaid those dreams with arid ideologies, and torpid bureau-
> crats drained our energies, at least we were spared the butchers. . . . But I am
> losing perspective. (273)

In another instance, when he describes a serene paradisal scene on the
Kenya–Tanzania border that was once an interimperial battlefield, Pius connects
colonial war savagery with neocolonial brutality: "What manner of men would
let these slopes be covered with guns, blood, guts? Alien, I say; then remind myself of the carnage our own leaders have wrought on the land" (179). Accordingly, through Pius's cautious critique, the novel's political discourse becomes
subtly and problematically formulated as a subtext.

Significantly, the conservatism of this truth-seeking Pius can be linked to a
cardinal character failing: he fears taking risks, ideological or personal. To his
credit though, Pius recognizes his own limitations and realizes that he has all
along been avoiding life's leading existential question posed by the poet Gregory,
his alter ego: "Would you do it again, has it been worth it?" (316). Lucidly, if
belatedly, Pius thus achieves his own epiphany, thereby mediating a profound and
exciting message about the transience and transcendence of being: "to live is to
take risk, and so you did not live" (317).

Pius's insights evolve in tandem with his awareness of the shift in his own attitude toward the "book": his impartial search for clues to solve the diary's intriguing puzzles assumes, in yet another astonishing twist in the narrative, a personal dimension. Rita, his former student and Ali's second wife, claims the diary in order to avoid revealing uncomplimentary aspects of her family's past. Rita's reappearance in Pius's life evokes his erstwhile silent, "impossible" love for her—a love that he dared not proclaim due to ethnic, religious, and social barriers. Now in his old age, Pius appreciates the significance of what his audacious schoolgirls used to reiterate to him: "the world belongs to the one who loves" (317), meaning to the one who risks engaging in a love forbidden by a repressive society. As the self-assured, now divorced, Rita impresses upon him, the present and the future can never be disentangled from the past; therefore, her children's nouveau riche status in Europe need not be jeopardized by "unnecessary" revelations about the past. In one sense then, Pius's surrender of the diary to Rita represents a compromise act, a gesture of genuine loyalty and love, signifying that our reading or telling of history is neither absolute, nor objective, nor out of context: we often proclaim and endorse that which is most convenient. A human construct, history, as with beauty, is in the eye of the beholder or reader. In another, it represents a compromising act, a betrayal of his commitment to truth, however tentative and partial that truth might have been: our narrator's pious pursuit of history veers to a self-gratifying indulgence in *his* story.

What we are witnessing here is the unmasking of the veneer of the aloof, impartial historian who hence has to admit and reconcile his own subjectivity. The surrender of "the book of secrets" is an act of silencing, a perpetuation of a lie. Ironically, in return for the diary, Rita gives him a gift of the newly published poetry book of his late colleague Gregory and an expensive pen that symbolizes the medium of depoliticizing Pius's future meditations while foreclosing the imperial dossier. Here it becomes obvious that the agenda of the neocolonial comprador class converges with the interests of the apologists for the colonial enterprise through the proactive agencies of discursive constraint, camouflage, silence, or amnesia. The challenge for the reader in such a situation is to recognize the merits and limitations of the novel's historian-narrator: sensitive and sympathetic yet vulnerable and collaborationist.

The impact of Vassanji's novel then is, to borrow an insight from Gayatri Chakravorty Spivak, to dislodge the metropolitan definition through "citation, reinscription, [and] rerouting the historical" (217). If what is academically labeled "postcolonial" (as distinct from postmodernist) literatures insist "on the historical as the foundational and all-embracing" (Gugelberger 584), then Vassanji's novel does that partly through interpolating Prospero's script "with a Calibanic viewpoint" (Gugelberger 581) despite the handicap in the narrator's representativity. The reader of *The Book of Secrets* is offered a site of an encounter, an interaction, with a colonial text that aches for a complementary or countertext; the Muslim, African, or "third worldist" text in English fills a lacuna and provides a setting not only to redress a balance but also to synthesize diverse discursive formations: the erstwhile oppressed, voiceless, or marginalized is now empowered to voice an alternative historiographical discourse that resists closure and "opens directly onto the fractures and contradictions of colonialist epistemology" (Spurr 2). Moreover, such an articulated text, operating well beyond derivative or conflictual praxes, demands new strategies for rereading, reevaluating, and reconstructing, and for taking risks with them—risks that are at once requisite and rewarding.

## ADIB KHAN'S *SEASONAL ADJUSTMENTS*

When awarding the 1994 Best First Book Award to Adib Khan's novel *Seasonal Adjustments*, the judges for the Commonwealth Writers Prize stated that "Khan has provided a Muslim voice to Australia's growing multicultural literature" (*Chimo* 40). Initially, one may wonder in what way does this engaging, elegant narrative represent a "Muslim" voice, especially when one finds such strong anticlerical statements in it and many of the characters who "claim" to be devout or practicing Muslims are seen acting lewdly, hypocritically, or exploitatively. As well, the references to the liberation war for Bangladesh and the evocative scenes of the 1971 massacres that the Pakistani army perpetrated against their Bengali coreligionists highlight the conceived notion of the collapse of Islam as an integrative force for the then two wings (East and West) of Pakistan. Maulana Abul Kalam Azad, the prominent Muslim politician and close ally of Jawaharlal Nehru, opposed the idea of the partition of the subcontinent as unworkable because geography was against it:

> Indian Muslims were dispersed in a way which made it impossible to form a separate state in a consolidated area. The Muslim majority areas were in the north-west and north-east. These two regions have no point of physical contact. People in these two areas are completely different from one another in every respect except religion. It is one of the greatest frauds on the people to suggest that religious affinity can unite areas which are geographically, economically, linguistically and culturally different. (248)

Presciently, Azad foresaw the breakup of Pakistan as early as 1957 when he wrote his autobiography: "No one can hope that East and West Pakistan will compose all their differences and form one nation" (248). The West Pakistani establishment considered the Bengali Muslims to be "half-Muslims," neither "true Pakistanis nor really pure Muslims" (qtd. in Moten 98). The Pakistani scholar Akbar Ahmed, who was a subdivisional officer in East Pakistan during the 1971 crisis, testifies,

"In East Pakistan I was horrified at the cultural insensitivity and plain arrogance of my colleagues. They were not only not seeing the coming storm but seemed to be inviting it. West Pakistanis in East Pakistan would routinely refer to the Bengalis as 'Bingo Bastards' or 'Black Monkeys'" (240). The carnage committed against the Bengali Muslims remains a stain on Muslim collective conscience and shakes one's faith in Muslim solidarity. It also foregrounds the triumph of ethnicity—rooted in linguistic, cultural, and regional concerns—over faith, especially when the latter was cruelly and conveniently exploited by the military and bureaucratic elites of West Pakistan.

More importantly, the narrator Iqbal's cynicism about Islam and his ignorance and revulsion of its rituals serve to dramatize the impact of time and distance on the analytical sensibilities of the hero and his current alienation from both his native Muslim/Bangladeshi culture and his adoptive, seemingly secularized Australian zeitgeist. However, one needs to focus on the discursive subtext as it reveals the narrator's reductive assumptions about Islam and its enduring values, especially when viewed "with borrowed eyes" (7). Caused by dislocation from his native land, alien views about Islam would only exacerbate the gap between the immigrant and his native land without necessarily endearing or reconciling him with his adoptive culture. The hero's confusion about Islam is an integral part of his overall disconnection from the family and friends whom he has left behind at the height of the Bangladeshi civil war. His flight has distanced him from his own people and created a void that he is trying to fathom without really being able to figure out how to fill it precisely since a satisfying alternative is not there.

*Seasonal Adjustments* is a novel about a *retour aux sources*, whereby the forty-three-year-old Iqbal returns to his native Bangladesh after an absence of eighteen years, during which he has married Michel, an Australian from a strong Catholic family, established himself as a teacher, and developed a small set of Australian friends. While his marriage is now going through a crisis of separation, his relationship with his twelve-year-old daughter, Nadine, who is accompanying him on his visit to Bangladesh, is the one shining constant in his life that is free from ambiguity and cynicism. Obviously, returning to one's roots connects closely with the concept of identity and the attempt to plumb the factors and forces that shape one's sense of self. Refined, conscious, and current sensibilities are influenced by a multiplicity of things emanating from transnational, transcultural sources. Insularity (whether ethnic, theocratic, or nationalistic) and purist versions of personhood are no longer tenable in a mobile, increasingly integrated, though not necessarily equitable, world. However, the return to one's roots to "go back to [the] source and find the past" (1–2) may seem futile, for one can never go "home" again and may never solve the riddles in one's life, yet it makes one, as Iqbal's case graphically illustrates, become acutely aware of the contradictions in one's constituent makeup, experience them, and by the end have a clear sense of their impact. Literature thus becomes a fertile terrain to explore emotional and cultural complexities through providing contexts, idioms, and themes to explore, articulate, and conceptualize.

The thematic framework of *Seasonal Adjustments* is informed by a binary conception of the hero's experiences shifting contrapuntally between two societies of diametrically diverse ethos. The narrative operates through a contrastive dialectic that foregrounds perceived irreconcilable polarities. In Bangladesh, feudal patriarchal structures and a corrupt antidemocratic military government dominate a nation afflicted with abject poverty, ethnic strife, and hypocrisy operating in the name of Islam. In Australia, success is measured by vulgar, vacuous commercialism and smug complacency that is often camouflaged in Christian rituals. While Iqbal's Australian in-laws want to baptize Nadine as a Catholic, Iqbal's family organizes a lavish ceremony to celebrate her *aqeeqa*, a Bangladeshi coming-of-age ceremony. Just as Iqbal's father-in-law, representing a "solid stalwart Church-and-Flag Establishment" (Liberman 12), maneuvers for a Catholic identity for his hybrid granddaughter, Iqbal's mother assumes a Muslim identity for her; just as Iqbal resists the imposition of Christianity on her, he tries to explain to his family in Bangladesh that she should not necessarily be assumed to be a Muslim. As well, the racism in Australia against immigrants and the Aborigines is paralleled by the racism in Bangladesh against the Biharis and the Hindus. In such a painfully polarized context, finding a harmonious, in-between terrain becomes a challenge.

*Seasonal Adjustments* is the most detailed narrative in English to date dealing with the alienation that the Muslim immigrant experiences on his return "home." Since the bulk of the narrative takes place in Bangladesh, it is instructive to observe the modulations of the narrator's feelings toward his native culture, religion, family, and friends. Iqbal admits that his alienation is caused by his "lack of communal empathy; a sense of non-belonging" (196), leading to his frustration with himself: "What upsets me most is my inability to slip back into a tradition I assumed was an integral part of me" (116). Spurned and self-consciously diminished in Australia, Iqbal feels detached, superior, and cynical, yet guilty and perturbed in Bangladesh. This mind-set becomes evident when he reflects on the abject decay and poverty in Bangladesh that he observes outside his privileged family surroundings:

> Are Bengalis, in some ways, naturally deficient? Do these deplorable conditions reflect a racial limitation which condemns us to perpetual abjection? As a race, are we destined to survive a technologically aggressive twenty-first century? I have made an effort to develop a mechanism of escaping the onslaught of such misgivings by reminding myself that I have adopted another country. These are not my problems. I shouldn't take them personally. The ploy does not succeed. I cannot remove the weight of this perturbation, this feeling of

frustrated sorrow and pain as if I were somehow on the outside of myself, watching my own slow death. (42)

Significantly, Iqbal, who in Australia refers to himself as a Muslim "in a way" (34), attributes the acceptance of the Bangladeshi poor of their sorry fate to the influence of Islam on them:

> It could have something to do with the acceptance of one's place in life deter-
> mined by the Almighty in His infinite wisdom. Who is man to dispute His
> Will? *We created man to try him with afflictions.* I recall the Koranic words I strug-
> gled to understand as a young boy. It was drummed into me from an early age
> that submission was the defining quality of Islam. I have never reconciled my-
> self to the notion of arbitrary suffering as a trial of faith. It must have been some
> form of genetic aberration which made me rebel against the acceptance of suf-
> fering and pain despite the assurances of a sublime meaning behind it all. That
> has not changed. I see as little dignity and purpose in the punitive harshness of
> life around me as I did when I was a practicing Muslim. (41)

Herein then lies Iqbal's complex confused attitude toward Islam. His equation of Islam with "submission" (which is a literal translation of the word *Islam*) is not accurate. Islam never suggests that one should blindly accept injustice or abject poverty. In fact, it induces agency toward righting wrongs. It urges believers to submit to no one but Allah. The Canadian Muslim scholar Jamal Badawi gives a lucid and concise definition of the key term *Islam*:

> It is derived from the Arabic root (SLM) which connotes "peace" or "sub-
> mission." Indeed, the proper meaning of "Islam" is the attainment of peace,
> both inner and outer peace, by submission of oneself to the will of Allah. And
> when we say submit, we are talking about conscious, loving and trusting sub-
> mission to the will of Allah, the acceptance of His grace and the following of
> His path. (2)

This surrender to Allah's supremacy, which in essence assumes an intimate inner authority that is abstract and nonfigurative, supersedes, theologically speaking, loyalty to state, race, party, and, in very exceptional cases, even fam-ily. This primary article of faith—universally required from Muslims irrespec-tive of ethnicity, class, or gender—frees the believers from fear or obligation to any authority that they do not willingly accept and gives an egalitarian va-lence to the faith that regards *all* as equal. In theory, this could be quite reas-suring: tyranny may prevail but for a while since Allah, the supreme sanctuary, will redress its ravishes. The same can be said about poverty, natural disaster, or personal affliction.

Iqbal's skewed interpretation of the phenomenon of poverty in Bangladesh is not only a misrepresentation of Islam, but is also a signifier of his lack of understanding of the cultural and political reality of his native society, toward which he cannot show the same degree of genuine, sacrificial involvement as Iftiqar, the journalist friend who functions as the novel's conscience. While Iqbal leaves his country shortly before the carnage preceding Bangladesh's independence in 1971—a departure that looks more like an abandonment than a flight for safety—Iftiqar joins the ranks of the freedom fighters. While Iqbal, caught between binary values and contrastive claims, has lost his grounding and resorts to flight, futile protest, or morbid cynicism, Iftiqar has no ambiguities about identity, values, or choices. A solid figure who does not compromise his principles or shirks from making daring, difficult choices, he is now a destitute, but committed and highly erudite, journalist whose writings expose the venality of a cruel military regime in Bangladesh. Iftiqar and his humorous friend, Zafar, the "martyr"/editor in chief of the journal he works for, are firmly rooted in the context of their culture, deeply care about their people, and selflessly risk life and personal comfort in a contestatory stance against a tyrannical military regime.

As foils to the narrator, Iftiqar and Zafar recognize the corrupt government, the exploitative elite classes, and the xenophobic cliques to be responsible for the disfranchisement of the people and both engage in praxis to right the wrong, yet Iqbal alone, by a morbid contrast, indulges in smug speculation by reductively blaming Islam for their abject condition. Indeed, his flawed fixation with Islam represents a significant segment of the narrative discourse. No passage shows his displeasure with Islam more provocatively than the description of the mosque he attends for an obligatory prayer:

> The mosque itself stands at the end of a *wretched* stretch of cemented *wasteland*, its massive dome rising like the *bald* head of a *helpless* giant, whose neck is *imprisoned* in concrete, to enshrine a landmark of *striking ugliness*. (187–88; emphasis added)

This short passage strikes the reader by its being devoid of any spiritual symbolism that a mosque usually evokes for a Muslim, especially for someone who has been away from his native land for eighteen years. More importantly, the quote is replete with distilled revulsion, suggested through the pejorative words italicized above. Such a choice of idiom reflects not only Iqbal's discontent, but also his sense of superiority over the people around him: it shows his disregard for the worshippers around him who may not see the mosque through Iqbal's "borrowed eye."

Iqbal's concern with Islam's staying power over his people, including to a certain degree himself, becomes a constant concern for him and occupies a significant portion of the novel's discourse. There are recurrent passages conveying Iqbal's harsh reflections about Islam and his arguments, albeit restrained and respectful, with his Bangladeshi family about his attitude toward Islam. His father's pontifical statement to him, hypocritical as it seems being uttered by an old man who keeps issues of *Penthouse* in his drawer, assumes, paradoxically enough, a certain validity and provides the reader, especially the non-Muslim, with an alternative referent:

> You are still a Muslim. You were born as one . . . you do not have a choice. You may have moments of private doubt about religion. We all do. But you cannot shake off your heritage. A tradition of 1300 years has shaped you. 1300 years! How can you deny yourself its riches. (249)

Significantly, Adib Khan in an interview with Rosemary Sorensen affirms this stance: "You may not be a practicing Muslim but there are certain fundamentals that are ground into you" (14). However, Iqbal does not seem to be interested in such a perspective: his exile in Australia has infused him with a new set of values that are revealed quite clearly early in the novel: "I am firmly entrenched in the self-centred ways of the world I have chosen to live in. I measure time not in terms of people and values but in relation to palpable achievements. I want to conquer life instead of live it" (8). Needless to say, this attitude is alien to the ethos of the Muslim world and does not endear him to his family who can discern callousness in him and openly criticize it, as his sister Nafisa does, qualifying it as "emotional stagnation":

> It is sad the way you have distanced yourself from people who should matter to you. You have always been so cautious about loving. Why do you treat love as an investable capital? If it doesn't pay handsome dividends, you want to withdraw your assets and go elsewhere. Why? (47)

Nafisa's diagnosis recalls the central statement in Iris Murdoch's novel *The Bell* that "all our failures are ultimately failures in love" (237). Significantly, Michel, Iqbal's wife, also points out this failure in love, when she confronts him by making a diagnosis similar to Nafisa's:

> You do not know how to love. . . . You never express your affections without appearing to be embarrassed. What is it with you? A severe congestion? Does love mean anything personal to you? Is it simply a four-letter world with vague philosophical meanings to titillate you intellectually? Does it ever come alive? Does it ever escape from the pages of books to become a living part of you? (48)

This "emotional stagnation" or "congestion" signifies spiritual paralysis, even death, which is emblematically illustrated by Iqbal's visit to the family graveyard and the senile caretaker's claim that "*Choto Babu* [i.e., Iqbal] is not in this life" (290). This suggests that to his family in Bangladesh he is, to all intents, dead: this macabre notion leads to an inevitable insight that dawns on him: "Despite my fears, I am afflicted with a morbid desire to finish here, near the house of my birth. To be buried in a foreign land is an inordinately cruel ending" (292). Interestingly, the novel's closure with the visit to the graveyard contrasts the opening with the visit to the river, which not only signifies flux but also evokes the potent Islamic symbolism of water being the source of life: the Qur'anic ayah states, "And we have created from water every living thing."

If Iqbal has returned to Bangladesh seeking solace and salvation, then he could be sadly disappointed. However, all is not wasted. His sojourn "home" as a detached visitor has endowed him with a rich set of observations and encounters that are bound to generate maturing insights. One such an encounter is with the assertive Nadira, his brother Hashim's friend, who impresses him by her oracular articulation of her vision of life as a former immigrant in England who, unlike Iqbal, has opted to return home and settle in Bangladesh:

> To regret would be to go back and rummage among the junk I have discarded. I am living with a new set of priorities. I am committed to them. Life can be such a creative act if you make the effort. I no longer treat living as if it is a treacherous enemy. It is subtle and full of obtuse meanings. I intend to devote my life to their discovery and understanding. (173)

As an alter ego or a feminine foil, Nadira's speech contrasts Iqbal's ambivalence and, like Ifiqar's choices and views, provides an alternative perspective in the discourse. It also creates a profound effect on Iqbal: "It makes me think that perhaps the terms of life are negotiable. Maybe life was not meant to be a linear, one-way motion. There may be opportunities for U-turns and diversions, for slowing down, for pausing to search for a previously missed niche in the haste to keep going" (173).

This is the locus of hope, if there need be such a pointer for the searching sensibility. Paradoxically, the conclusion also affirms the ambiguity of the immigrant's attempt at affiliation: ever locked on the horns of a dilemma, the immigrant copes with the malaise of his complex contemporary reality through brave recognition of his own ambivalent affiliations toward extended family, Islamic tradition, and Bangladeshi politics on the one hand, and nuclear family, fluid values, Catholic ceremonials, and Australia's evolving cross-culturalism on the other. If the intent, as the novel's prologue suggests, is for the narrator-hero to "go home" where he "really" belongs so as to "heal" in his "spiritual womb" (1–2), then a healing of sorts is achieved, but with the realization that home could be anywhere, yet the restless/resilient soul can belong nowhere. There are only temporary homes whose comfort and convenience are contingent on situational contexts. No wonder then that the narrative concludes on raised questions and eyebrows.

Adib Khan's depiction of Iqbal's ambivalent affiliations foregrounds at once the narrator's one-dimensionality when interpreting the life of his people, due largely to his geographical and emotional detachment from them, and the comprehensive relevance of Islam in all matters practical, interpretative, and spiritual. Islam's dominant sway accords individuals a context of meaning and a hopeful, if fateful or confining, sense to survive. Iqbal's oscillation between denial and acceptance of his Muslim identity suggests an affiliation of sorts: throughout, he is preoccupied with Islam's impact on his life. Thus, the novel's consummate depiction of the narrator-hero's ambivalent affiliation with Islam and through its constant engagement with its ethos, idioms, and metaphors affirm that Adib Khan has indeed "provided a Muslim voice."

## CONCLUSION

The twentieth century is not only the century of exiles, but also the century of multiple identities. Humanity's diverse heritages have "broken loose" (to use the title of Vassanji's story) of ethnic and geographic hegemony: cultural cross-pollination is a forceful facet of life in the age of globalization and instant communication. As Salman Rushdie puts it so colorfully, we need to celebrate "hybridity, impurity, intermingling, the transformation that comes of new and unexpected combinations of human beings, cultures, ideas, politics, movies, songs"; we need to rejoice "in mongrelization and [fear] the absolutism of the pure. *Mélange,* hotchpotch, a bit of this and a bit of that is *how newness enters the world.* It is the great possibility that mass migration gives the world" (*Imaginary Homelands* 394).

If Vassanji's discourse is consumed by community consciousness, Khan's is focused on the individual's sensibility. If Vassanji's narrative engagement with the ethos of Islam is indirect and subtle, Khan's is preoccupied with its impact on his characters' lives. While Vassanji and Khan each projects a distinctive style, context, and perspective, the appeal of their narratives resides in their ironic ridicule of the claim of ethnic or religious purists: half-castes, mixed ancestries, syncretic ideologies and beliefs, and cross-cultural encounters, relationships or marriages become dynamic occasions of challenge and potential. For instance, esoteric Shamsi rituals, being a blend of Hinduism and Islam, celebrate "thundering Allah as simply a form of reposing Vishnu" (*Gunny Sack* 7). As Vassanji lucidly puts it, "ultimately, I see myself as everything that's gone into me—Africa, India, Britain, America, Canada, Hinduism, Islam. The search for essences I find deeply offensive, it's a kind of fundamentalism" (qtd. in Kanaganayakam 130). Despite the characters' instinctive equivocation toward "others," and despite their justifiable gravitation toward their ethnic shelter, the narrative discourse suggests that the human in us is too outgoing, resilient, and receptive to be boxed into a single, tribalistic identification, snug as that may be. Gone then are the days of narcissistic unicultures, monoidentities; in come the ethos and mores of multiplicity and cross-culturalism. This brave new world may induce ambivalence, at times even confusion, but that is its challenging outlook.

The works of both M. G. Vassanji and Adib Khan demonstrate that immigration/exile away from *Dar al-Islam* (the world of Islam) creates not only metaphysical problems relevant to faith and spirituality, but also identitarian problems. Sharply and elegantly, they convey not only the contrastive values between the culture of Islam and that of exile, but also the characters' aching concern to find a safe, stable terrain to accommodate their hybridized, evolving sensibilities. These works do not offer definitive answers, nor are they to be expected. It is quite satisfying that they provoke polemics in humane and engaging ways. In such conditions of flux and ambivalent affiliations no neat discursive closure is possible.

# SIX

# Crisis Reading/Reading Crisis: The Polemics of Salman Rushdie's *The Satanic Verses*

Colonialism is not satisfied merely with holding people in its grip and empty-
ing the native's brain of all form and content. By a kind of perverted logic, it
turns to the past of the oppressed people, and distorts, disfigures and destroys it.
—Frantz Fanon

READERS MAY BE SURPRISED TO FIND SALMAN RUSHDIE'S *THE
Satanic Verses* included in a book about Muslim narratives in English, when the
author has unequivocally declared "to put it as simply as possible: *I am not a Muslim*" ("In Good Faith" 405). Moreover, how could it be a "Muslim" narrative
when the majority of Muslims who cared to read it felt offended by it? Others
who have not read a word of it are lividly revolted by the mere mention of the
book and its author.[1] However, since the novel's content and concern involve
crucial moments in the emergence of Islam, excluding Rushdie's narrative from
the discourse of this book would be an error of both omission and commission.
Paradoxically, yet understandably, Rushdie himself admits being a product of the
culture of Islam, despite belonging to a nonpracticing Muslim family: "religion
for me," he affirms in his short-lived, well-publicized "embrace" of Islam, "has
always meant Islam" ("Why I Have Embraced Islam" 430). Rushdie's most impressive work, *Midnight's Children*, is seen, by at least one critic, as "a Muslim
novel" because it "conveys the sensibility of Islamic alienation from the rest of
India" (Jussawalla, *Family Quarrels* 117). The name Rushdie has become so intertwined with the literary representation of Islam that no discourse on one
would be complete without referring to the other. Moreover, no text in the
twentieth century received such notoriety due to its religious content and the
angry response to it: banning and burning the book and condemning its author

to death. Thus, life in the literary world has never been the same since the book's publication in 1988. What we witnessed was an overwhelming crisis of reading, interpreting, and responding to a troubled, troubling text.[2]

Daringly and ambitiously, *The Satanic Verses* presents itself as a historiographical metafiction, deploying various tropes and encompassing multiple layers of signification, while operating within a postmodernist, counterculture context. Rushdie's strategy involves "pitting levity against gravity" (*Satanic* 3); its narratological slogan, inspired by *The Thousand and One Nights*, declares "it was and it was not . . . it happened and it never did" (35). Transcending time and space, the hybridized narrative moves synchronically (between England, India, and Argentina) and diachronically (between the present and the early days of Islam). Yet this impressively expansive narrative is consciously bounded by the doppelgänger motif, embodied by two survivors of a blown-up plane: Saladin Chamcha and Gibreel Farishta. These dual "angeldevilish" (5) heroes experience a series of tragicomic, fantastic-realistic episodes narrated in the usual Rushdiesque multilayered, multitoned fashion.

While Rushdie's two preceding novels, *Midnight's Children* (1981) and *Shame* (1983), touched off some controversy in India and Pakistan, respectively, the crisis caused by *The Satanic Verses* excessively and intensely surpassed the previous reactions; it assumed an unprecedented violence whose universal implications were/are bound to be damaging. Deplorably, the crisis, which "has been long, bitter and deep" (Rushdie, "Why I Have Embraced" 431), has resurrected ancient cultural enmities (if ever they were dormant), provoked an ugly orgy of accusations, name-calling, and racism, in the midst of which the West (to use those grand, binary divides) has once again misread the East, and the East has once again misrepresented itself. More seriously and closer to my concerns, we risk, in this sorry situation, contaminating our discourse—whether literary or religio-political— with intolerance, transgression, and disturbingly presumptuous assumptions about the superiority of *one* value system over another, *one* reading response over another. What we acutely need in the process of reading (and hopefully riding) the crisis is a genuine, mutual (at times heroic) exercise of sympathetic imagination, whereby the concerns and sensitivities of the Other are recognized.

When the controversy broke out, many readers wondered about the risks, rewards, and rationales for such a product of "levity." What does Rushdie or anyone gain from such a polemical, postmodern representation? Can a postmodern line of inquiry calm nerves? Can it shed light on the aesthetic and epistemological roots of Rushdie's narrativization of the emergence of Islam?

## A POSTMODERN PERSPECTIVE

In attempting to gauge our response to a complex text such as *The Satanic Verses*, we need to recall the Bakhtinian notion that fiction is a process, not a final product, and that a novel is quintessentially polyphonic; that is, it cannot be reduced to a single voice: authorial, privileged, or otherwise. Moreover, many would suggest that the driving energy that propels the narrative in Rushdie's work is guided by postmodern views of history that "confront the problematic nature of the past as an object of knowledge for the present" and that history and literature constitute "systems of signification by which we make sense of the past" (Hutcheon, "Postmodern Problematizing" 367). Here, history does not mean final, definitive renditions, nor does it involve the "customary fetishizing of facts" (Hutcheon, "Postmodern Problematizing" 377); rather history is a selective, re-constructive, narrative discourse that challenges the dominant versions of representation and provokes a counterdiscourse. Moreover, if history, as the new historicists argue, is a form of narrative, the postmodern fiction that deploys and dramatizes historical figures or events can claim to be yet another version of the past that is entitled to legitimacy. The net result is that the postmodern version rivals or at least destabilizes the seemingly immutable master narrative: self-consciously, tentatively, yet transgressively. Thus, the postmodern historiographer reworks his material with paradoxical hubris and humility, affection and aversion, care and cruelty. Consequently, if the text affirms anything, it affirms its ambivalence, tentativeness, and mutability.

Such a paradoxical manner in configuring and reshaping of history parallels, in Rushdie's oeuvre, a hesitant view toward history itself as an epistemological phenomenon to be contended with. On the one hand, history assumes a frightening kaleidoscopic totality over the individual's fate; as with Saleem Sinai, one is "handcuffed to history" (*Midnight's Children* 9). Likewise, Gibreel Farishta's obsession with history takes the form of a series of dreams that disturbingly infiltrate taboo territories. On the other hand, history represents a valuable source of inspiration, a liberator that can edify and enlighten us on complex, current issues. It functions as a crucial ideological ally that ultimately enriches the narrative of tentativeness and enhances the discourse of ambivalence: the primary aim is to probe rather than propound, question rather than confirm, doubt rather than dictate. History is in the eye of the beholder or projector; we do not have one history but histories. And Rushdie does not hide his hostility toward any belief system that posits "history" on fixed, sanctified grounds. As a postmodernist, he sees reality (whatever it may mean) as an unfinished project, a flux phenomenon that resists containment or closure and remains open to multiple renditions and projections; as Rushdie puts it, for him fiction involves "radical reformulations of language, form and ideas" and "attempt[s] to do what the word *novel* seems to insist upon: to see the world anew" ("In Good Faith" 393).

To prove his point, Rushdie selects his target most riskily and attacks relentlessly—some would say sensationally and immaturely—the driving, enduring, cohesive center of Muslim history and civilization, symbolized in the figure of Prophet Muhammad. This may explain why the portrayal of the

Prophet appears so inflammatory and offensive, since it entails parodically ridiculing Islam's most sanctified figure. To Rushdie, as to all postmodernists, no one is sacred, nothing is static, and everything is open to question, parody, and subversion. Hence the clash of cultures and the conflict of representations.

## A MUSLIM PERSPECTIVE

Any reader of Rushdie's earlier works, especially his critically acclaimed *Midnight's Children*, has, like myself, looked forward with excitement and eager anticipation to reading another novel by a writer of proven imaginative energy. However, anyone who has even a rudimentary knowledge of the culture and civilization of Islam would immediately realize on encountering certain passages in the text that the book contains a bombshell. The most offensive part of the novel centers on the historical portion in which the narrative turns into a roman à clef, depicting in a deliberately convoluted way the life of the Prophet Muhammad, referred to as "Mahound." Obviously the choice of this name is anything but innocent. According to *The Oxford English Dictionary, Mahound* signifies, especially for Western medievalists, four meanings, all being corrupted derivatives of Prophet Muhammad's name: "false prophet," "a false god," "a hideous creature," and "a name for the devil." Rushdie's choice of historical names is tantalizingly selective, alternating between real and suggestive ones, as well as double and triple usage of the same name throughout the narrative. For instance, Abu Simbul, the actual name of a Pharaonic temple, stands for Abu Sufyan, a wealthy man and one of the Prophet's strongest opponents, who was later forced to convert to Islam; and Salman the Persian, one of the Prophet's companions fictionalized as Mahound's scribe, evokes the author's first name. However, "Mahound" is the most troubling name whose choice Rushdie tried to justify rather unconvincingly in his article "In Good Faith," his most detailed defense against the accusations leveled at him. It is instructive to quote him at length here:

> *I must have known,* my accusers say, that my use of the old devil-name 'Mahound', a medieval European demonization of 'Muhammad', would cause offence. In fact, this is an instance in which de-contextualization has created a complete reversal of meaning. A part of the relevant context is on page ninety-three of the novel. 'To turn insults into strengths, wigs, tories, Blacks all choose to wear with pride the names they were given in scorn; likewise, our mountain-climbing, prophet-motivated solitary is to be the medieval baby-frightener, the Devil's synonym: Mahound.' Central to the purpose of *The Satanic Verses* is the process of reclaiming language from one's opponents. . . . 'Trotsky' was Trotsky's jailer's name. By taking it for his own, he symbolically conquered his captor and set himself free. Something of the same spirit lay behind my use of the name 'Mahound'. (402)

While one sees the innocent, indeed noble, intent claimed here, one can retort that Blacks and Trotsky themselves chose to appropriate the pejorative names concocted for them and they did that in their own time while resisting their contemporary opponents. Muhammad neither chose the appropriation option, indeed nor does he need it, nor did he delegate Salman Rushdie to claim it on his behalf, especially when Rushdie himself declares in the same article quite emphatically that he is "*not a Muslim*" (405). Rushdie cannot have it both ways. Also why does Rushdie, in his self-styled incarnation as a defender of Muhammad, dredge up a name that has long been ridiculed and rejected as a symptom of medievalist anti-Muslim hysteria and as a disgrace only to those who invented it? In other words, there is no contemporary relevance or reward for appropriating an already discredited name. Moreover, Rushdie's professed claim to "reclaiming and unpoisoning" the name Mahound in order to "transform it" ("Interview" 56) could have been justified had his portrayal of Mahound as a character been appealing enough to reflect, at least partially, the generosity and compassion of the historical Muhammad. Matching the demonic evocation of his name, Mahound, though charismatic, is unscrupulously power-hungry and profit-motivated (as the play on the homonym "prophet-motivated" suggests); self-focused, he is calculating and, at times, quite murderously cruel. One is then hard-pressed to see how the "unpoisoning" and "transformation" can be achieved through the portrayal of such an unpleasant and vengeful character who murders writers and prostitutes: Rushdie's Mahound is made to proclaim while ordering the beheading of the satirist poet named Baal, itself an intriguing name, "Writers and Whores. I see no difference here" (392). Indeed, when one does contextualize the choice of the name Mahound with the other transgressions operating in the offensive parts of the narrative, one has to conclude that Rushdie's defense, in this instance, is disingenuous.

The offensive parts are contained in chapter 2, "Mahound" (89–126), and chapter 6, "Return to Jahilia" (357–94). Rushdie's deliberate discourse, couched in a thinly veiled dream sequence, suggests three offensive things about this "Mahound-Mahon-Muhammad" (401). First, Mahound, a calculating businessman-turned-prophet, founds a religion called "Submission" (a literal, decontextualized translation for the Arabic word *Islam*) in the desert city of Jahilia (which literally means "ignorance" but here stands for pre-Islamic Mecca). Charismatic and determined, Mahound seems mainly engaged in a personal pursuit of power. This "fit man, no soft-bellied usurer he" (93) has three powerful opponents: the poet Baal, "the precocious polemicist" and one of Jahilia's "blood-praising versifiers" (98); the wealthy businessman Abu Simbel, the plutocrat whose manipulative skills enable him to "make his quarry think he has hunted the hunter" (98); and Abu Simbel's wife, Hind, a towering, lustful figure whose seductive powers are rooted in wealth, status, and physical charm.[3] Nevertheless, Mahound's crafty, at times cruel, schemes triumph over these formidable foes, since he has "no scruples . . . no qualms about ways and means" (363).

Second, this businessman-turned-prophet cunningly contrives "those matter-of-fact revelations" (366), claiming them to be delivered to him by the archangel Gibreel (Gabriel). These speculations are uttered by Mahound's intoxicated scribe, Salman the Persian, an irreverent depiction of one of the Prophet's loyal companions:

> And Gibreel the archangel specified the manner in which a man should be buried, and how his property should be divided, so that Salman the Persian got to wondering what manner of God this was that sounded so much like a businessman. This was when he had the idea that destroyed his faith, because he recalled that of course Mahound himself had been a businessman, and a damned successful one at that, a person to whom organization and rules came naturally, so how excessively convenient it was that he should have come up with such a very businesslike archangel, who handed down the management decisions of this highly corporate, if non-corporeal, God. (364)

Rushdie's narrative here echoes the anti-Islamic cliché about the apocrypha of the Qur'an and about Muhammad being an imposter who fabricated a falsely sacred text to match a Christlike holiness. In *Orientalism*, Edward Said astutely reveals a striking parallel strategy between Orientalism's portrayal of the Orient as the alien Other and its depiction of Muhammad as an imposter:

> What it [Orientalism] is trying to do, as Dante tried to do in the *Inferno*, is at one and the same time to characterize the Orient as alien and to incorporate it schematically on a theatrical stage whose audience, manager, and actors are *for* Europe, and only for Europe. Hence the vacillation between the familiar and the alien. Mohammed is always the imposter (familiar, because he pretends to be like the Jesus we know) and always the Oriental (alien because although he is in some ways "like" Jesus, he is after all not like him). (71–72)

Said's elaborate argument goes further in unmasking the arrogance of claims that are often made declarative and self-evident:

> Thus, Mohammed *is* an imposter, the very phrase canonized in d'Herbelot's *Bibliothèque* and dramatized in a sense by Dante. No background need be given; the evidence necessary to convict Mohammed is contained in the "is." One does not qualify the phrase, neither does it seem necessary to say that Mohammed *was* an imposter, nor need one consider for a moment that it may not be necessary to repeat the statement. It *is* repeated, and he *is* an imposter, and each time one says it, he becomes more of an imposter and the author of the statement gains a little more authority in having declared it. (72)

Elegant and erudite, Said's argument is nonetheless surprising in that he does not acknowledge Thomas Carlyle for being perhaps the first Western intellectual of caliber to debunk the prejudicial notions about the Prophet. Despite Carlyle's incapacity to understand the Qur'an meaningfully and appreciatively, his famous lecture about Muhammad, entitled "The Hero as Prophet," is quite an adulatory piece. According to Montgomery Watt, Carlyle's "great originality" is shown in his being "the first writer in either east or west to attempt to fathom the inner experience of the founder of Islam" (253) and in his lecture being "the first strong affirmation in the whole of European literature, medieval and modern, of a belief in the sincerity of Muhammad" (247). Carlyle condemns the reference to Muhammad as "a scheming Imposter, a Falsehood incarnate, [whose] religion is a mere mass of quackery and fatuity. . . ." Conscious of his exclusively "Christian" audience and thoughtfully engaged in his own terms of reference, Carlyle, gingerly yet unequivocally, affirms that "the lies, which well-meaning zeal has heaped round this man, are disgraceful to ourselves only" (Carlyle 50). By depicting his Mahound as a self-serving pretender and a fabricator of a holy text, Rushdie's narrative echoes that Orientalist tradition and thus places himself, consciously or inadvertently, within its orbit. Has Rushdie metamorphosed himself into a Trojan horse inside the Muslim camp?

Proceeding with this implicit/explicit notion of the apocrypha of the Qur'an, "the central theophany of Islam" (Nasr 37), Rushdie revives an obscure issue of the so-called Satanic Verses from which the novel's title is derived. The title alludes to an incident in which Muhammad, allegedly, made a concession to the oligarchy of pre-Islamic Mecca, accepting three idols as divine intercessors. The incident is reported by two classical Muslim historians who are separated by about two and three centuries, respectively, from the Prophet's era between 570–632 CE: the two are al-Waqidi (747–823 CE) and al-Tabari (c. 839–923 CE). The two report that the "satanic verses" had been declared in *Surat* (Chapter) al-Najm (the Star) then rescinded by the Prophet as being a fabrication by Satan. In his commentary of Surat al-Najm, one of the Qur'an translators, Maulana Muhammad Ali, argues that this incident was quite unknown to Muslims prior to al-Waqidi: "There is not a trustworthy hadith [the Prophet's saying] that lends support to this story. Muhammad ibn Ishaq, who died as early as 151 A.H. [721 CE], does not mention it" and "when questioned about it, Ibn Ishaq called it a fabrication of the *zindeeqs* [infidels]" (1003 n. 238). Part of Maulana Muhammad Ali's repudiation of the whole incident is based on the fact that throughout his life, the Prophet has perseveringly preached against idolatry. Furthermore, he casts doubt on the reliability of the two classical historians:

> And the famous Bukhari, the most trustworthy authority on the sayings of the
> Holy Prophet, was Waqidi's contemporary, and his collection of sayings contains
> no mention of the story. As regards Waqidi, all competent authorities entertain a

very low opinion of his trustworthiness. The *Mizan al-I'tidal*, a critical work on
the lives and characters of the reporters of Hadith, speaks of Waqidi as unreliable
and even as a fabricator of reports. As regards Tabari, [Orientalist Sir William]
Muir himself represents him as guilty of "indiscriminate reception." (1003 n.)

It should be noted here that almost all modern Muslim scholars, with perhaps the
notable exception of Fazlur Rahman (Ruthven 39), refute the story. And even
among modern Orientalists the opinion is divided: some like Sir William Muir,
Montgomery Watt, and Maxime Rodinson accept it, while others like Count
Caetani and John Burton "question its authenticity" (Ruthven 39). In the course
of the novel, the wily Mahound becomes partly tempted, partly pressured into a
deal with Abu Simbel to compromise the new religion's categorical monotheism
by accepting three idols (al-Lat, al-Uzza, and Manat) as intermediaries between
God and worshipping, revenue-generating pilgrims. The deal gives crucial political and practical advantages to Mahound's new religion, giving it official sanction
and secure circulation for adherents; simultaneously, it secures profit for Jahilia's
business establishment. However, Mahound revokes the deal and recants the *ayāt*
(verses) that endowed the idols with intercessory powers, claiming that the verses
were deliberately altered, falsified, and delivered to him by Shaitan (Satan). By
adopting and dramatizing this episode, Rushdie highlights it as a version of truth
that may have been deliberately ignored by the sanitized and "sanctified" chronicles of history. The ultimate implication of this narrativized incident is that the
Qur'an is not the holy, definitive book that all Muslims believe to be God's exact
words, *ipsissima verba*, but a text conveniently faked by the Prophet. Needless to
say, such a suggestion by Rushdie causes a gross offense to Muslims.

Third, and more seriously, Rushdie portrays, through Gibreel Farishta's de-
generating dream sequence, an elaborate scene at "the most popular brothel in
Jahilia" (376) called The Curtain, "Hijab" (which also means in Arabic "veil," a
provocative suggestion that Muslims treat their women, some of whom may
wear veils, as prostitutes). The female workers at The Curtain impersonate the
Prophet's wives to improve business. The idea is the fruit of Baal's depraved
poetic imagination:

> How many wives? Twelve and one old lady, long dead. How many whores be-
> hind the Curtain? Twelve again; and, secret on her black-tented throne, the an-
> cient Madam, still defying death. Where there is no belief, there is no
> blasphemy. Baal told the Madam of his idea; she settled matters in her voice of
> a laryngitis frog. "It is very dangerous," she pronounced, "but it could be damn
> good for business. We will go carefully; but we will go." (380)

In this segment of the novel, the real names of the Prophet's wives (whom
Muslims reverentially call "Mothers of the Believers") are used. Even a dead wife

is not spared in this puzzling, bizarre segment, since catering to necrophilic customers can create profit:

> Strangest of all was the whore who had taken the name of "Zainab bint Khuza-imah", knowing that this wife of Mahound had recently died. The necrophilia of her lovers, who forbade her to make any movements, was one of the more unsavoury aspects of the new regime at The Curtain. But business was business, and this, too, was a need that the courtesans fulfilled. (382)

Believers would legitimately consider such a wantonly contrived episode as the most vicious of Rushdie's offenses. To them Rushdie's blend of blasphemy and pornography tastelessly verges on the obscene. Defending himself, Rushdie justi-fies this scene by putting it into the context of the opposition between the sacred and profane: "It is always clearly stated that the Prophet's wives are not being de-scribed as getting up to anything improper. But this profane world, the world of the terrible poet Baal, and of bought sex, turns into a kind of distorting mirror of the sacred world at the moment at which the two worlds have come together" ("Interview" 64). Earlier, in his article "In Good Faith," Rushdie gives a more de-tailed explanation whereby, if I am reading him correctly, he views the Prophet's harem in at once similar and contrastive terms to that of the brothel and vice versa:

> Both are places where women are sequestered, in the harem to keep them from all men except from their husband and their close family members, in the brothel for the use of strange males. Harem and brothel are antithetical worlds, and the presence in the harem of the Prophet, the receiver of a sacred text, is likewise contrasted with the presence in the brothel of the clapped-out poet, Baal, the creator of profane texts. The two struggling worlds, pure and impure, chaste and coarse, are juxtaposed by making them echoes of one another; and, finally, the pure eradicates the impure. (401)

One is really amazed by the naïveté and insensitivity of such a response matched by a gloss over the offense that he caused to Muslims, whose culture he claims to have known and studied. Novelist and prominent journalist, Khushwant Singh, who had advised against publishing the book in India, comments on this scene: "There is no doubt that there are passages in the book that would offend Mus-lim sentiments. He has used the same names in the book as the Prophet's family. You can write anything you want and justify it as being a dream sequence" (1). Singh's reference to the dream sequence has been Rushdie's initial line of de-fense, blaming it on the fantasy of a character's, Gibreel Farishta, deranged mind. Later, in a revealing answer to a pointed question that connects this scene with the issue of the Prophet's many marriages and "sexual life," Rushdie repeats one of the favorite mantras for anti-Muslim Orientalists:

It has often been said that the Prophet was a very highly sexual man. At the same time it was also the case that a lot of these marriages were political marriages. The harem of Mohammed was a very important political location at a time when different tribes, different clans, made alliances with early Islam through marriage. Yes, I think it would be fair to say that he liked girls. He often liked them very young. ("Interview" 63)

While he seems to be defending the necessity behind those partly political, partly philanthropic marriages, some of which were only formal, he evokes an image of an oversexed pedophile. The best rebuttal to such a slur is the one articulated by Thomas Carlyle, whom none would accuse of being a "Muslim fundamentalist":

Mahomet himself, after all that can be said about him, was not a sensual man. We shall err widely if we consider this man as a common voluptuary, intent mainly on base enjoyment, —nay on enjoyment of any kind. His household was of the frugalest; his common diet barley-bread and water: sometimes for months there was not a fire once lighted on his hearth. They record with just pride that he would mend his own shoes, patch his own cloak. A poor, hard-toiling, ill-provided man; careless of what vulgar men toil for. (81)

Any believer in freedom of expression and in the function and validity of literature can appreciate why a Western reader, educated in a presumably secular, liberal-humanist culture, may be bedeviled by all the fuss and furor about a mere book, a work of fiction containing a troubling dream sequence. However, in order to understand the enormity of what has been done, a circumspect, tolerant reader needs to appreciate what the Prophet Muhammad means to Muslims across the Muslim world and throughout their immigrant communities in the West. The Prophet is not only a religious figure (the Messenger of the Faith) but also the symbol of the heroic tradition, the figure who epitomizes virtue, wisdom, compassion, and courage. Fully human as he repeatedly affirmed, the Prophet has admirably and endearingly become for over fourteen centuries a constant cultural focus in the collective consciousness of the masses. In short, he is the holiest figure that represents for over one-quarter of the earth's population the luminous, enduring, cohesive center. Is it any wonder then that Muslims (including liberal and secular Muslims) become puzzled, offended, or outraged when such a figure is so gratuitously and relentlessly ridiculed in a work of fiction?

Had Rushdie written a nonfictional work about the Prophet in which he engaged in a metaphysical or spiritual speculation, the anger would not have been so intense, nor would it have had such a regrettable level of demonization and countervilification. Rushdie's narrative strategy involves using subterfuge in the guise of fictionality. He cleverly immunizes his text against external charges by associating the offensive passages with the obsessive imagination of a mentally tortured character. Moreover, he can always deploy the classic claim of authorial distance or inviting/inventing multiple layers of meaning of an ambivalent text whose "act of creation is not a rational and a conscious one" ("In Good Faith" 408). Here then is the sore point for the protesting Muslims: they feel frustrated and furious because the assault on the Prophet can be easily denied as a mere work of fiction, a mere dream sequence, or a mere statement uttered by a deranged, drunken character who does not represent the author's views: "the waking Gibreel is a coarse-mouthed fellow, and it would be surprising if the dream-figures he conjures up did not sometimes speak as rough and even obscene a language as their dreamer" ("In Good Faith" 399). They see little room for meaningful, factual, point/counterpoint debate.

## THE CRITICAL RESPONSE

In the clamor that ensued after the publication of *The Satanic Verses*, a varied range of responses emerged, most of which was emotional from both sides of the sharply marked binary divide, thus unfortunately feeding "a fable of Western freedom vs. Oriental fanaticism" (Brennan 144). While academic criticism was generally immune from the acrimony of the mediatized reponses (print and electronic), it nevertheless was not entirely immune from the binary opposition. It is not within the scope of this discussion to survey all that has been written about the novel, being perhaps the most intensely and widely discussed postmodern/"postcolonial" novel within a relatively short span of time after its publication, thanks largely to the fatwa. However, one cannot help but wonder first at the diversity of critical idiom used to describe Rushdie's historiographical deconstruction/reconstruction. Was it blasphemy? Offense? Self-hate? Racism? Or simply bad taste? *Blasphemy* and *offense* are the two most commonly used labels. However, throughout my discussion of the novel I used exclusively the word *offense* for two reasons. First, *blasphemy*, loaded as it is, pertains to the realm of theology, while *offense*, as I conceptualize it, relates to the realm of cultural politics and praxis, which are my primary concerns. Second, the term *offense* emits the most measured degree of gravity yet is free from the extremities of sensationalism or flippancy. If *offense* is an appropriate term, was it then deliberate or inadvertent? Michael Thorpe affirms that "one cannot doubt Rushdie offended deliberately" and that "Rushdie's satire is seen as especially pernicious because it feeds Western prejudice and adds to a literary tradition hostile since Dante consigned Muhammad to the Ninth Circle of the *Inferno* and Pope Innocent III dubbed him 'the Beast of the Apocalypse'" (30). To put matters into a balanced perspective, the novel offers its own version of the issue, through the satirist poet

Baal, Rushdie's profane mouthpiece, who lucidly and luxuriously articulates the writer's role: "[A] poet's work [is] . . . to name the unnamable, to point at frauds, to take sides, start arguments, shape the world and stop it from going to sleep" (97). Thus, Rushdie, most probably, took a miscalculated risk that, to his surprise and spleen, backfired.

The term *blasphemy* has been used by Rushdie's most vociferous opponents, especially those who support the fatwa, sanction the burning of the book, or support its banning. In his sensationally entitled book *Be Careful with Muhammad: The Salman Rushdie Affair*, Shabbir Akhtar, who candidly refers to himself as a "fundamentalist Muslim" (49) and who regards Rushdie as "a *literary* terrorist" (11), sounds breathtakingly categorical: "That *The Satanic Verses* is blasphemous should be, for the Muslim conscience uncontroversial." In a regrettably presumptuous—indeed rather disturbing—tone, he adds:

> Any Muslim who fails to be offended by Rushdie's book ceases, on account of that fact, to be a Muslim. *The Satanic Verses* has become a litmus-paper test for distinguishing faith from rejection. The test applies to all shades of opinion— orthodox, heretical, indifferent; it applies to all Muslims—good, bad, practising, lapsed. . . . These contentions are completely conclusive; there is no room here for private sophistication rooted in hypocrisy and schooled in dishonesty. (35)

In contrast to Akhtar's uncompromising stance about the book's blasphemy, many academic critics in the West handle its "blasphemy" with a clever twist. Sara Suleri, for instance, gives the term a "schooled" and "sophisticated" nuance by recasting it as an "act of archaic devotion" and "curious faith":

> for readers both familiar and unfamiliar with Islamic culture, one of the most seductive imperatives that *The Satanic Verses* exudes is an acute consciousness of its status as blasphemy. Even before the fundamentalists descend to burn the published text, the book itself inflames, unfolding an act of archaic devotion to the cultural system that it must both desecrate and renew. The desire to desecrate must here be disaligned from more simplistic [*sic*] perspective over whether or not Rushdie has been "offensive to Islam"; instead, it perversely demands to be read as a gesture of wrenching loyalty, suggesting that blasphemy can be articulated only within the compass of belief. In the context of such ambivalence, Rushdie performs an act of curious faith: his text chooses disloyalty in order to dramatize its continuing obsession with the metaphors Islam makes available to a postcolonial sensibility. (191)

On the other hand, Ali A. Mazrui not only confirms the accusation of blasphemy but also invokes the charge of racism in Rushdie's irreverent portrayal of Bilal, the Prophet's black loyal companion and Islam's first *mu'azzin* (caller for prayer), and of Bilal X, the fictional African-American convert to Islam that evokes the figure of Malcolm X. Mazrui poses a number of rhetorical questions:

> Is Rushdie making fun of African-Americans *generally*? Or is he satirizing Afroamerican *Muslims*? Or is he ridiculing the significance of Malcolm X? But since many Afroamerican Muslims regard Islam as one route back toward re-Africanization, and therefore a point of return to Roots [*sic*], is Rushdie simply continuing his contempt for his own roots? (367)

More seriously and rather surprisingly, Mazrui compares *The Satanic Verses* to Adolf Hitler's *Mein Kampf*:

> To question whether *The Satanic Verses* is as racist as *Mein Kampf* was, the answer is *not*. But there is an undercurrent of Negrophobia in both books. The two books are also anti-Semitic—but directed at different sections of the Semitic peoples. While Hitler was primarily anti-Jewish, there is an undercurrent of anti-Arabism in Rushdie. (367)

Mazrui concludes his acerbic evaluation of the book by making yet another accusation when he states that "Rushdie subordinates the real anguish of Muslim believers to the titillation of his Western reader" (368).

Going beyond "offense" and "blasphemy," D. C. R. A. Goonetilleke, in his thoughtfully balanced study of Rushdie's oeuvre, raises the issue of taste or rather bad taste in Rushdie's naming the Prophet as Mahound and the prostitutes after Muhammad's wives:

> Rushdie betrays a deep insensitivity to the fact that he will thus bruise the religious susceptibilities of the Muslims and his arguments in his defence reveal that he is unaware of his own insensitivity. Such susceptibilities are perhaps more acute in the case of Muslims than those of the adherents of other religions: Muslims are enjoined to engage in formal worship five times a day; they view the Koran as the direct word of God (not the gospel "according to" Mark, Matthew and so on). (104)

Goonetilleke attributes Rushdie's "insensitivity" to his upbringing in a secular family and to spending most of his life in Britain, making him ultimately a "lapsed Muslim" (104).

The debate about the book, in its various forms, made literary circles and academic communities pay sudden accrued attention to the culture and tradition of Muslims and their religion; this could create a positive result because it raises awareness and responds to the need of caring and curious minds to understand the context within which the text functions. Regrettably, not all that has been written was accurate or serious; some scholars did not demonstrate due diligence or depth in the way they made general statements about Islam and its traditions. As an illustration, let me choose two works whose authors I deem to be serious and well-meaning academics. In his otherwise informative book on Rushdie, Jim Harrison states, "In reality the Qur'an existed for some time in fragmentary disorder and was not assembled into its present form and 'canonized' until some time after Muhammad's death" (102). Astonishingly, the reference that Harrison gives to this imprecise statement is page 82 in Rushdie's *Midnight's Children*, in which Saleem Sinai reports, with tongue-in-cheek, about his father's, Ahmed Sinai, "ambition" to rearrange "the Quran in accurately chronological order." More seriously, Harrison proceeds from Saleem Sinai's statement to conclude hastily thus: "in other words, it [the Qur'an] was in part the work of ordinary human labors and human judgment and therefore subject to a human capacity for error, just like any holy book" (102). The irony in this carelessly formulated statement cannot fail to escape an observant reader: it begins in reality, then becomes trapped in fiction, and concludes in hasty generalization. If one needs to make serious statements about the Qur'an, can one not find more authoritative works than Rushdie's *Midnight's Children*? Are Saleem Sinai and Ahmed Sinai (both fictional constructs) authorities on Islam? Even when we make allowance for Saleem Sinai as being a quasi-autobiographical alter ego for Rushdie, is Rushdie himself an authority on Islam? According to Akbar Ahmed, Rushdie is "unreliable on Islam" (115), because his "knowledge of Islam is limited and usually derived from cursory reading of the orientalists" (164). On the other hand, Feroza Jussawalla claims that Rushdie is "deeply rooted in Muslim culture" and is "deeply knowledgeable about Islamic history and theology" ("Rushdie's" 58; n9). Perhaps based on such an assumption, Jussawalla commits an error similar to Harrison's: she quotes a historically erroneous statement made by Saleem Sinai on page 61 of *Midnight's Children*: "Zulfikar is a famous name amongst Muslims. It was the name of the two-pronged sword carried by Ali, the nephew of the prophet Muhammad" ("Rushdie's" 63). Any grade-six Muslim pupil knows that the Prophet had no siblings and that Ali was his cousin and son-in-law, yet Jussawalla quotes without pointing out this error in Rushdie's text. More seriously, Jussawalla makes an additional error of her own when she misrepresents the origin of the Muslim call for prayer and declaration of faith *Allahu Akbar* (God is Great), which Muslim fighters metamorphosed during battle into a rallying cry, declaring their readiness for martyrdom. Astonishingly, she attributes the call to the syncretistically tolerant Mughal emperor Akbar: "It is ironic that the Islamic war cry 'Allahu Akbar' generates from Akbar's court, where it meant not only 'God is great' but 'Akbar is God' and was the motto of Akbar's court's reform of Islam" ("Rushdie's" 57). Jussawalla acknowledges the source of this grossly erroneous assertion in her statement to page 132 in Stanley Wolpert's *A New History of India*. However, on checking the source, one can easily discover that Jussawalla has misrepresented Wolpert's statement, which reads:

> The motto of that [Akbar's] court religion, used as a salutation by its devotees, was *Allahu Akbar*, which could mean either "God is great" or "Akbar is God." It was doubtless interpreted both ways, depending whether the person using it was more of a devout Muslim or an imperial Mughal. (132)

While Wolpert, a historian on the subcontinent but no scholar on Islam, does not reference his statement about the punning twist of *Allahu Akbar* in Akbar's court, he does not claim that the call generates from Akbar's court. Any Muslim adult knows that *Allahu Akbar* dates back to the Prophet's days: that is more than nine centuries before Akbar's birth. Following the same pattern, Jussawalla makes another hasty generalization without basing it on any reference when she claims that "the story of Salman, the scribe, leaving in the 'Satanic Verses' is a specifically Islamic tale told in all Muslim cultures" ("Rushdie's" 53). This generalized, unsupported, misinformed statement contains three errors: the historical Salman the Persian was not a scribe, but a barber (Ruthven 39); Salman the Persian has nothing to do whatsoever with the "Satanic Verses"; and the story of the "Satanic Verses" is not a tale told in *all* Muslim cultures because, while it is reported by only two Muslim historians (al-Waqidi and al-Tabari), many classical Muslim scholars doubt its reliability and authenticity, and "many modern Muslim writers regard it as 'apocryphal gossip' dredged up from the past by Western orientalists to discredit Islam" (Ruthven 38–39). To disentangle the crafty Rushdiesque narrative web, into which Jussawalla has fallen, regarding the historical role of Salman the Persian, it is useful to quote at length the clarification articulated by Malise Ruthven:

> In his novel Rushdie links the incident with other episodes in the accounts of early Muslim annalists which cast doubt on the divinity of the Qur'an: for example, according to a story, also recorded by Tabari, one of the Prophet's scribes, Abdullah ibn Sa'ad, temporarily lost his faith after a mistake he had made in transcription went unnoticed by the Prophet. In Gibreel's dream the part of Abdullah is given to Salman al Farisi. Salman is an important figure in the early history of Islam. A barber of Persian birth who was adopted into the Prophet's household, he masterminded one of Muhammad's victories over the Meccans by persuading Muhammad to build a defensive ditch around the city of Medina. . . . Much revered by the Shi'a, he is also regarded as one of the founders of Sufism, the mystical tradition in Islam. He is not named as one of Muhammad's scribes. Rushdie's use of this character suggests ironic endorsement of Abdullah's doubt. (39)

Jussawalla makes a legitimate plea for "localized interpretations that study the history of the contexts of the texts" undertaken by "an intermediary interpretative community" ("Rushdie's" 71), yet when those intermediaries themselves add to the confusion, we really have a reading crisis on our hands. It is not my concern to go over all the other contextual and conceptual errors that are to be located in Jussawalla's rather lengthy article; however, there is one intriguing issue that I have to point out because it relates to the sequence of Rushdie's many metamorphoses during the painful postfatwa saga. Jussawalla's contention, as her title suggests, is that Rushdie's *The Satanic Verses* is his "love letter" to Islam; she thus distances herself from Suleri's blasphemy interpretation, yet curiously the two critics converge: Suleri sees the novel as "an act of archaic devotion" and "curious faith" that "desecrate[s] and renew[s]" (191), while Jussawalla argues that Rushdie undertakes "a reformist retelling of the history of Islam" through "the rewriting of a sacred book not to target and satirize, not to create a counterhegemonic discourse, but to correct a wrong out of the love for his religion" (63). This might have been Rushdie's intent, but Ali Mazrui would retort that "Rushdie should have known that no great culture can be reformed by abusing it" (368). Interestingly, Jussawalla bases crucial points in her argument by quoting from Rushdie's article "Why I Have Embraced Islam," which he wrote after his short-lived "conversion" to Islam on Christmas eve of 1990. The article appeared in the 1991 first edition of his collection of essays, *Imaginary Homelands: Essays and Criticism 1981–1991*. However, after rescinding his declaration of faith, Rushdie wrote an article, entitled "One Thousand Days in a Balloon," in which he partly explains that "embrace" to his then being "in a state of some confusion and torment" (436). More importantly, Rushdie expunges "Why I Have Embraced Islam" from the book's 1992 edition and replaces it with "One Thousand Days in a Balloon." Is Rushdie invalidating the "Embrace" article to correspond to his rescinding the conversion? At any rate, Jussawalla does not touch on the subsequent developments critically germane to her claims, even though her article was published in 1996 in *Diacritics* and reprinted in 1999 in a collection of essays on Rushdie.

## SALMAN RUSHDIE'S *THE SATANIC VERSES* AND NAGUIB MAHFOUZ'S *CHILDREN OF THE ALLEY*

One erroneous association critics and journalists make involves invoking Naguib Mahfouz's novel *Children of the Alley* (serialized in Arabic in 1959) in the context of the so-called The Rushdie Affair, or at least they try to draw a parallel between Mahfouz's tribulations with writing his *roman phare* and Rushdie's condemnation for writing his *The Satanic Verses*. Mahfouz's narrative involves genealogical allegorization of humanity's search for meaning through narrativizing the Biblical/Qur'anic story of Adam's expulsion from paradise and the genesis of the three monotheistic religions: Judaism, Christianity, and Islam. It concludes with the emergence of science as the imperfect rival to religion that accidentally leads to the death of God, represented in the novel by the Alley's great ancestor, Gabalawi; however, Mahfouz has told the novel's first English translator, Philip Stewart, that Gabalawi does not represent God "but a certain idea of God that men have made" (vii). The heroes of this fascinating *roman à clef* are the founders of the three Abrahamic religions: Gabal (as Moses), Rifaa (as Jesus), and Qassem as (Muhammad), as well as the magician/chemist Arafa, representing modern knowledge or science. Discursively, Mahfouz's narrative underscores humanity's double needs for spirituality, an abstract anchor for existence, and justice, a concrete concept for governance that enables individuals and communities to survive with dignity and serenity. Only genuine self-sacrificing saviors with heroic qualities can respond to the Alley's, that is, the world's, aching needs and put an end to any deviation from what the Qur'an describes as "the straight path." Being an agnostic at the time of writing *Children of the Alley*, Mahfouz's introduction of Arafa as a latter-day savior dramatizes the notion that when science becomes a tool in the hands of an exploitative oligarchy, it becomes tainted and harmful: Arafa gets corrupted and joins the service of the estate's overseer, replacing the erstwhile terror tool, the gangsters.

Ambitious in its historical and metaphysical dimensions, Mahfouz's narrative is more accessible to the reader than Rushdie's. Uninhibitedly playful with metaphors and idioms whereby inventively expanding the boundaries of the English language, Rushdie's narrative is more daring in its diverse experimentation with technique than Mahfouz's. More importantly, one needs, however, to clarify the supposed similarity between the two novels by highlighting the fact that Mahfouz, unlike Rushdie, writes cautiously and respectfully and from within the culture and civilization of Islam. Indeed, the major sources of Mahfouz's narratives are the Qur'an—which tells in glowing terms the stories of Moses and Jesus as holy prophets, precursors of Muhammad—and the *Sira*, the compendium of episodes inscribed from the oral traditions chronicling Muhammad's life: as if to acknowledge his indebtedness to the Qur'an, Mahfouz divides his novel into 114 chapters to match the same number of Surahs in the Qur'an. More specifically, Mahfouz adopts the Qur'anic version of the prophetic chain linking the three monotheistic faiths by establishing a conceptual connection between Qassem and his two heroic predecessors in the Alley's cosmic history: Gabal and Rifaa. At a crucial moment in his struggle against the usurpers of Gabalawi's heritage, Qassem affirms this linkage and counts on it: "Why do they [the followers of Gabal and Rifaa] call me a liar, when they should be the first to believe me and support me" (311). Moreover, Mahfouz articulates the Islamic view about the distinction in spiritual strategies of the three prophets, presenting Qassem's teachings as the wise incorporation of the teachings of his two predecessors: a follower puts a question to Qassem: "So will you use force like Gabal, or love, like Rifaa?" Qassem's hand explored his turban: "Force when necessary, and love at all times" (296). Later, just before going to battle, Qassem affirms this distinction and thus exhorts his followers: "We will raise clubs the way Gabal did, but to achieve the mercy that Rifaa called for. We will use the estate for everyone's good, until we make Adham's [i.e., Adam's] dream come true. This is our mission—not gang rule" (330).

Rushdie, in contrast to Mahfouz, writes parodically from a supposedly secular tradition that queries the concept of sanctified holiness and probes selective, sanitized history, by "pitting levity against gravity." Mahfouz, being a religious skeptic at the time of writing *Children of the Alley* in 1959, tries to dramatize the conflict between religion and science; more specifically, he is trying to explore the notion of how science's conception of the world could lead to God collaterally becoming irrelevant, absent, or accidentally dead. However, Mahfouz has always revered and admired Islam as one of his inspirational sources, moving toward a Sufic appreciation of Islam later in his life. Indeed, in his acceptance speech of the 1988 Nobel Prize for Literature, he affirmed that he is the proud product of two rich, if different, civilizations: one is ancient Egyptian and the other Islamic.

It is therefore brazenly ignorant of the die-hard blind cleric, Umar Abdul Rahman, to issue a death fatwa against Mahfouz during the controversy surrounding *The Satanic Verses*—that is, almost twenty years after Mahfouz serialized his novel in the semiofficial newspaper *al-Ahram*—saying that had Mahfouz been condemned to death at the time of the serialization of *Children of the Alley*, "Rushdie would never have dared to publish his blasphemies" (Ruthven 116). It is also a gross injustice to link Mahfouz with Rushdie or to accuse Mahfouz of being anti-Islamic without even having read either Mahfouz's or Rushdie's work. While Mahfouz opposed the fatwa against Rushdie's life, he criticized him for seemingly ridiculing Islam.

## CONCLUSION

Let me then close by advancing the following five propositions:

1. If the "Rushdie Affair" proves anything, it affirms the inseparability of text and context. Any previous notions we might have had about the insularity of literature have been proven false. For, as Linda Hutcheon cogently argues, "gone now is the belief that art is, or can be, autonomous, separate from the world. Post-modernist art situates itself squarely in the context of its own creation and reception in a social and ideological reality" ("Challenging" 34). In his article "Outside the Whale," Rushdie himself emphasizes the notion that "works of art, even works of entertainment, do not come into being in a social and political vacuum; and that the way they operate cannot be separated from politics, from history" (130). We thus cannot divorce text from context. Put differently,

the production of any literary work is culturally conditioned; subsequently, the responses to the literary work are likewise culturally conditioned.[4]

2. The postmodernist impulse to articulate, parody, or subvert the contexts encompassing its texts has included foraying into the politics of culture and religion. *The Satanic Verses* does exactly that. It delves daringly into various current religious and political issues, because—as Rushdie lucidly and unequivocally argues—"politics and literature, like sport and politics, do mix, are inextricably mixed, and . . . that mixture has consequences" ("Outside the Whale" 137). Accordingly, one can qualify *The Satanic Verses* as a text permeated by religio-political issues starting from its first two pages (e.g., terrorism, the politics of the subcontinent, racism in Britain), and "anyone reading the table of contents alone, with chapter headings such as 'Ayesha' and 'Mahound,' could see that the novel was a 500-page parody of Muhammad's life" (Brennan 144). The responses to such a polemical text are bound to be religio-political too. We may not like some of the responses, but the text itself elicits and provokes them. An engaged reader is indifferent neither to Rushdie's text nor to the response it generates.

3. Starting with its title, *The Satanic Verses* unearths and copies some of the spurious, or at least disputable, claims that a few Orientalists, be they missionaries or affiliates of colonial enterprises, have unearthed, magnified, or fabricated about the history and culture of Islam. Edward Said's compelling arguments in *Orientalism* (1978) and his subsequent works measure the weight and mass of what those "experts" have propagated about Islam. The impact of their writings is still to a large extent dominant in Western views of Islam. Any conscientious, fair-minded person needs to pause and reflect before jumping to essentialist, categorical conclusions about Islam, especially when it has often been seen reductively as the perennial hostile Other. Germane Greer, to her credit, went against the prevailing mood in the West by declaring, "I . . . feel a bit nervous about basing a book upon a sacred text, because it seems to me you appeal to all the people who hate that creed and would like to suppress those people. And there is so much anti-Islamic feeling. It is just too easy, and that worries me" (qtd. Kirchhoff C2). Rushdie's utilization of Orientalist fabrications seems to the ordinary Muslim reader not only flattering to those prepackaged stereotypes about Islam, but also to signal the burning of bridges between the author and his own cultural roots. Rushdie's post-*Satanic* writing confirms this view. Regrettably, Rushdie is no longer the voice of "third world" agonies and an activist for persecuted minorities. Now a celebrity lavishing in elite lifestyle, he, to borrow José Marti, no longer "casts his lot with the wretched of the earth"; the Jaguar in Nicaragua must indeed be smiling. With the exception of his charming novella, *Haroun and the Sea of Stories*, his post-*Satanic* writing, whether creative or journalistic, has disappointingly veered into other directions that reveal a slippage into paths away

from the countercolonial narrative of India and the fascinating blend of its Hindu–Muslim metaphors.

4. By copying this reductively edited version of Islamic history, Rushdie, who should have known otherwise, has made his motives seem suspect to Muslims. Whether deliberately or inadvertently, he has turned his literary product into an attractive item (hot and rare) for anti-Muslim consumers. Yet by doing so, Rushdie, the erstwhile leftist polemicist, may have qualified himself for what Gayatri Chakravorty Spivak calls "the privileged native informant" (256); she means by that those "third world" writers who exploit their intimate knowledge of their culture to present unflattering images that endorse Western stereotypes, with her two models being V. S. Naipaul and Bharati Mukherjee. Rushdie's narrative, if my contention is valid, becomes in the final analysis alien to the "third world" view of itself. Regrettably, he has, to apply Said's comment on Naipaul, "allowed himself quite consciously to be turned into a witness for the Western prosecution" ("Intellectuals" 53), and has thus rendered himself inoperative within the "third world" literary discourse. As I see it, the dialectic of that discourse is critical (at times severely critical) of its cultural roots, yet remains actively committed to them. I am thinking of such engaged writers as Egyptian Naguib Mahfouz, Kurdish-Turkish Yashar Kemal, Kenyan Ngugi wa Thoing'o, Chilean Pablo Neruda, and Pakistani Faiz Ahmad Faiz.

5. While one may mildly or severely critique *The Satanic Verses*, quibble with its troubling discourse, impute all sorts of mercenary, conspiratorial, or blasphemous motives to its author, the book remains, within its own right and term of reference, impressive. As Janette Turner Hospital colorfully puts it, this novel is "a firecracker of a work whose every page fizzes with linguistic acrobatics and exuberance, with cross-language puns, with clichés suddenly rinsed and new[ly]-minted so that they shock and shimmer" (C17). Given its profound literary value, depth, density, and, above all, humor, *The Satanic Verses* does not deserve to be banned. It demands debate, not destruction. I am taking this stance while I am quite distressed and saddened by the regrettably gratuitous deaths that took place during the height of the crisis. It would not be fair to lay the blame for those deaths squarely on Rushdie or his book. I am also mindful of the vexing question that Germane Greer courageously raised when she responded to a question about why she did not sign a petition to support her friend, Rushdie: "I didn't presuppose that a book that got people killed should be allowed to go on being published. I think that no book is worth a single person's life. Not one, I do not care what it is. If anybody dies because of a book, then that book is miscalculated, aimed in a wrong direction" (qtd. in Kirchhoff C2). While one would shudder to ponder the options in such a situation, banning books is not a choice. Needless to say, burning books is not only civilizationally repugnant but is also

quite injurious to the ethos of Islam, whose heritage abounds with shining examples of tolerance, fair hearing, and respect for books. Islam's spirit of tolerance is steeped in theological and epistemological confidence rather than weakness, in a refined aesthetic vision rather than closed-mindedness, in a receptive intellectual agility rather than refractory rejection. Ayatollah Khomeini's fatwa, extraliterary, extrajudiciary as it was, is not valid. A masterful political legerdemain, it was a carefully calculated response to a riskily miscalculated piece of writing. One transgression (Rushdie's) does not justify another (Khomeini's).

# SEVEN

# Muslim Women's Autobiographical Narratives: Fatima Mernissi's *Dreams of Trespass* and Che Husna Azhari's *The Rambutan Orchard*

Paradise is under the feet of mothers.

—Prophet Muhammad

ACCORDING TO THE SOMALI NOVELIST NURUDDIN FARAH, WOMEN represent "the symbol of the subjugated self in each one of us. Wherever you go in the world, woman's fate is worse than man's" (1828). Fatima Mernissi's autobiographical narrative *Dreams of Trespass: Tales of a Harem Girlhood* chronicles the history of the discrimination against her and other female members of her family perpetrated by a male-dominated, tradition-shackled society. The site is the Muslim cultural city of Fez, Morocco. In this narrative of the first ten years of her life, Mernissi paints portraits of resourceful, courageous women confined in the secluded women's quarters of the extended family's home, who nevertheless rise above an imposed environment of exclusion and seclusion. The confinement of women here evokes Foucauldian notions of borders and boundaries, erected in prisons or mental institutions, as symptoms of power relationships. By its very nature, power intrudes, divides, and imposes: any imposition is a brutalization of the victim's volition. The prohibition on women to leave their quarters, except on special occasions and only when accompanied by a male relative or guardian, represents not only a limitation on freedom but also an asphyxiation of creative potential. As in all of Mernissi's other books, Islam is at the center of the discourse. Male appropriation, interpretation, and self-serving implementation of the teachings of Islam have established, in Mernissi's view, a complex set of rules, prohibitions, and boundaries (*hudud*) that relegates women to marginalized, powerless entities to be guided and controlled by men, at times to extremes of exploitation, abuse, even violence and slavery.

As a central concept consuming the narrator's consciousness, *hudud* becomes the book's dominant metaphor that defines and delimits women's destiny. As a young child, Mernissi is told by the headmistress at her Qur'anic school that "education is to know the *hudud,* the sacred frontiers," and "[t]o be a Muslim was to respect the *hudud.* And for a child to respect the *hudud* was to obey" (3). Naturally, to a child, *hudud,* despite its centrality in ethics and education, remains a nebulous, slippery term; she therefore seeks the help of an older female cousin to show her the location of *hudud*: "She answered that all she knew for sure was that everything would work out fine if I obeyed the teacher. The *hudud* was whatever the teacher forbade. My cousin's words helped me relax and start enjoying school" (3). It is emblematic that *hudud* is defined to a young girl of an inquisitive mind according to what the whip-wielding teacher forbade, creating a lasting, lifelong impact: "But since then, looking for the frontier has become my life's occupation. Anxiety eats at me whenever I cannot situate the geometric line organizing my powerlessness" (3). By the book's last page, *hudud* is thrown into sharp focus through an adult's metaphorical voice, as

> a cosmic frontier [that] splits the planet into two halves. The frontier indicates the line of power because wherever there is a frontier, there are two kinds of creatures walking on Allah's earth, the powerful on one side, and the powerless on the other. (242)

Thus, a "*surveiller et punir*" (discipline and punish) institution takes shape here in which the powerless (i.e., the women) end up with a lower status, less mobility, and fewer privileges. One's fate is sealed and becomes recognizable according to the book's last Kafkaesque caveat: "if you can't get out, you are on the powerless side" (242).

Deliberately drawing a parallel between the division of the national homeland and the domestic household, Mernissi underscores the fact that Morocco, during the narrative time in the early 1940s, was divided and occupied by the two colonial powers of France and Spain. This sundering of the country is replicated in the partition of the Mernissi household between men's quarters and women's: the harem. The suggestion here is that the women were doubly colonized: as citizens of a foreign-occupied country and as secluded inhabitants of a male-controlled household. Since the word *harem* of the title has acquired titillating nuances in some Western mind-sets, Mernissi's narrator, to her credit, makes a clear distinction between two concepts of harem: imperial and domestic. Imperial harem has excited many a prominent Orientalist's penchant for the twin pursuits of erotica and exotica as reflected in several European paintings and narratives; it reached its pathological pinnacle with the Turkish Ottoman dynasty: places with fearsome eunuchs guarding female sex slaves and nights of intrigue and debauchery are all part of that sordid saga.[1] According to Mernissi, imperial harem began "with the territorial conquest and accumulation of wealth of the Muslim imperial dynasties, starting with the Omayyads, a seventh-century Arab dynasty based in Damascus" (34). On the other hand, Mernissi associates domestic harem with extended families "with no slaves and no eunuchs, and often with monogamous couples, but who carried on the tradition of women's seclusion " (34). The institution of domestic harem critiqued here is very much similar to that of purdah in India/Pakistan that has been dramatized and critiqued by the three Muslim women writers from India discussed in chapter 2: Rokeya Sakhawat Hossain in "Sultana's Dream" and *Avarodhbasini*, Iqbalunissa Hussain in *Purdah and Polygamy*, and Attia Hosain in *Sunlight on a Broken Column*. While the world of domestic harem that Mernissi describes is not as oblique and crippling as the purdah world of Bengali Muslim women in the 1900s that Rokeya Hossain describes in *Avarodhbasini*, Mernissi's confinement is still restrictive and ridiculous. Happily, owing to progressive social developments and the efforts of Muslim feminist activists, the two institutions of purdah and harem are heading toward the exit, to be replaced by the often voluntary practice of hijab (head scarf) especially among young women who "appear to be responding favorably to the invitation to return to the roots of their heritage" (Haddad 70).[2] Of course, hijab generates a debate of its own that shall continue throughout the twenty-first century. In her subsequent book, *Schehrezade Goes West*, Mernissi once again foregrounds male power as the arbiter on women's dress codes through a comparison between Muslim and European women: "Power manifests itself as theater, with the powerful dictating to the weak what role they must play. To veil on the Muslim side of the Mediterranean is to dress as the ruling Imam demands. To be considered beautiful on the European side of the Mediterranean is to dress as the market-Imam demands" (114).

The secluded women in Mernissi's *Dreams of Trespass*, though cornered, are not defeated, though controlled are not paralyzed, though hurt are not broken. They devise means to connect mentally and imaginatively with the wider world denied to them. Reading (for those who could or who taught themselves how to) and listening to the radio (normally a man's privilege but the women find ways to have access to it when the men are out) are two cleverly symbolic acts of resistance that strengthen their spirit of subversion, whose manifestations can be seen in the resort to humor, dramatic productions, and storytelling. For the agitators and activists among the women in the household, humor becomes an authority-defying strategy, a tension-releasing outlet, and a hope-sustaining instrument. It enables them to endure a cheerless environment and survive sanely their powerlessness. Despite very limited resources and experiences, the dramatic productions—concocted and based on the lives of pioneering feminists from the Muslim world such as Aisha Taymour, Zaynab Fawwaz, and Huda

Sha'raoui—testify to their daring creativity and thirst for affiliation with emblematic figures of survival, resistance, and reform. Demonstrating active audience participation, the women function simultaneously as actors, audience, and commentators on the plays that are scripted and directed by the narrator's favorite female cousin, Chama. Storytelling signifies their stirred imagination and identification with heroic role models such as Shahrazad of *The One Thousand and One Nights*. One of the narrator's favorite relatives, the unjustly abandoned wife, Aunt Habiba, is a resourceful modern-day Shahrazad who spins numerous inspiring tales of courage and hope that excite the imagination of her enchanted young listeners. The stories enable the listeners to combat fear, expand the imagination, and inculcate in them the spirit of tolerance and openness:

> Riding on her words, we traveled past Sind and Hind (India), leaving Muslim territories behind, living dangerously, and making friends with Christians and Jews, who shared their bizarre foods with us and watched us do our prayers, while we watched them do theirs. Sometimes we traveled so far that no gods were to be found, only sun- and fire-worshippers, but even they seemed friendly and endearing when introduced by Aunt Habiba. Her tales made me long to become an adult and an expert storyteller myself. I wanted to learn how to talk in the night. (19)

In this context, *The One Thousand and One Nights* represents the prototype for narrative excellence. Shahrazad, the resourceful heroine, is the inspiration and model for feminine self-preservation in the face of male mania. Shahrazad wisely chose neither confrontation (as futile as it would have been) nor escape (equally futile but also undignified) but art or artfulness in storytelling, whereby, according to E. M. Forster, she wielded "the weapon of suspense—the only literary tool that has any effect upon tyrants and savages" (28). Shahrazad's artfulness signifies confrontation by other means. In a telling footnote, Mernissi debunks the view of "many Westerners" of her as "a lovely but simple-minded entertainer"; Mernissi sees her as

> a strategist and a powerful thinker, who uses her psychological knowledge of human beings to get them to walk faster and leap higher. Like Saladin and Sindbad, she makes us bolder and more sure of ourselves and of our capacity to transform the world and its people. (15)

Accordingly, in spite of numerous restrictions, prohibitions, and put-downs, the women turn the harem into a vibrant character-building world, while maintaining self-respect and nourishing hope for a better alternative, if not for themselves then for their young offsprings. In an insightful moment, the narrator's mother articulates her "dream of trespass":

"At least my daughters will have a better life, full of opportunities," she would
say. "They will get an education, and travel. They will discover the world, understand it, and eventually participate in transforming it. As it is, the world is
most definitely rotten. For me at least. Maybe you ladies have found the secret
to being happy in this courtyard." Then she would turn to me and say, "You *are*
going to transform this world, aren't you? You are going to create a planet without walls and without frontiers, where the gatekeepers have off every day of the
year." Long silences would follow her speeches, but the beauty of her images
would linger on, and float around the courtyard like perfumes, like dreams.
Invisible, but so powerful. (200–01)

Significantly, the women have an entrenched belief that in Islam "everyone is
equal. Allah said so. His prophet preached the same" (26); even animals, perceptively explains Yasmina, the narrator's feisty maternal grandmother, are equal to
humans: "Animals are just like us; the only thing they lack is speech" (35). Such
an inclusivist attitude affirms the potential of turning their current, crippling
life into "a cascade of serene delights" (81). What emerges from the series of vignettes, anecdotes, and exposés is a composite image of strong women who, despite their confinement, are at once conscious of the denial of their Islamic
rights and remain devout in their faith. They underpin their resistance on the
concept of *'Adl* (justice) in Islam and anchor their vision on the brightest and
most tolerant elements of Islam, such as the Prophet's call for respect for one's
mother: "to get to paradise, a Muslim had to pass under his mother's feet" (239).
The women's evocation of the Prophet's name in the Mernissi household interlinks with Nawal El Saadawi's astute pronouncement in her article "Women
and Islam":

> Prophet Mohammed was more emancipated with respect to women than most
> men of his time, and even most Muslim men nowadays. He gave his women
> the right to stand up to him, rebuke him, or tell him where he had gone
> wrong. (75)

However, among the women in the household, the attitude toward *hudud* is not
uniform. The narrator contests and complains about it. Aunt Habiba, "who had
been cast off and sent away suddenly for no reason by a husband she loved
dearly," accepts it (3). She includes *hudud* within a conceptual frame of justice
that involves obligations on both men and women; in her eyes, *hudud* was not
meant to privilege men, but to safeguard women's rights, that is, their frontiers:
"When you hurt a woman, you are violating Allah's sacred frontier. It is unlaw-
ful to hurt the weak" (3). If Aunt Habiba's statement suggests that she regards
women as weak, her own resourcefulness and occasional daring acts prove that
she is far from being such a person. Her views on women as being weak are,

moreover, qualitatively different from those of the narrator's rebellious mother who "had always rejected male superiority as nonsense and totally anti-Muslim—'Allah made us all equal,' she would say" (9). One can see that both Aunt Habiba and the narrator's mother refer to Islam as the definitive recourse whose foundational principles of justice and fair play have been over the years modified and/or manipulated by those who wield power in society so as to suit their own agendas.

Registering the diverse angles from which these sincere, sympathetic women approach Islam somehow reflects the unsettled, at times contradictory, positions that Mernissi expresses in a number of her other published works. In her first book, *Beyond the Veil,* she makes a categorical claim that the "Muslim system" is antiwomen because of its fear of women adulterating men's allegiance to God:

> It appears to me that the Muslim system is not so much opposed to women as to the heterosexual unit. What is feared is the growth of the involvement between a man and a woman into an all-encompassing love, satisfying the sexual, emotional and intellectual needs of both partners. Such an involvement constitutes a direct threat to the man's allegiance to Allah, which should be the unconditional investment of all the man's energies, thoughts and feelings in his God. (viii)

Mernissi's statement here is quite problematic because her reading of Islam is quasi-celibatical, approaching a monastic tradition. In other words, it projects on Islam a perspective that is alien and irrelevant to its context. (Nevertheless, her suggestion elsewhere in the same book that the liberation of women is not only a "spiritual problem" but "predominantly an economic issue" (99) assumes greater validity.) In her other book *Doing Daily Battle: Interviews with Moroccan Women,* she pronounces "our heritage as I have experienced it as a child, adolescent, and adult, [sic] is an obscurantist and mutilating heritage" (13). On the other hand, the preface to the English edition of her *Women and Islam: An Historical and Theological Inquiry* reveals a radically different position, expressed in equally categorical terms:

> Any man who believes that a Muslim woman who fights for her dignity and right to citizenship excludes herself necessarily from the *umma* and is a brainwashed victim of Western propaganda is a man who misunderstands his own religious heritage, his own cultural identity. The vast and inspiring records of Muslim history so brilliantly completed for us by scholars such as Ibn Hisham, Ibn Hajar, Ibn Sa'ad, and Tabari, [sic] speak to the contrary. We Muslim women can walk into the modern world with pride, knowing that the quest for dignity, democracy, and human rights, for full participation in the political and social

affairs of our country, stems from no imported Western values, but is a true part of the Muslim tradition. Of this I am certain, after reading the works of those scholars mentioned above and many others. They give me evidence to feel proud of my Muslim past and to feel justified in valuing the best gifts of modern civilization: human rights and the satisfaction of full citizenship. (vii–viii)

This affirmative position recalls Naila Minai's argument that Islam came with a "feminist bill of rights":

> It was a religion that concerned itself heavily with women's rights, in a surprisingly contemporary manner. A woman was to be educated and allowed to earn and manage her income. She was to be recognized as legal heir to her father's property along with her brother. Her rights in marriage were also clearly spelled out: she was entitled to sexual satisfaction as well as economic support. Nor was divorce to consist any longer of merely throwing the wife out of the house without paying her financial compensation. (4)

In her sociohistorical writings, Mernissi goes over the same track time and again, at the risk of repeating herself. This is arguably justifiable given the heat and ferocity of the debate, the delicacy and complexity of the issues involved, and the stiff resistance from conservative quarters. Murad Hofmann, a German diplomat who converted to Islam, deems Mernissi "not competent in Islamic history, philosophy, and theology. Yet she dabbles in all these" (69 n. 94). Significantly, she makes one crucial distinction between political Islam and what she calls "*Islam Risala*": by political Islam she refers "to Islam as the practice of power, to the acts of people animated by passions and motivated by interest" while *Islam Risala* means to her "the divine message, the ideal recorded in the Koran, the holy book" (Mernissi, *Forgotten Queens* 5). That ideal was put into practice during "the Prophet's splendid days at Medina, when women took part, as disciples, in the building of an initially egalitarian Islam" (Mernissi, *Women's Rebellion* 87). While Mernissi engages in a serious debate against patriarchy within the Muslim tradition, she, like Leila Ahmed in *Women and Gender in Islam*, argues, with a tinge of irony, against the notion that Arab women, being "subservient, obedient slaves," owe their awareness of patriarchal hegemony to Western feminists:

> But if you carefully ask yourself (as I often have) why an American or French feminist will think that I am less clever than she in grasping patriarchal degradation schemes, you realize that it gives her an immediate control of the situation; she is the leader and I the follower. She, in spite of her claimed desire to change the system and make it more egalitarian for women, retains (lurking deep down in her subliminal ideological genes) the racist and imperialist

Western *male* distorting drives. Even when faced with an Arab woman who has similar diplomas, knowledge, and experience, she unconsciously reproduces the supremacist colonial pattern. Every time I come across a Western feminist who thinks I am indebted to her for my own development on feminist issues, I worry not so much about the prospects of an international sisterhood, but about the possibility of Western feminism's transforming itself into popular social movements able to produce structural change in the world centres of industrialized empires. (*Women's Rebellion* 15–16)

With such shifting grounds and complex milieux to operate from, *Dreams of Trespass* retrieves, reconstructs, and re/presents lived experiences; such an autobiographical pursuit is no random recall but a deliberate, selective, and structured exercise of memory. Shaping the narrative with such a methodical coherence represents, in Georges Gusdorf's views, the "original sins of autobiography" because

the narrative is conscious, and since the narrator's consciousness directs the narrative, it seems to him [or to her] incontestable that it has also directed his [or her] life. In other words, the act of reflecting that is essential to conscious awareness is transferred, by a kind of unavoidable optical illusion, back to the stage of the event itself. (41)

The narrative's appealing merit is thus gained at the expense of the sense of spontaneity and unpredictability that is a constituent of our ontological comprehension of life. Moreover, these crafted exposés of the narrator's private experiences are quite skillfully and persistently contextualized into wider, more public levels of signification, that is, gender politics in a tradition seemingly and arguably rooted in religion. If, according to James Olney, autobiography "might fairly be seen as a very daring, even foolhardy, undertaking—a bold rush into an area where angels might well fear to tread" (3), Mernissi's discourse on her awareness of sexuality, seclusion, and suppression in their various shapes is indeed admirably daring. One detects an aching need to open up space to discuss gender politics away from the rigid boundaries and taboos erected by patriarchy and reified notions perpetrated by some Western feminists.

As a subgenre, autobiography is a variegated form as diverse as St. Augustine's *Confessions* and *Roland Barthes* by Roland Barthes. Since the "I," as our sole source, attempts to recover an absence, our reading is focused on its pronouncements, articulations, and temperamental shifts. In such a context, total veracity and absolute fidelity to detail, though dearly valued by some, may assume a secondary importance—or no importance at all if one were to accept Paul Valéry's famous dictum "En littérature, le vrais n'est pas conceivable" (in literature, truth is not conceivable), meaning that literature is concerned only with the impact of language and does not care about the truth of its speculations. However, it does not suffice to treat the text merely as an autonomous, verbal construction; no text, even the most narcissistic, can be totally self-reflexive. While trusting the integrity and insights of the "I" is important in an autobiographical narrative, the narrative's situatedness in specific spatial and temporal foci becomes equally crucial. Part of the success of Mernissi's narrative is its recurrent outward trajectories toward sociopolitical events that extrapolate beyond the immediate concerns of the female child toward the concerns of the mature, erudite woman who was once that child.

In the book's first two sentences, an adult's voice thus begins the narrative by concisely specifying three things at once: time/history; the locale in terms of East–West geography; and the two thematic conflicts involving (1) gender politics as manifested in the seclusion of women in the harem (the foreground), and (2) religious nationalism against the "Christian" colonizers (the background):

> I was born in a harem in 1940 in Fez, a ninth-century Moroccan city some five thousand kilometers west of Mecca and one thousand kilometers south of Madrid, one of the dangerous capitals of the Christians. The problems with the Christians start, said father, as with women, when the *hudud*, or sacred frontier, is not respected. (1)

With such loaded idioms, the reader's expectations are heightened and pointed in various directions, within which the "I" becomes only one, if the leading, component/indicator out of many. Gender and nationalist aspirations are immediately aligned in a parallel fashion so as to become the narrative's major and minor motifs:

> When Allah created the earth, said father, he separated men from women and put a sea between Muslims and Christians for a reason. Harmony exists when each group respects the prescribed limits of the other; trespassing leads only to sorrow and unhappiness. But women dreamed of trespassing all the time. The world beyond the gate was their obsession. They fantasized all day long about parading in unfamiliar streets while the Christians kept crossing the sea bringing death and chaos. (1–2)

Counterbalancing this simplistic, if benign, weltanschauung, there are, throughout the narrative, recurrent references to the positive impact of Moroccan nationalism on family life, especially regarding dress code, educating girls, and encouraging (or tolerating) women to participate in anticolonialist demonstrations. Mernissi's stance here acknowledges the salutary impact of the male- and elite-led nationalism and differs from that of other Arab feminists. For instance, Evelyne Accad argues:

In the Middle East, nationalism and feminism have never mixed very well. Women have been used in national liberation struggles—Algeria, Iran, Palestine to name a few—only to be sent back to their kitchens after "independence" was gained. (238)

Interestingly, Moroccan nationalism in *Dreams of Trespass* assumes an Islamic context with no mention of Arab nationalism, which became prominent in the 1950s and 1960s in *Mashriq* (the eastern part of the Arab world). In fact, solid pan-Islamic sentiments are expressed when reflecting on intra-Muslim marriage; according to Chama, "A young Moroccan lady could marry as far away as Lahore, Kuala Lumpur, or even China. 'Allah made Islam's territory immense and wonderfully diverse,' she said" (194). The pan-Islamism expressed here is Mernissi's manner of highlighting one of the fascinating features of Islam that gave it cohesion and consistency throughout time and across geography, enabling it to establish roots wherever it spread.

Mernissi's *Dream of Trespass* represents a gendered social discourse articulated through the medium of autobiographical narrative. It not only recalls selective episodes from childhood memories but puts those incidents into a politicized, interpretive historiography of family domestic practices projected from within the larger context of nationalist politics. As a text with an agenda, it succeeds in exposing male double-talk and appropriation of the theological argument to be utilized toward the enforcement of the codes of confinement. As a blend of life-writing and gender polemic, the book militates for testing, trespassing, and breaking down the boundaries of seclusion and for discussing and celebrating human sexuality and healthy male and female awareness of their bodies. At the same time, Mernissi's discourse demystifies an institution (the harem) that has been part of the deformed mythology of exoticized Islam, for, to use Barbara Harlow's phrase, "the secret tantalizing recesses of the harem" has been teasing and feeding Western fixation (xvi). This obsessive fantasia represents not only a misinformed reductionist construct of an entire culture, but also a harmful contamination of vision that damages the intrusive, defiling gazer. Ultimately, the victimizer runs the risk of victimizing himself.

It is instructive to compare Mernissi's autobiographical narrative with that of Che Husna Azhari's recollection of her childhood experiences as a precocious young girl growing up in a religious Muslim environment in rural Malaysia. Azhari's narrative is contained in a slim book entitled *The Rambutan Orchard*, published in 1993, a year earlier than the publication of Mernissi's *Dreams of Trespass*. Both Mernissi and Azhari are established academics in their own countries: Mernissi is a sociologist who has published several books about the status of women in Muslim cultural heritage and contemporary society; Azhari is a scientist whose literary writings, in prose and poetry, are strongly autobiographical, with an engaging penchant for humor. Azhari's *The Rambutan Orchard* contains five interlinked episodes that relate to her life as a Malay Muslim girl growing up in Melor, a village in rural Kelantan, the northeastern state of the Malaysian peninsula, where the author grew up. While the events are experienced by a child, the discourse, like Mernissi's, is voiced by an adult who was that child. In contrast to Mernissi's autobiographical reconstruction of her Moroccan childhood experiences, shaped and animated by an ideological drive, Azhari's is prompted by the joy of telling stories retrieved, reconstructed, or reinvented for the pleasure of the exercise itself. This contrast can be construed from the title of each book. Mernissi's *Dreams of Trespass: Tales of a Harem Childhood* immediately forecasts a concept, an idea of some subversive resonance, invoking resistance to gender-biased boundaries; concurrently it flaunts the exotically charged term *Harem* that recalls, to borrow Rana Kabbani's subtitle, one of "Europe's myth[s] of orient," to be deflated later in a footnote. On the other hand, Azhari's simple title, *The Rambutan Orchard*, suggests an attachment to a place, an affiliation with an environment, "an orchard," which explicitly evokes the concept of "Jannah," a reference to the Muslim concept of "Orchard-Paradise" (5) often mentioned in the Qur'an. The rural environment assumes a critical formative factor in the young heroine's life. For Muslims, harmony and affiliation with nature are so central that the color green has symbolically become identified with Islam. While Mernissi foregrounds the word *dreams* in her title and throughout the text as a subversive metaphor, Azhari too articulates her own dreams, not of "trespass" but of a regenerative, cross-generational signification:

> a verdant garden of beautiful dreams. . . .
> Because we are all keepers of Dreams,
> Transmuters of Dreams
> In unbroken chains.
> For our children, and our grandchildren.
> We pressed it into their reluctant hands. (79)

Described in idyllic terms, nature, like everything else in Azhari's discourse, is steeped in the rituals of Islam combined with a mother's care:

Whatever tree there was in my rambutan orchard, it grew and flowered and bore the most succulent, worm-free fruits. All the fruits could only be described in superlatives. There were reasons for this. First, the trees were planted by my mother. Anything my mother touched and placed in the earth would sprout and grow, as if she had a pact with the ground. Then she watered them and carried chicken and duck's droppings from under the house to these plants as nutritional offerings. But we also knew there was another reason for their zealous growth. My mother constantly talked to the trees and often recited Quran to them. It was the most potent fertilizer of all. The trees grew and grew, the fruits too became agricultural wonders. We took everything for granted and later took whatever was in the orchard as the measuring stick for everything. (8–9)

Apart from conveying a secure set of values, the mother's identification with nature parallels that of grandmother Yasmina's in Mernissi's narrative, and the heroines of both books register ardent allegiances to their strong, devoted mothers, while the fathers are either absent or of marginal impact.

Both Mernissi's and Azhari's reconstructive narratives resort to humorous vignettes as a means to convey poignant points. The heroines of both books can laugh with others and laugh at themselves. However, unlike Mernissi's *citadine* heroine who progressively becomes aware of the confining male-constructed boundaries, Azhari's rural heroine spends her childhood in an open environment, even though the latter's milieu is just as dominated by the ethos and rituals of Islam as the former's. The heroine's life seems unrestricted by any visible boundaries, at least not at this early stage covered in the narrative. This may explain the divergent discourses articulated in Mernissi's and Azhari's narratives. Ever the diligent polemicist, Mernissi often interjects an incisive feminist thrust into the episodes; conversely, following a lucid, straightforward design, Azhari is keen on recuperating past experiences to spin engaging narrative yarns out of them. Given the young age of the heroines in both narratives, there is a deliberate ellipsis of sexuality, even though Mernissi's delves combatively into the politics of sexuality, while Azhari avoids this issue altogether. Capturing the rhythm of her rural community, Azhari's stories are at once steeped in the rituals of Islam and in Malay popular mythology. Time is punctuated by the calls of prayers, while space is inhabited by folkloric spirits of peninsular collective imagination concocting stories about ghosts, bandits, and "children eaters." Endearingly, Azhari mentions her village custom of greeting strangers, whomever they may be, a practice that she has carried with her "till [her] old age, all over the continents that [she] travelled to," even though "sophisticated human beings" might scoff at it as odd or naive (13).

Azhari's narrative operates through vignettes fashioned after the oral tradition of storytelling, common in many Muslim societies. The audience here is assumed to be "everybody, adults and children alike" (5). As the preface points out, Azhari has grown "on a diet of Jannah stories" (5), affirming them as a potent formative factor in the child's imagination. This religion-rooted inspirational "diet" of conventional Shahrazadic tales[3] is astutely modified by a touch of postmodernist skepticism mentioned in the book's epilogue, when the author-narrator admits the "fabrication" and fictional embellishment of events and details of childhood recollections: "Memories tend to be personalized and historically incorrect. Dates jumbled, black becomes white, white becomes black; events, people, tastes, emotions, tinged and foreshadowed by experiences in faraway places" (77).

An astute observer of her village's characters, customs, and minor conflicts, she is deeply sensitive, indeed protective, about her Malay Muslim culture and the image her writing is projecting about it. Her style is scant and simple, yet moving and engagingly poetic. In a touching conclusion to a story entitled "The Boy Who Spoke Sparingly," she writes about a mute poor playmate who falls ill and dies:

> And now my friend Mat Hussein has gone to God, I wish that he might have all the things he did not have in this world. I wish that he might have an opulent house built in marble and pearls, large, cool, and airy. But most of all I wish that he may be strong and tall and when he opens his mouth, he may be silver-tongued, beautiful words flowing from his mouth. Those who hear him speak will be spellbound by the eloquence and beauty of his words. (75–76)

This paradisical image with which she concludes the last story brings her narrative full circle: it began with her being fed Jannah stories and ends with her constructing one to house her deceased friend. In the world of Azhari's imagination, the ethos of caring and compassion is anchored in the creeds and conventions of Islam that represent the formative social and spiritual factors in the heroine's growth to mature adulthood.

# EIGHT

# Arab-Muslim Feminism and the Narrative of Hybridity: The Fiction of Ahdaf Soueif

No one today is purely *one* thing.
                            —Edward Said, *Culture and Imperialism.*

For me the world is a garden of cultures where a thousand flowers grow. Throughout history all cultures have fed on one another, being grafted onto one another and in the process our world has been enriched.
                    —Yashar Kemal, Kurdish-Turkish novelist, in his trial speech

AS AN ARAB-MUSLIM WOMAN WHO WRITES IN ENGLISH, AHDAF SOUEIF connects with two currents in contemporary Arab and Muslim literatures: Muslim women from diverse parts of the world who write in English (writers such as Mena Abdullah from Australia, Attia Hosain from India, Zaynab Alkali from Nigeria, and Farhana Sheikh from England) and the feminist literature in Arabic represented by such writers as Nawal El Saadawi, Hanan al-Shaykh, Ahlam Mosteghanemi, and Salwa Bakr. I foreground these two currents as contradistinctive factors to another corpus of writing that becomes relevant when analyzing Soueif's fiction—namely, Western texts with prominent female heroines such as *Madame Bovary, Anna Karenina, Wuthering Heights*, and, most importantly, *Middlemarch.*

As a hybrid of numerous East–West, classical–modern, and, to a lesser degree, urban–rural literary trends, the writings of Ahdaf Soueif reveal features in contemporary Arab and Muslim literatures produced in English and deal with crucial motifs in "postcolonial"/"third world" literatures such as representation, migration/exile, and colonial/neocolonial/postcolonial transitions. Her work fuses a number of discursive trajectories involving such complex polemics as Arab and Egyptian nationalisms, gender politics, and Muslims' response to both modernity and hegemonic prejudices emanating from the West.

To date, Soueif has produced four works of fiction: two collections of short stories, *Aisha* (1983) and *Sandpiper* (1996); a dense epic novel of almost eight hundred pages, *In the Eye of the Sun* (1992), demonstrating a "combination of scrupulous deliberation and formidable narrative energy" (Kermode 19); and a second novel entitled *The Map of Love* (1999), a tour de force of revisionist metahistory of Egypt in the twentieth century. These four works are interlinked by characters, episodes, and cross-references that suggest a quasi-autobiographical slant to the narrative whose instigating impulse is to highlight the process of emotional and intellectual growth of its privileged, upper-middle-class heroines: Aisha, Asya, and Amal.

## AISHA

Soueif's first book, *Aisha,* contains an uneven collection of eight stories—the dust jacket refers to them as chapters—that deal with such issues as marital tension, feminine sexuality, and rape in narratives that shift settings between Egypt and Europe. Significantly, the well-read, well-traveled narrator-heroine, Aisha, refers to herself as a "Westernized bourgeois intellectual": "I loved Maggie Tulliver, Anna Karenina, Emma Bovary, and understood them as I understood none of the people around me" (27). The bourgeois lifestyle (though not necessarily the mentality) is unapologetically illustrated in various acquisitions and souvenirs purchased in different cities of the world; Aisha reflects on her numerous travels: "What city was left that she could not go to and not find memories?" (20). Indeed, travel becomes an initiation process toward hybridity whereby cultures coalesce, compete, and conflict simultaneously. The resulting mélange of diverse values causes confusion and clarity, contest and collaboration, enrichment and impoverishment. Apart from the heroine's cosmopolitan concerns and marital worries, two narratives in the collection give us rare, fascinating, if disturbing, images of life in rural Egypt. One, "The Wedding of Zeina" (the title evokes parodically Tayeb Salih's Arabic novel *The Wedding of Zein*), deals with the trauma that the servant Zeina has undergone many years earlier on her wedding night at the age of only fifteen: not only does the young bride not comprehend the choice of a husband the family has made for her, nor the tiresome, painful wedding preparations she has to undergo, but she is also shocked by the violence and force used by female family members present at the wedding chamber to help the groom penetrate her with his bandaged finger so that the blood-soaked bandage can be exhibited as a sign of the virginity of the bride—a proof of a prized commodity. As Zeina recalls, "My uncle wound it around his head, blood and all, and danced slowly and proudly into the crowd using his gun like a cane to dance with and calling out 'Our Honour, Our daughter's Honour, Our family's Honour'" (82). In the following story entitled "Her Man," a continuation (though not a sequel) of the preceding one, the husband marries a second woman over Zeina, thus creating a tense, if silent, rivalry between the two wives. The disturbing turn in the story occurs when Zeina resorts to deceit and dishonesty to betray the second younger wife to the husband, claiming that the latter has dishonored him while he was away. Immediately, the impetuous husband divorces the second wife. While this story reveals the rash credulity of the foolish husband, it, more significantly, highlights the treachery of the first wife who unscrupulously manipulates a trusting rival so that she, Zeina, keeps "her man." The foregrounding of women betraying women signifies that, for Soueif, apportioning blame in the dynamics of sexual politics cannot be gender-specific. Moreover, one cannot disavow or condemn the entire culture of Islam, in whose name several cruel practices are done against women. This attitude in Soueif's writing is a shared feature with the works of other Arab and Muslim women writers in English that reveal an unequivocal sense of affiliation with their Islamic culture, while at the same time condemning and combating the abusive excesses of patriarchy when it appropriates and exploits the religious argument to preserve its own spiritual and material hegemony. Edward Said would say that "such works are feminist but not exclusivist . . . engaged but not demagogic, sensitive to but not maudlin about women's experience" (*Culture* xxiv).

Alternatively, the discourse of these writers strives, with varying degrees of militancy, for an agenda that is quite distinct from Euro-American feminism, however we may perceive that to be. In her 1992 study, *Women and Gender in Islam: Historical Roots of a Modern Debate,* Leila Ahmed cautions against the attitude of some Western feminists who adopt and "uncritically reinscribe the old story . . . that Arab men, Arab culture, and Islam are incurably backward and that Arab and Islamic societies indeed deserve to be dominated, undermined, or worse" (246–47). Earlier, Nawal El Saadawi, in her 1979 preface to the English edition of her book *The Hidden Face of Eve,* takes a similar stance emanating from a lucid, leftist perspective:

> Influential circles, particularly in the Western imperialist world, depict the problems of Arab women as stemming from the substance and values of Islam, and simultaneously depict the retarded development of Arab countries in many important areas as largely the result of religious and cultural factors or even inherent characteristics in the mental and psychic constitution of the Arab peoples. For them underdevelopment is not related to economic and political factors, at the root of which lies foreign exploitation of resources, and the plunder to which national riches are exposed. For them there is no link between political and economic emancipation and the processes related to growth, development, and progress. (i)

Moreover, in a critique of reductionist generalizations about Arab and Muslim women, Chandra Mohanty exposes certain feminist a priori Eurocentric assumptions: "This mode of feminist analysis, by homogenizing and systematizing the experiences of different groups of women, erases all marginal and resistant modes of experience" (80). She further argues:

> Not only are *all* Arab and Muslim women seen to constitute a homogeneous oppressed group, but there is no discussion of the specific *practices* within the family, which constitute women as mothers, wives, sisters, etc. Arabs and Muslims, it appears, don't change at all. Their patriarchical family is carried over from the times of the Prophet Muhammad. They exist, as it were, outside history. (70)

## IN THE EYE OF THE SUN

Ahdaf Soueif's *In the Eye of the Sun*, a quasi-autobiographical bildungsroman, develops several of the motifs introduced in *Aisha,* except here more densely and expansively, whereby "high politics and domestic minutiae are juxtaposed" (Mantel 28). As with Aisha, the titular heroine of Soueif's first book, the liberated, privileged, cosmopolitan heroine of *In the Eye of the Sun,* Asya, is portrayed candidly and sympathetically. According to the Egyptian novelist, Sonallah Ibrahim, Soueif "is the only [Egyptian] novelist who has dared to treat the topic of sexuality with such courage and clarity, sparing nothing and describing everything in the minutest detail" (viii).

Significantly, the heroine's name, Asya, is a multilayered hybrid. In one of the stories in *Sandpiper,* entitled "Mandy," whose events and characters interlink with the novel, the following explanation of the Arabic name is given to Mandy, a metonym for the mundane non-Arabic reader of the English text: "It actually means Asia in Arabic . . . it can also mean 'the Cruel One' and 'she who is full of sorrow'" (93). Apart from the duality of emotions that the name suggests, the fact that an Egyptian, whose country is situated in Africa, is given a name that recalls another continent while the explanation is given in a third continent suggests that Asya's feelings, experiences, and worldviews extend beyond her geographical borders. Also Asya, in the Muslim tradition, is the name of the Pharaoh's childless wife who adopted and loved the baby prophet Musa (Moses), found adrift in a basket in the Nile near her palace; she saved the baby from a certain death and raised him to healthy youth. Asya is thus a name that integrates Pharaonic Egypt with Judaism and Islam.

Moreover, Soueif's *In the Eye of the Sun* integrates the private history of a woman and her family with the political history of the nation between the years 1967 and 1980, done with detailed ideological depth and definition. We

feel the pulsating drama of the senseless defeat of the Egyptian army during the
Six Days' War of June 1967, together with the puzzlement and despair of ordinary Egyptians who were initially led by President Nasser's monstrous propaganda machine to believe that Egypt was winning, to be told later that the loss
had been immense and humiliating. The image of Nasser, the anticolonialist pa-
triarch-dictator, is complex: tyrannical, mysterious, but charismatic, popular, and
dedicated.[1] This integration of the private and the political has been a fascinating feature, as we have already witnessed, in the works of other Muslim writers
in English: Attia Hosain, Nuruddin Farah, M. G. Vassanji, and Adib Khan. What
is particularly engaging about the heroine, Asya, is that her sharp political sensitivity extends beyond Egyptian nationalist concerns to embrace other dispossessed peoples of the Middle East such as the Kurds, Palestinians, and
Armenians. To further nuance the novel's political discourse, Soueif uses dis-
ease/surgery as a metaphor for the crisis/cure of the tyrannical regimes in the
Arab world. The incident in which an Egyptian army truck, heading for the
front shortly before the Six Days' War, maims Asya's beloved uncle is yet another potently symbolic signifier of a self-injurious army that damages the same
people it is supposed to defend.

While Asya reveals an acute political awareness, derived from an active, hybridized intellectual life straddling Middle Eastern and European cultures, she
is not without paradoxes. She espouses Marxism, yet belongs to a privileged
class: "we see how privilege shackles those who enjoy it, and how restrictive
are the expectations placed on women of this stratum" (Booth 204). She is a
woman of conscience, yet she loves and is married to a man who installs the
computer system for the Syrian secret service. More important, the feminist,
sexually liberated Asya finds "under certain circumstances . . . polygamy ac-
ceptable." She says "I don't 'believe' in polygamy . . . but I don't condemn it out
of hand" (401). She defends her position by deploying the cultural relativist argument: "I wouldn't judge a cannibal by criteria other than those of his own
society" (401). Asya's complex stance here is, to borrow Alfred Arteaga's reinscription of Bakhtin, "inherently polyglot" whereby her "hybridized discourse
rejects the principle of monologue and composes itself by selecting from competing discourses" (18). By the novel's conclusion, the author, to her credit,
feels no compulsion to "quick fix" the conflicts in the heroine's life: back in
Egypt, Asya reconnects symbolically with her two civilizational inspirations: Islamic and ancient Pharaonic,[2] without necessarily disowning her acquired
Western values and experiences. Accordingly, for the modern Arab and Muslim woman, Soueif suggests, the task is not to deny conflicts or paradoxes, but
to accept, comprehend, and even, when possible, fuse them. Such ambivalence
and tentativeness, and such a set of complex, composite paradoxes evoke what
Homi Bhabha calls "the Third Space of enunciation" that "destroys this mirror
of representation in which cultural knowledge is customarily revealed as an

integrated, open, expanding code" (37). In one sense, the roots of these paradoxes seem to stem from the ambivalent affiliations to Arab-Muslim cultural
ethos on the one hand and to acquired European intellectualism on the other:
often Asya reads the "West" from an "Eastern" perspective and she sees the
"East" through "Western" eyes. For instance, walking along the Thames evokes
scenes from the Nile for her; and the recurrent references to *Middlemarch* give
us the impression that she sees herself as Dorothea, except, as Said observes, "in
many ways Asya is her own Casaubon" ("Anglo-Arab Encounter" 19). Conversely, in an engaging segment of the novel, the narrator describes a peasant
family from the heartland of the Egyptian countryside through references to
figures in the Western "canon":

> The mother is a silent, still-faced, black-clad figure out of Lorca: small but the
> centre of power. Her domain is the large, crumbling farmhouse and her voca-
> tion is to keep the family going. The two sisters, married into neighbouring
> farming families, are sometimes from Grimm and sometimes from Louisa May
> Alcott. The brothers are a couple of well-meaning buffoons out of Dickens or
> Fielding: they are dogged by disaster. . . .
>
> The father, a dreamy, expansive sort of man from Tolstoy, a failed and im-
> poverished Levin, owns the only pair of long rubber boots in Beheira
> Province—if not in the whole of agricultural Egypt. (26)

Here, Mikhail Bakhtin's dialogic notions become germane. In his seminal
essay, "Discourse in the Novel," Bakhtin incisively articulates one of his original
ideas about the double-voicedness of the linguistic hybrid as illustrated in novels: "What is hybridization?" he asks:

> It is a mixture of two social languages within the limits of a single utterance,
> an encounter, within the arena of an utterance, between two different linguis-
> tic consciousnesses, separated from one another by an epoch, by social differ-
> entiation or by some other factor. (*Dialogic* 358)

Bakhtin furthermore posits that "the novelistic hybrid is *an artistically organized
system for bringing different languages in contact with one another,* a system having as its
goal the illumination of one language by means of another, the carving-out of a
living image of another language" (*Dialogic* 361). Bakhtin's astute dialogical notion of linguistic, novelistic hybridity can be extended to the spheres of politics,
culture, and commerce in our postindustrial era. As individuals cyberlink,
economies "globalize," and cultures cross-fertilize, hybridity manifests an inevitability that at once destabilizes entrenched exclusionist ethos and entails a
*métissage* of competing or conflicting values that interbreed and give birth to, in
Rushdie's flamboyant phrase, "bastard [children] of history" (*Imaginary Homelands*

394). It is within this flux of cultural hybridity that the fiction of Egyptian-British Ahdaf Soueif is examined here.

Significantly, in the "Epilogue," when Asya returns to Egypt, Soueif chooses an excerpt from Rudyard Kipling's "Song of the Wise Children" to signify a resolution of sorts of the East–West, North–South binary oppositions in the form of a *retour aux sources* "to undo what the North has done" (737). In a published interview with Soueif, a provocative question is put to her claiming that "Asya is not really Egyptian, is she?" The author's Rushdiesque response is tellingly revealing:

> Yes, she is, in the sense that I am Egyptian. There are so many hybrids now, people who are a little bit of this and a little bit of that. The interesting thing is what we make of it, what kind of hybrid we become and how we feel about it. (Pakravan 275)

In other words, despite all appearances to the contrary, Asya—polyglot, well-traveled, and academically accomplished—is simultaneously Egyptian, Arab, and Muslim, as well as other things. Of course, Asya's return to Egypt does not entirely resolve her paradoxes of hybridity; it shifts the locale to allow for other paradoxes to emerge, while enabling her to face and (de)fuse them maturely.

These paradoxes notwithstanding, Soueif's daringly candid portrayal of her heroine makes her, as Edward Said observes, "one of the most extraordinary chroniclers of sexual politics now writing" ("Anglo-Arab Encounter" 19). With Ahdaf Soueif's impressive achievement in *In the Eye of the Sun,* Muslim fiction in English and Middle Eastern women's writings break taboo terrains, one of whose manifestations is that the female characters in her fiction often discuss, uninhibitedly and minutely, complex sexual matters among themselves. Articulate and protective, the nurse Dada Zeina, who appears in both *Aisha* and *In the Eye of the Sun,* discusses in detail with Asya the coital conundrum between the heroine and her husband, Saif Madi, whose sexual paralysis, it seems, is due to his phobia of causing her pain during intercourse. (An ironic signifier of the husband's phallic failure, the name Saif Madi in Arabic means a "piercing sword.") This openness is also reflected in the affectionate, instructive relationship between Asya and her mother; indeed, the mother, in both *Aisha* and *In the Eye of the Sun,* represents a figure of comfort, stability, and guidance in crisis situations.[3] In one significant instance, Asya, after the emotional and sexual estrangement from her Egyptian husband, dabbles in an extramarital affair with an insecurely possessive Englishman who never calls her by her real name and constantly addresses her as "baby," "babe, or "man."[4] Characterized by an ambivalent dynamics of attraction/revulsion, this bizarre, hostile liaison between the sophisticated Egyptian Asya and the crude English Gerald typifies the antagonistic structure of the racial model that Robert Young describes, in which

> the races and their intermixture circulate around an ambivalent axis of desire and
> aversion: a structure of attraction where people and cultures intermix and merge,
> transforming themselves as a result, and a structure of repulsion, where the differ-
> ent elements remain distinct and are set against each other dialogically. (19)

Asya does not hesitate to let her mother know about this damaging affair, a gesture that is quite exceptional when put in an Arabic cultural context. While the
mother does not approve of the extramarital affair, she stands by her daughter
and, as ever, gives emotional and moral support, while the aloof, meticulous, but
not uncaring, academic father is kept in the dark. The mother, who is a prominent
university professor of English literature in her own right, astutely highlights one
of Asya's fundamental failings by reminding her that life is more messy and complex than the plots and characters of the European novels with which she identifies herself and that Asya needs to develop a discerning perspective over her
reality: "This is life, not a novel: you can't sit around being in a dilemma. Things
move, people change" (578), the mother exhorts Asya. This statement echoes an
earlier observation made by Asya's close friend, Chrissie: "It's never the 'right
time.' This is not a novel; you can't time things in life. This is how things happen"
(263). This dislocation between the realm of Western literature and the reality of
the Middle Eastern world constitutes a leitmotific feature that runs throughout
Soueif's fiction. We see an earlier manifestation of it in the short story "Nativity"
in *Aisha*: in an intensely focused, psychologically charged moment the heroine,
Aisha, admits her tendency to see events and figures in her life through literary al-
lusions. In a stream-of-consciousness mode, she reflects thus upon her sinister se-
ducer and subsequent rapist in terms of Samuel Taylor Coleridge's "Kubla Khan":

> It is due to his presence that this dance is palpably more charged than the pre-
> vious ones. "And all shall cry Beware! Beware! His flashing eyes, his—" Well,
> his hair *isn't* floating, she interrupts herself—stop being so silly. It's true. She
> shakes her head. Aisha, you know so much more about Art than Life. Here is
> Life. Life surrounds you, clamours at your ears and eyes and nostrils and you
> crouch in your corner beside your nurse and quote poetry. (136)

Ironically, even Gerald, the crude caricature of a figure, lectures Asya on her most
glaring fault: "The trouble with you . . . is that all your ideas are second-hand;
they are derived from art—not life. . . . O.K. You're intelligent, you're bright,
you're good at taking things to pieces, but you're not good at putting them
together again. You're not clever enough for that" (706).

The most pointed awareness of reality comes to Asya on her return to Egypt
as a professor of English literature at Cairo University. She becomes immediately
conscious that a visible number of her female students, whose class affiliations are
not as privileged as hers, wear the conservative Islamic dress, hijab. An Islamist

female student among them refuses to participate in class discussions because she considers her own voice as 'awra (literally means a private body part not to be revealed). This, of course, is a revealing moment for the aspiring neophyte woman professor fresh from Europe:

> The voice of woman a 'awra. Of course, she'd always known that theoretically, but she'd never come across anyone for whom it was a living truth before. So, as far as this girl—and the others who thought like her—were concerned she was doing a sort of porno-spread up here on the podium for the world to see. So now it was not only a class that wasn't bothered about literature, that didn't know English, that didn't know about sentences, that was too numerous to be taught properly anyway, but also a class holding people who were sitting and scrutinizing her and thinking she was doing something shameful by merely being there—something worse than shame something for which the fires of hell were being stoked in readiness. What if they knew—what if they had looked through the window of the cottage and had seen a blond, blue-eyed man kneeling, his head between her thighs—. (754)

It seems here that Asya, privately preoccupied with her image, misses the wider social and symbolic implications of a woman silencing her own voice. This self-censoring, whether a result of genuine theological conviction or misogynous manipulation, is an acute epiphanic moment that the narrative regrettably does not fully explore. In other words, the discourse here takes a solipsistic significa-tion rather than a collective concern existing within a Muslim cultural context. In her concise review, Leila Ahmed critiques this segment in the novel by high-lighting the social divide between Asya and her students:

> Asya is of middle-class background; the Islam of the middle and upper classes, an urbane, cosmopolitan, secular or near-secular Islam, is of course not the only Islam there is. Moreover, it is an Islam that differs from the Islamic habits and attitudes of other classes. While it is entirely appropriate for the middle-class heroine to direct a hostile and Western-like gaze toward the habits, attitudes and political perspectives of other classes, it might have been more satisfying if the author, as distinct from the heroine, had shown some awareness of Asya's class biases. ("Woman" 6)

## THE MAP OF LOVE

In Soueif's second novel, *The Map of Love*, the privileged-class perspective be-comes even more dominant, yet it is sensitized by humane refinement and con-textualized within a profound preoccupation with history. Indeed, this landmark novel is so steeped in the discourse of history/histories that it would be instructive to probe in some detail its handling of the subject. To begin with a basic concept, history and the discipline of studying it represent a polyphonic, open-ended argument. History involves versions and visions, strategies and styles, details and destinations. Such a perspective entails regarding history as a text, a form of fiction, and assumes that objective history is all but impossible. In fact the French word *histoire* suggests, among other things, the tellingly double meaning of referring to the system of chronicling, analyzing past events, and also to the imaginative genre of fiction. The process of retrieving and fictionalizing certain historical moments in the destiny of any nation, or what Mikhail Bakhtin would call "the novelization of history," gets even more complex because the writer's creative imagination assumes free reign in selecting events, shaping situations, coloring ambience, and charting the terrain often according to subjective criteria governing motives and predilections. For this reason, intriguingly enough, Bakhtin has consistently associated the historical novel with "precisely objectified and finalizing, that is monological, forms of artistic cognition" (*Problems* 271). Happily, the new historicists enrich this debate with their foundational formula about "the historicity of texts and the textuality of histories" (Montrose 5). So when one fictionalizes history, one then creates fiction upon fiction or fiction permeated with fiction; this layering of complexities makes the reader's task both challenging and fascinating.

To problematize the issue further, the history of Western colonialism in the Arab and Muslim worlds is wrought with painful memories whose relics still haunt us in various shapes to this day and possibly for generations to come. Many issues are still agonizingly outstanding, caused—mainly but not exclusively—by cavalier colonial mapping, artificial borders, and states being planted or concocted that do not respond to indigenous national aspirations but to serve long-term, imperial, geopolitical schemes. What makes it even more frustrating is that the discourses—whether political, mediatized, or literary—have been and still are efficiently dominated by the technologically advanced hegemonic Euro-American powers. To focus specifically on the literary domain, and more pertinently to the variegated discourses in English, the representation of the culture and civilization of Arabs and Muslims has predominantly been shaped by Western literary figures of diverse persuasions, such as Richard Burton, T. E. Lawrence, and V. S. Naipaul—the latter is not without dark irony (no pun intended). This quasi-definitive describing of the Other, a nasty practice hotly protested by the majority of contemporary "third worldist" intellectuals, was done while this "Other" remained silent, unaware, or unable to respond in an equally effective way, all the while the pernicious *discours dominant* has created stereotypical images about diversely rich and cosmopolitan civilizations like those of the Arabs and Muslims. Accordingly, if novelizing history, that is, fictionalizing fiction, is ontologically layered with complexity, then it becomes even more daunting when an Arab-Muslim novelist like Ahdaf Soueif undertakes producing in English a revisionist metahistory to articulate her nationalist version of Egypt's modern history. So the Other, the erstwhile invisible, silent, or marginalized can now speak and speak well in the "step-mother tongue" of English, to borrow a term from Bharati Mukherjee (31)—in fact so eloquently well that *The Map of Love* was short-listed for the prestigious Booker Prize in 1999.

To make the situation even more meaningful, the Egypt-born, England-resident Soueif creates in this novel the character of England-born, Egypt-resident Anna Winterbourne, a recently widowed young aristocrat who, while on a visit to Egypt in the early decade of the twentieth century, marries an Egyptian and becomes integrated into a Cairene household. Through this skillful setup and through extensive excerpts from Anna's private journals, Soueif not only reclaims an Egyptian nationalist perspective, but also appropriates an "English" voice, Anna Winterbourne's, and transposes onto it statements and testimonials regarding British atrocities in the Sudan in 1898, British colonial arrogance in controlling Egypt in the 1900s including a detailed description of the massacre of the fallaheen in the village of Denshwai in 1906, and the emergence of Zionist colonization schemes in Palestine during the dying days of the Ottoman empire. The English lady thus becomes a medium for transmitting messages to an English readership in a text that is keenly audience-conscious.

One risks being a reductionist when trying to sketch such a complex novel, yet the task is quite necessary. The novel covers two historically charged periods in Egypt, covering the first and the last decades of the twentieth century. The narrative interlinks three carefully delineated female characters: Anna Winterbourne, Amal al-Ghamrawi, and Isabel Parkman, and foregrounds two cross-cultural love affairs separated by almost a century. In the symbolic dawning year of 1900, the English Lady Anna Winterbourne visits British-controlled Egypt where she falls in love with the Egyptian nationalist-aristocrat Sharif Basha al-Baroudi, a landowning lawyer and Amal's granduncle, and spends eleven years of matrimonial bliss with him in Cairo. In the mid-1990s the young American Isabel Parkman, the divorced great-granddaughter of Anna and Sharif's, falls in love in New York with Amal's brother, Omar al-Ghamrawi, with whom she has a son, named Sharif. Through this tightly knit web of a hybrid family extended over three continents, the novel focuses on Amal who has separated from her British husband, after spending twenty years in England with him, and opted to return to Egypt. Amal's encounter with Isabel in Cairo involves receiving a trunk that contains, among other symbolically significant contents, Anna's diaries, whose discovery initiates a fascinating recall of both personal and political histories, anchored on a warm, empathetic affinity between Amal and Anna across time and text.

Anna's trunk, now an heirloom to Isabel, involves a multitude of objects and documents: apart from Anna's detailed diaries of her life in Egypt, it contains period newspaper cuttings in both English and Arabic covering the first two decades of the twentieth century; a testimony from Layla al-Baroudi, Amal's grandmother, on family events concerning her brother Sharif Basha's marriage to Anna; and a tapestry, made by Anna in Cairo, symbolically conjoining Pharaonic and Islamic ciphers. The trunk, which has traveled from Egypt to Europe to the United States and then back to Egypt, represents not only an inventive plot device to interlink characters, situations, and discourses but also a signifier of the novel's salient cross-cultural appeal: it is a repository, a national archive from which the genealogy of nation building can derive inspirational data.

Through Amal's engaged and informed filing and filtering of the historical materials, and, significantly, her grounded awareness of current politics in Egypt, the novel's solid, sophisticated structure takes an almost symmetrical shape through an analogical pattern of events, ethos, and discourses shifting between the two decades at the dawn and dusk of the twentieth century. To borrow two terms from Gérard Genette, Soueif's narrative here operates through proleptic and analeptic trajectories, that is by anticipatory forward movement and by retrospective backward movement (40). These strategies of prolepsis and analepsis crown the novel's quintuple layers of complexity, with the other four layers involving history as fiction, fictionalizing fiction, an Arab fictionalizing Egyptian history in English, and the metamorphosing of an "English" character to a purveyor of Egyptian nationalist ethos.

Initially, Anna is politically neutral but inquisitive; her first husband, Edward, has willingly served in the British war in the Sudan, but has returned to England stunned into silence. Anna suspects that Edward, sensitive and ethical, must have been shocked by the enormity of the carnage inflicted by General (later Lord) Kitchener's highly mechanized, well-equipped army upon the followers of 'Abdullah al-Mahdi, among whom ten thousand were mauled in the battle of Omdurman in September 1898 ("Omdurman"). A motive is thus established for Anna to know more about what caused the traumatic scars to Edward, who becomes such an emaciated recluse that he withers into guilt-ridden death.

The following are two entries from Anna's diary registered in the narrative through which one can see Soueif's crafty style in trying to capture the idiom of a refined English lady but also her subtle strategy to prompt the character, Anna, and by extension the reader, to sharpen her curiosity about British politics in Egypt and the Sudan:

> Caroline Bourke tells me that Sir William Butler, meeting General Kitchener upon his arrival at Dover, said to him, "Well, if you do not bring down a curse on the British Empire for what you have been doing, there is no truth in Christianity." And Kitchener simply stared at him. I asked her what he meant. What had they done beyond taking the Soudan and restoring order? And she

> said she did not know—but with such dark looks as left me full of foreboding.
> I long to ask my husband what this means, for my instinct is that there is a key
> here to what ails him, but I am afraid. He is so changed and now is unable to
> take any nourishment but the thinnest broth and some crusts of bread. (31)

What we have in this second- and thirdhand reporting is the official line, or what
Noam Chomsky would call the "manufactured lie," about "taking the Soudan
and restoring order." However, there is also a strong sense that there is something
more to this than what people are being told, yet this elision, this gap, is left tantalizingly open. The reader here shares the inquisitive character's foreboding that
there is another, darker, dimension that needs to be explored. The second quote
gives a glimpse of the type of information that is elliptically left unreported or
unpublicized in colonial officialese:

> Caroline came to visit and told me how they say Kitchener's men desecrated
> the body of the Mahdi whom the natives believe to be a Holy Man and how
> Billy Gordon cut off his head that the General might use it for an inkwell. It
> cannot be true, for if it were—I truly fear for Edward now. (33)

Here once again, this Caroline Bourke, Anna's reliable reporter, becomes what I
would term as our "metropolitan informant," leading to an instinctive formation
of creative curiosity as well as a foreboding sense of horror and condemnation.
We realize that "restoring order" of the previous passage is a euphemistic code
name for gory barbarity. Furthermore, the passage adroitly links the atrocity
committed against al-Mahdi with Anna's private concern about her husband; the
private becomes political and vice versa. After Edward's death, Anna's inquisi-
tiveness spurs her to travel to Egypt, partly as a holiday trip, partly as a fact-
finding mission.

Once in Egypt, Anna's process of politicization begins, and it becomes
quite engaging to observe how Anna starts as neutral in the heated political
conflict between Egyptian nationalists and the British colonizers, led then by
the de facto ruler of Egypt and the bully of an administrator, Lord Cromer. She
reports faithfully but uneasily what the colonizers say about the "inefficient"
Egyptians who are not fit to rule themselves and how the British are there to
civilize them. One of the British, in a striking illustration of a Foucauldian-di-
agnosed syndrome of power presuming knowledge, even claims that "it would
take generations before the Natives were fit to rule themselves as they [have]
neither integrity nor moral fibre, being too long accustomed to foreign rule"
(99). This statement, which many colonial functionaries throughout the British
Empire assumed to be Bible-truth, echoes and encapsulates a speech given on
June 13, 1910, in the House of Commons by Arthur James Balfour, making a
number of claims about how crucial Britain's presence in Egypt was for Egypt's

own sake and self-knowledge. In *Orientalism*, Edward Said quotes Balfour's speech in detail in order to deconstruct it by unmasking its subtext:

> England knows Egypt; Egypt is what England knows; England knows that Egypt cannot have self-government; England confirms that by occupying Egypt; for the Egyptians, Egypt is what England has occupied and now governs; foreign occupation therefore becomes "the very basis" of contemporary Egyptian civilization; Egypt requires, indeed insists upon, British occupation. (34)

Ironically, the British characters in Soueif's novel make their statements while having a picnic in the shadow of the pyramids, the composite symbol of Egyptians' suffering and sacrifice as well as their ingenuity and civilizational energy, which these unwelcome intruders are incapable of ever appreciating. Anna asks pertinent questions that eventually make her ready to sympathize with and espouse the nationalist argument. She wonders, for instance, "whether it is possible for a conquering ruler to truly see into the character of the people whom he rules" (99). The British in Egypt, cocooned in smug elitist gatherings, want no contact with the Egyptians, except the servants, yet they do not hesitate to make totalizing statements and assumptions about them. Anna realizes later that many of the assumptions that the British made about the Egyptians turn out to be wrong. She discovers that the nationalists are not merely "talking classes" and "professional malcontents" (97) as the British officials degradingly refer to them, but serious and dignified people who care about the fate of their country and are willing to sacrifice dearly for it. When on her way to the Khedive's ball at 'Abdin Palace, she sees from her carriage a group of Egyptians marching in a procession assuming, as she is told, that they must be "celebrating some events" (93); she discovers later that it was actually an anti-British demonstration that ends with the arrest of the demonstrators. When Sharif Basha's family meet Sabir, the Egyptian servant assigned by the British to be her bodyguard, they immediately know about his personal life; Anna is shocked to realize that it is through her Egyptian hosts who have barely met Sabir and not through the British for whom the servant has been working for years that she learns that he had a wife and a family; the British neither knew nor cared to know about him, loyal and diligent as he has been to them.

Anna ultimately adopts the nationalist position and becomes a supporting activist within the limits allowed for a woman in the period. It is tempting to suggest here that Anna, as a fictional construct, is intended to represent open-minded readers in English or in the West in general. Once they go beyond the stereotypes regarding the Other and begin to see for themselves the specificity of contexts from an unprejudiced angle, alternative versions and perspectives are bound to emerge. More importantly, this shift in Anna's sympathy makes her quite appealing to Amal, who, throughout the narrative, is scrutinizing the strikingly emblematic items contained in the trunk and reading and reflecting upon all the statements contained in Anna's diary. Structurally, the affectionate, imaginative bonding between the two pivotal female characters and the consequent conflation of ethos scaffold the novel and cohere the form that is critical to this multilayered narrative; it also renders the shift between the political issues of the past and the present smooth and meaningful. Amal writes, "I got to know Anna as though she were my best friend—or better" (43); enchanted and immersed in her reading, she later wonders, "Who else has read this journal? And when they read it, did they too feel that it spoke to them? For the sense of Anna speaking to me—writing it down for me—is so powerful that I find myself speaking to her in my head. At night, in my dreams, I sit with her and we speak as friends and sisters" (306). There are recurrent voice-overs merging Anna's engaged reports about Egypt's struggle for independence with Amal's current concerns with Egypt's and the Arab world's agonizing politics:

> Each week brings fresh news of land expropriation, of great national industries and service companies sold off to foreign investors, of Iraqi children dying and Palestinian homes demolished, fresh news of gun battles in Upper Egypt, of the names of more urban intellectuals added to the Jama'at's hit list, of defiant young men in cages holding open Qur'ans in their hands, of raids and torture and executions. And next door but one, Algeria daily throws up terrible examples; and when people—people like Isabel—put the question, we say no, that can't happen here, and when they ask why, we can only say: because this is Egypt. (101)

The perspectives of the two women, separated by almost a century, converge effortlessly and empathetically. The analogical schematization of political issues in the 1900s and the 1990s enables the reader to situate the conflicts of the present within the context of the past and to understand the problems of the past within the perspective of the present. This contrastive contextualization yields a depressing insight about current political deformities in Egypt and the Arab world, whereby the political issues of the past seem, by hindsight, simple and discernible: the enemy was known and the aim of national sovereignty was clear, even though there was a divergence of opinions about the best ways to achieve it. To Amal al-Ghamrawi, the novel's "central intelligence" to use Henry James's term, the issues in present-day neocolonial Egypt seem to be complex and unwieldy, with no clear sight for a genuine national agenda. As one of Amal's friends puts it, " In Nasser's time—for all its drawbacks, all the mistakes—there was an Idea. A national project. Now what do we have? The Idea of the Consumer? Trying to hang on to America's hem—" (229). Another friend endorses this statement yet rectifies it by arguing that "a national project comes about as an embodiment of the will of the people" and that "Nasser's project finally did not work because for the people to have a will it has to have a certain amount of space and freedom, freedom to question everything: religion, politics, sex—" (229). More specifically, decent and dedicated individuals seem powerless or hopeless; some become cynical, and one commits suicide.

As the conscience of the novel, Amal's sensitivity and humane politicization become the novel's moral anchor. Unlike the eponymous Aisha of Soueif's first book, who is portrayed as apolitical and passive (she is ritualistically raped at the end of the book), and unlike Asya the heroine of *In the Eye of the Sun*, who is shown to be politically conscious yet is snarled in a near-neurotic sexual imbroglio, Amal maturely sublimates her marital malaise, reveals an agonized empathy with the marginalized and the downtrodden, and even engages in limited agency. The scene with the caged political prisoner movingly highlights her humanity:

> As she waits at the traffic light she becomes aware of somebody looking at her and glances up. From the high window of the police van next to her, a young man stares intently. His beard is thick and black, his dark eyes are intense, his hands grip the iron bars of the window. Amal averts her eyes and looks straight ahead. But she feels ashamed. Ashamed that she should be free, here in her car, free to drive wherever she wishes, while this young man is caged like an animal. Whose country is it? That is what it amounts to now. The light turns green and she accelerates forward. She had cried when she told 'Omar over the phone about the men she had seen, tied together and huddled in the roadside kiosk, when she had told him the stories the fallaheen had told her.
>
> "It's an ugly world," he'd said, "on the whole." (298)

Perceptive, confident, and caring, Amal—supposedly representing, as her name suggests, hope—oscillates between optimism and despair, agency and helplessness, angered activism and resigned fatalism. In a corrupt political system, marked by nepotism, cronyism, and cruelty, the concerned individual feels diminished and ineffectual. By the novel's conclusion, a sense of despair overshadows the narrative, conveyed through clever conflation of Anna's narrative and Amal's voice:

> In the living room Amal picks up the newspaper she had not had a chance to read. Monica Lewinsky and her blue dress take up two pages. Sudan should not be partitioned. Clinton vows to avenge America on Ben Laden. Albright threatens action against Iraq. Torture in Palestinian jails—she folds the newspaper and throws it into the big wastepaper basket. *It feels very hard,* Anna had written a hundred years ago, *not to feel caught up in a terrible time of brutality and* we—Amal edits—*are helpless to do anything but wait for history to run its course.* She

puts the tape her brother had brought back from Ramallah into the tape player, stretches out on the sofa under the ceiling fan and lights a cigarette.

'I have a ship
In the harbour
And God's forgotten us
In the harbour—.' (512–13)

Significantly, as Amal rearranges and deciphers the contents of Anna's trunk, echoing the domestic life of the Egyptian elite in the 1900s, and as she reflects on the political problems of Egypt in the 1990s, a pattern of juxtaposition and analogy emerges involving the dual history of life in Egypt in the first and last decades of the twentieth century. In the 1900s, Anna's initially neutral reporting graphically details the arrogance of the British colonialists and their smug self-serving mentality to justify their hegemony over the Egyptians. In the 1990s, a parallel situation is intimated about neocolonial corporate domination over the Egyptian economy: blaming the country's economic hardships on the United States, a woman farmer in Amal's ancestral village expresses it simply but poignantly by asking rhetorically, "Isn't Amreeka the biggest country now and what she says goes?" (176). In the 1900s, religious traditionalists oppose all aspects of cultural modernity in Egypt such as establishing a national university or educating women; Sharif Basha decries their mentality by pointing out that "their interventions are always in a negative direction—everything in their book is haram" (265). In the 1990s, the Islamist militants, while adopting the political idiom of the left, manifest a similar rejectionist stance: as one of Amal's friends puts it, "They have no political programme beyond 'Islam is the solution'. Ask them any detailed question and they don't have an answer" (227). In the 1900s, ordinary Egyptians, but especially the fallaheen, bore the brunt of British domination with the most brutal act being the massacre and hanging of the villagers of Denshwai in 1906—an episode that has left its mark in the folkloric imagination of Egyptians to this day. In the 1990s, the descendants of those same fallaheen are once again paying the heavy penalty of being caught in the cross fire between armed Islamist militants and the government's cruel security apparatchiks whose motto is "everybody is a suspect" (439). After his release and the other men in his village from jail on suspicion of being "terrorists," 'Am Abu el-Ma'ati, the overseer of Amal's family farm, wisely but sadly describes their plight as disfranchised citizenry: "we are neither the first nor the last village to have this happen to it. And this is not the first nor the last government to terrorise the people—" (450).

Another pattern that also emerges in this novel is the skillful blending of fictional and historical characters. Thoroughly and thoughtfully researched, *The Map of Love* portrays dramatically some of the prominent political players in Egypt of the 1900s, such as Lord Cromer and his entourage of colonial functionaries, and Egyptian princes and aristocrats, as well as leading cultural and nationalist figures of the period, with special endearing attention given to the enlightened Sheikh of al-Azhar (the Grand Imam), Muhammad 'Abdou—Sharif Basha's friend who happily officiates his wedding to Anna. 'Abdou's disciple, the French-educated Kurdish-Egyptian intellectual Qasim Amin wrote a book entitled *The Liberation of Women*, in which he called for respecting women's rights and the necessity of their education. At a gathering at Sharif Basha's, Amin makes his point firmly but politely, linking women's liberation with the nationalist movement:

> We cannot claim to desire a Renaissance for Egypt . . . while half her population live in the Middle Ages. To take the simplest matters, how can children be brought up with the right outlook by ignorant mothers? How can a man find support and companionship with an ignorant wife? (380–81)

Significantly, Amin's pioneering book is still celebrated as a landmark in Egyptian cultural history, and Soueif's reference to his passionate plea in the 1900s for liberating women and educating them—modest demands by the norms of the twenty-first century—signifies, in the novel's inclusivist discourse, that Arab-Muslim feminism solicits and embraces support from enlightened men of the caliber of Amin; indeed, the agency of progressive men as feminist allies is an inspirational phenomenon in many "third world" societies. Moreover, the novel's discourse suggests that Arab-Muslim feminism can find nourishing sources from within the culture and civilization of Islam, as the pioneer Amin was pursuing in his polemic. From the series of encounters that Elizabeth Warnock Fernea conducted with a number of women activists in diverse Arab and Muslim communities, she registers a similar conviction among these women *sur place*:

> In Egypt, Turkey, Kuwait, and the United States, Islamic women begin with the assumption that the possibility of gender equality already exists in the Qur'an itself; the problem, as they see it, is malpractice, or misunderstanding, of the text. For these Muslim women, the first goal of a feminist movement is to re-understand and evaluate the sacred text, and for women to be involved in the process, which historically has been reserved to men. (416)

Soueif not only succeeds in her dramatic and discursive integration of the fictional characters with the historical ones like 'Abdou and Amin, but she also models one character, Amal's brother 'Omar, as a converse Edward Said figure. 'Omar is a famous musical conductor in New York who writes books on politics and culture. Having both Egyptian and Palestinian family ties, 'Omar is a member of the Palestinian National Congress and a ferocious opponent of the Oslo Accord; on a visit to Jerusalem, he decries the venality of Arafat's Bantustan-like mini-state "with eleven security services" (356). For his activities in the United States on behalf of the Palestinians, 'Omar earns the derogatory badges of the "Molotov Maestro" and the "Kalashnikov Conductor" (17); this is an obvious ironic evocation of the infamous label of "Professor of Terror" that appeared in *Commentary*, referring to the late Said's supposed "double career as a literary scholar and ideologue of terrorism" (qtd. in Shohat 125). In yet another instance of analogy, the contemporary figure of 'Omar parallels the figure of Shukri Bey, Sharif Basha's cousin in the 1900s, who passionately militates against the colonization of Palestinian land by the richly financed Zionists. Shukri Bey pays for his indefatigable activism with his life; similarly, we are obliquely told that 'Omar has been eliminated by his too many powerful enemies.[5]

The fashioning of 'Omar's agency as an uncompromising activist endows the novel's political discourse with a political dimension beyond past and current Egyptian concerns toward wider regional issues such as the plight of Iraqis and Palestinians. While Asya in *In the Eye of the Sun* reveals a remarkable political awareness by reflecting dejectedly on the suffering of other persecuted peoples of the Middle East, her sympathies seem confined to the abstract level. In *The Map of Love*, Amal makes a conscious attempt to shift from concern to at least partial praxis. We witness her meeting with human rights activists, Palestinian sympathizers, and supporters of the Iraqi people—being betrayed, brutalized, and taken hostage. As Deena al-'Ulama (a recall from *In the Eye of the Sun*: Asya's sister) articulates it forcefully:

> What normalization is possible with a neighbour who continues to build settlements and drive people out of the land? Who has an arsenal of nuclear weapons and screams wolf when someone else is suspected of having a few missiles? And it *is* our business—because what is happening to the Iraqis or the Palestinians today will happen to us tomorrow. (230)

Interestingly, the mature, self-assured Amal, when compared with Asya, seems not only more acutely committed to her nationalist ideals, but is also less preoccupied with her marital separation and sexual concerns. In a marked departure from *In the Eye of the Sun*, the handling of sexuality seems remote, restrained, and refined. Unlike Asya's sexual frustrations, Amal, while not entirely impervious to sexual attraction, sublimates the preoccupation with the body toward a genuine concern for those she could help in her ancestral village, Tawasi. Her taking residence in the village is more than a sentimental *retour aux sources*, but a sign of committed agency that tries to shield the villagers whom she loves from the transgression of a callous, cruel government, frightened by village volunteers running a school and a clinic, labeling them as "terrorists." (One may object to Amal's resort to cronyism to liberate the imprisoned innocent villagers, including 'Am Abu el-Ma'ati, from police brutality; however, her utterly selfless, well-intentioned act is urgently prompted by pragmatism rather than idealism.) Indeed, Amal's emotional closeness to the fallaheen—especially to 'Am Abu el-Ma'ati who, as his name suggests, is a caring avuncular figure and one of the novel's most memorable constructs—foregrounds her serious attachment to the village not only as an escape from crowded Cairo, but as an edifying, empowering source for coping with the dislocations of her private and public reality. (Once again analogy becomes the operative term here: Amal's affectionate admiration and warmth toward 'Am Abu el-Ma'ati parallels Anna's love for her two fathers-in-law: the anticolonialist Sir Charles in England and the saintly, ex-revolutionary al-Baroudi Bey.) As well, Amal's friendship with the down-to-earth Tahiyya, the doorman's wife in her building in Cairo, and with the female fallaheen in the village redresses the balance in the novel by allowing space and forum for figures outside the privileged political and cultural elite. In other words, there is a conscious design operating here to give voice to ordinary, yet intuitively astute, people and to let them air their concerns directly, effectively, and, at times, even humorously.

Moreover, Soueif's conscious attempt in *The Map of Love* to capture the linguistic patterns of the fallaheen of Upper Egypt parallels her attempt to capture the idiom of an educated English lady of the caliber of Anna Winterbourne writing her diaries in the 1900s. Soueif's rendition of Anna's intelligently inquisitive sensibility revealed in diaries and letters recalls the English literary tradition of epistolary fiction, especially Samuel Richardson's two eponymous novels *Pamela* and *Clarissa*. One can easily detect fascinating double or triple layers of translation operating in a text written by a polyglot woman author, whose first language is Arabic, capturing in English the nuanced thoughts and emotions of a female English character, with an imaginary gap of a century "separating" author and character. Thus, the novel, as a text in English, becomes in effect hybrid on multiple levels, involving not only two rich and resilient languages, Arabic and English, but also different social, class, period, and geographical variations within each of them. To further enrich the layered pattern of juxtaposition and analogy, Soueif skillfully establishes a motif of Muslim metaphors harmoniously hybridized with other religious traditions: Anna's tapestry with Islamic and Pharaonic imprints; a 1919 Egyptian flag emblazoned with the Crescent and the Cross, symbolizing the unity of the Egyptian Muslims and Christians in their uprising against British occupation; the mosque nestling inside a monastery, a heartwarming image of each holy sanctuary protecting the other from demolition at times of tension; and the three calendars followed simultaneously in Egypt: Gregorian, Islamic, and Coptic. The novel's ambitious hybridization process is not only linguistic or textual but also discursive, leading subtly toward humane, positive perspectives on Arab-Muslim culture in its most tolerant illustrations and in its openness toward the Other. Despite its potent anticolonial discourse, the novel reveals a conscious progression toward a reconciliatory universalist stance. In an article addressed to readers in Europe, Sharif Basha sums up his vision: "Our only hope now—and it is a small one—lies in *a unity of conscience* between the people of the world for whom this phrase itself would carry any meaning" (484; emphasis added). The novel reveals numerous instances of this "unity of conscience," but one moving moment of warmth and generosity suffices: on his wedding day to Anna, Sharif Basha's mother instructs her strong, adoring son about how to treat his English bride:

> You will be everything to her. If you make her unhappy, who will she go to? No mother, no sister, no friend. Nobody. It means if she angers you, you forgive her. If she crosses you, you make it up with her. And whatever the English do, you will never burden her with the guilt of her country. She will be not only your wife and the mother of your children—insha' Allah—but she will be your guest and a stranger under your protection and if you are unjust to her God will never forgive you. (281–82)

More importantly, Soueif uses the hybridity of the text to advance a woman-friendly Muslim perspective through the two most empathetic non-Muslim voices in the novel: the American Isabel and the British Anna. After studying the linguistic structure of the Arabic language, Isabel observes that the etymology of words with positive and dignified connotations is often associated with a feminine root; she asks rhetorically, "So how can they say Arabic is a patriarchal language?" (165). Anna registers in her diary that a Muslim woman "does not take her husband's name upon marriage" (137). Anna is also informed by Layla that when a Muslim woman is married, "her money is her own and her husband, if he is able, is obliged to furnish her with all the money she needs for her personal expenses as well as any household expenses she might incur" (352). Anna's integration into Egyptian culture becomes so solid that she, when describing her invisibility in a situation requiring her to wear the veil, sounds like an apologist for it: "Still, it is a most liberating thing, this veil. While I was wearing it, I could look wherever I wanted and nobody could look back at me" (195).

The hybrid, history-steeped text, composed by an Arab-Muslim woman author writing in English by choice, thus becomes a site for foregrounding, gently but assertively, a potently positive image about Arab-Muslim culture that is seldom witnessed in such an appealingly humane and cogent context. In essence, what we are witnessing here is an elegantly poised novelist who demonstrates her mature control of craft and clarity of vision. Significantly, her loving, lively depiction of the idiom and perspective of the fallaheen of Upper Egypt proves that she can enlarge her canvas with figures beyond the type of the "Westernized bourgeois intellectual" that the heroine of Soueif's first book, Aisha, identifies with. Accordingly, in *The Map of Love*, the author bridges the dislocations between a hybridized, privileged intellectual like Amal and the reality of her people. Ahdaf Soueif thus circumvents a common critique that is directed at Arab feminist writing of the 1960s and 1970s, specifically as it pertains to its ellipsis or dim, distant depiction of serious social problems facing contemporary Muslim women, problems such as polygyny, crimes of "honor," and the denial to women of equal rights in matters of divorce, education, and employment. Interestingly, Evelyne Accad in her pioneering 1978 work *Veil of Shame* registers these omissions in the fiction of men and women of the Arab Middle East and of North Africa, observing that "the literature of these areas, whether in French or in Arabic, failed to present the same picture as that reflected in the data of the social scientists" (12). While the creative process of producing literary works veers, as indeed it should, from pamphleteering and socioanthropological documentation, the mostly mimetic mode deployed in the fiction of Arab and Muslim women provokes our eager anticipation of a candid, courageous unveiling of some of the chilling acts of violence perpetrated against women in several Muslim societies, at times even in the name of religion, acts such as the hideously gruesome custom in Africa of female circumcision or genital mutilation, "which [has] nothing whatsoever to do with Islam" (Kabbani 16), even though, as Amitav Ghosh observed during his stay in rural Egypt, "it still continues to be widely practiced, by Christian and Muslim fellaheen [*sic*] alike" (203).[6] As we have seen, in Soueif's oeuvre a few of these issues are indeed treated, but in a secondhand fashion, through the refracted narrative of family servants. The inability or reluctance to convey such grisly realities (as reported to us, at times not without prejudice, through Western travelogues, journalistic reports, and anthropological studies) may be attributed partly to the fact that these women writers belong to privileged, urban elites. Muslim women from poor, rural families are usually worse off than their counterparts who come from urban, middle-class families who have better access to education: Rana Kabbani points out that "in Islamic society as in the West, the oppression of women is usually more the result of poverty and lack of education and other opportunities than of religion" (16). Besides, some Muslim and Middle Eastern women may, consciously or otherwise, be self-censoring and cautious so as not to antagonize the often politically powerful religious purists or radical Islamists who militate to impose by force a medievalist theocracy. In this respect, Michel Foucault's insights about the prohibitive, indeed nullifying, nature of power over sexuality becomes illuminating:

> Power acts by laying down the rule: power's hold on sex is maintained through language, or rather through the act of discourse that creates, from the very fact that it is articulated, a rule of law. It speaks, and that is the rule. The pure form of power resides in the function of the legislator; and its mode of action with regard to sex is of a juridico-discursive character. (83)

Foucault's astute pronouncement about power's "juridico-discursive character" recalls Simone de Beauvoir's tenacious statement about patriarchy's self-serving deployment of the law for codifying the politics of sexuality and delimiting its discourse:

> History has shown us that men have always kept in their hands all concrete powers; since the earliest days of the patriarchate they have thought best to keep women in a state of dependence; their codes of law have been set up against her; and thus she has been definitely established as the Other. (15)

Despite the limitations and lacunae (if these are the right appellations), and however we may perceive their causes, one should not underestimate the solidity and sincerity of the gender and cultural allegiances of Arab and Muslim women writers. Their works reveal an acute awareness of their own distinct and delicate exploration of a troubling terrain; their critique and/or combat of patriarchy is conjoined with a loyalty to abstract, at times even romanticized, ideals of either Islam or national identity, or both. They all recognize that religion and nationalism are active forces to engage with: for them, the discourse of liberation passes not through ridiculing or rejecting their Islamic heritage, but through appealing to its most enlightened and progressive tradition. In this context, change and progress are arguably possible not through current institutional and traditionalist practices, but through certain retrieved, reinterpreted, or revised theological or political frameworks that are sympathetic to women's aspirations. To assert their will, to claim a space for themselves, and to achieve their liberation, Arab and Muslim women, as suggested in their writings, need not only to maintain courage and perseverance but must also be ready to compromise. In essence then, the agenda propounded is relatively reformist, not radical. Nevertheless, we may see a more militant and confrontational response, as currently manifested in some Muslim women's writings in Arabic and French, to the alarming discourse of the religious zealots and fanatics—such as we witnessed with the horror of the Taliban regime in Afghanistan and such as we discern from the statements of those who call for male-made theocracies. As well, the feminist discourse of younger women that emerged in the 1980s and 1990s has "come to realize that the male revolutionary discourse, which tied women's liberation to national liberation and the growth of democracy, has failed to produce any concrete results" (Moussa-Mahmoud 213). This situation becomes specifically pronounced in the Algerian, Iranian, and Palestinian revolutions. Moreover, we are even witnessing a few feminist writers enlarge their focus beyond mainly urban, mainly middle-class concerns. Accordingly, one can see no closure to this refreshingly assertive, writerly process that keeps evolving.

The fiction of Ahdaf Soueif is an integral part of this evolving Arab-Muslim feminism or "womanism that is not at all a replica of Western feminisms"

(Ghazoul), and the fact that it is written in English carries with it specific characteristics. The hybridized English that Soueif deploys allows the conscious feminist narrative voice to infiltrate taboo terrains, both sexual and political, which might be inaccessible when handled in Arabic. Removed emotionally and culturally from the local scene, the English language accords a liberating medium to the author to broach and delve into issues such as feminine sexuality, the politics of power and economic dependency, and the disfranchisement of the poor: English here accords a liberating lexical storehouse and semantic sanctuary. While the hybridized English provides this idiomatic advantage, it maintains the distinctiveness of the composite cultures, ethos, and predilections involved. As Robert Young astutely observes, "hybridity is itself an example of hybridity, of a doubleness that both brings together, fuses, but also maintains separation" (22). While the author's, as well as most of her characters', first language is Arabic and the action in her fiction takes place in mostly non-English-speaking settings, the reader feels that the English text is actually a translation whose original, once existing in the author's mind, is now nonexistent. This palimpsestic process indicates at once erasure, reconstitution, and reorientation, thus straddling cultures, interfacing texts, and re(de)fining enunciations to fit the requisites of the reinscribed version in English. Of course, this complex discursive reconstruction stretches beyond the Bakhtinian model of linguistic, novelistic hybridization toward the politics of gender, identitarian religion, nationalism, and "postcolonial"/"third worldist" representation of the erstwhile silent, marginalized, or misrepresented colonized subject. Accordingly, even though the English language is readily associated in the collective memory of many "third world" nations with the colonialist and neocolonialist experiences, Soueif's adoption of it as a medium of expression dehegemonizes it and transforms it into an instrument of resistance to the discourses of both arrogant colonialism and exclusionist ultranationalism. Soueif's polyphonic discourse thus dramatizes complex and messy situations that are at once provocative, challenging, and inspiring.

# Conclusion

Come, come, whoever you are.
Wanderer, idolator, worshipper of fire,
Come even though you have broken your vows a thousand times,
Come, and come yet again.
Ours is not a caravan of despair.

—Jalâluddîn Rumi

## TOWARD NEW PARADIGMS

IF THERE IS ONE MAJOR IDEA TO EMERGE FROM THIS BOOK, IT IS THAT Muslim narratives in English, in the ways I have dealt with them here, are not, indeed cannot be, a monolithic discourse; witness the refreshing diversity of voices and visions articulated in them. Geographically diverse and with no defining or definitive influences as yet interlinking the majority of them, they thus reflect the specificity of each writer's sociohistorical milieu, intellectual progress, and artistic development. However, from the cumulative concert of these voices, discernible sensibilities, idioms, and motifs emanate pointing unequivocally to an engagement with the world and the values of Islam. This engagement, attachment, or allegiance to Islam has been a dimension worth probing and deconstructing.

Since we already have enough categories streamlining academic and intellectual discourse, the argument presented in this book should not be construed as a call for a new category, but only for an alternative, enabling paradigm, a fresh perspective that can operate through several of the existing categories, prefixed or suffixed with "post" or "ism." Ideally, a "category" suggests a somewhat cohesive set of concepts or activities that are neatly prescribed, notwithstanding Trinh T. Minh-ha's astute observation that "categories always leak" (94). On the other hand, a "paradigm" suggests a flexible pattern of diversity that keeps shifting while maintaining certain core concerns and common qualities. The paradigm proposed here foregrounds the cultural and civilizational contexts of Islam as revealed in Muslim narratives in English. This religion-oriented paradigm and all its identitarian and aesthetic corollaries are often overlooked or viewed with suspicion in Western secular discourses. However, foregrounding it becomes germane and illuminating when dealing with literary works inspired by the culture of Islam, whose rituals, metaphors, and values still hold aesthetic and spiritual sway.

Many Western, so-called experts sometime make presumptuous claims about Islam and Muslims, projecting often negative, stereotypical images and labels that are deployed regularly and systemically. Regrettably, little endeavor is made to question these clichés and stereotypes, perhaps due to laziness, sloppy professionalism, or sheer indifference. In an effort to dismantle one stereotype, we need to recognize, once and for all, the obvious fact that there is no grand monolith called "Islam." The Islam of outsiders, like that of some influential contemporary Orientalists, is different from the Islam experienced and expressed by many of the Muslim writers in English. More importantly, Muslim themselves have divergent views about the details and dogmas of the faith. When applied indiscriminately, clichés such as "moderate," "liberal," and "fundamentalist" are often more confusing than clarifying, because these are subjective, value-laden, context-specific terms that are conditioned by cultural norms and individual predilections.

If some Westerners make hasty generalizations about Islam and its people, some Muslims commit the same error, categorizing all Westerners as being racist and anti-Islamic. Curiously, some of them make such claims while actually living in Western societies and enjoying the privileges of their secular, democratic institutions. The fact that they (the Westerners) did or do it to Islam and its culture is no excuse for Muslims to retaliate likewise, succumbing to shortsighted prejudices. As civilizations encounter and embrace, the option should be for debate not denigration, cooperation not clash, harmony not hegemony.

Muslim literatures in English and in other European languages could be one such site of stimulating encounter. After being engaged with the narratives discussed in this book, one becomes exposed to a rich culture mediated by diverse versions, perspectives, and experiences, indeed as diverse as each writer reveals her or his specific moment and locale in the evolving world of Islam. It becomes abundantly clear that living Islam is not merely a spiritual practice or theological adherence, but also an intellectual and emotional engagement that cannot be escaped or elided. Often there is little choice with regard to this engagement not only because Islam and its institutions dominate the culture in a structural and organic way, but also because Islam, however one conceives it, commands affection even from its own dissenters: Islam's values of justice and generosity, of courage and creativity, endow it with endearing and enduring loyalty. This loyalty is one of Islam's hallmarks that many outsiders miss, misunderstand, or misrepresent. Reciprocally, Islam awards a sense of belonging to a grand Ummah, despite the multiplicity of its cultures and ethnicities. This identitarian affiliation with Islam, claimed by such diverse writers as Mena Abdullah, Nuruddin Farah, Ahdaf Soueif, and Fatima Mernissi, is not and can never be a monopoly of purists and radicals who claim Islam in the most vociferous fashion, or take a narrow, intolerant stance on it that excludes others who do not share their views.

## THE NEED FOR A CONTEMPORARY MUSLIM CULTURAL THEORY

Postmodernism, postcolonialism, or its alternative term *tricontinentalism* advocated by Robert Young (5), and, to a lesser degree, deconstruction represent major matrices in which contemporary Western intellectuality operates. New concepts in ethics, aesthetics, and epistemology are constantly emerging because nothing is static and everything is in constant flux. One can never step in the same river twice, as Heraclitus once observed. Consequently, issues such as canonicity, voice, the correlation between discourse and power (Foucault), heteroglossia and polyphony (Bakhtin), approaches such as new-historicism, neo-Marxism, and feminism, in its numerous incarnations, as well as emerging, exciting concepts in hermeneutics, astrophysics, and social sciences have created a challenging intellectual ecology in which Muslims have to operate. Serious Muslim thinkers cannot afford ignoring phenomena that are making constant inroads into humanity's political, economic, and social behavior. Muslims need to offer responses: confident, current, dialogical. There will never be easy answers, but the engagement could be exciting and rewarding. Whether in academe or the world at large, fads and fashions come and go, but only genuine things can last. What better metaphorical motto can one find than the Qur'anic verse, "As for the foam, it shall be jettisoned as scum, and *whatever benefits people abides in the earth*" ("Thunder" 17; emphasis added). Muslims need to develop discourses that connect with the impressive achievements of medieval theoreticians such as Ibn Khaldoun, al-Farabi, and Ibn Rushd. Edward Said eloquently points out that "one of the great hallmarks of Islamic culture is its rich and vastly ingenious interpretive energy. . . . Whole institutions, whole traditions, whole schools of thought are built out of such things as a system of commentary, a linguistic theory, a hermeneutical performance" (61–62). We need to celebrate the work of original Muslim thinkers of the twentieth century who tried to revive and reconnect with this rich heritage and relate it to contemporary contexts: thinkers such as Muhammad 'Abdou, Taha Hussein, Ali Shari'ati, Muhammad Baqir al-Sadder, and Ali al-Wardi, to name a few.

## INTO THE FUTURE

Except for Salman Rushdie, most of the works discussed in this book are quite serious, often sad, sometimes with tragic tones, but seldom humorous. This dearth in humoristic writing comes somewhat as a surprise given a tradition of humorous narratives from al-Jahidh, *The Thousand and One Nights*, and the folktales of Juha (Khoja Nasruddin). As the works of Milan Kundera and Rohinton Mistry attest, humor is an invaluable instrument for discursive subtlety and multiplicity, and we may see humor becoming prevalent in the future. A new generation is emerging of young men and women writers such as Fadia Faqir (*Pillars of Salt*), Jamal Mahjoub (*In the Hour of Sings*), Nadeem Aslam (*Season of the Rainbirds*), Aamer Hussein (*Mirror to the Sun*), and Leila Aboulela (*Coloured Lights*). For reasons of space, they were not dealt with here, but they certainly have the potential to imprint their mark on the literary landscape.

## ISLAM THE CRITICAL FACTOR

Anyone who studies the history of Islam would acknowledge that Islam has experienced periods of stress and strife as well as periods of ascendancy and triumph. It survived serious schisms from within starting with the carnage of Karbala in 680 CE through to the gratuitous criminal butchery of the Iran–Iraq war (the first Gulf War, 1980–1988) and the destruction and bloodbath of the second Gulf War (1990–1991) and its aftermath. It has also withstood external battles: the Crusades, the expulsion of Muslims from al-Andalus (Spain), colonialism, and the loss of Palestine in 1948. Yet Islam not only survived these trying periods but also at times even triumphed. Islam, whether undergoing moments of grief or glory, has thus remained for over fourteen centuries a potent, primary force, shaping world history significantly. This staying power, dynamism, and resilience shall capably continue into the future. Those claiming foresight and clever calculations cannot dismiss Islam; as the shocking horrors of September 11, 2001, prove, they can ignore it at their peril or loss. In *Islam: Religion, History, and Civilization*, Seyyed Hossein Nasr underscores the notion that the study of Islam is "of great significance for the West" not only because it creates a better understanding of a "major world civilization" but also because

> the Islamic revelation is the third and final revelation of the Abrahamic monotheistic cycle and constitutes a major branch of the tree of monotheism. It is, therefore, a religion without whose study the knowledge of the whole religious family to which Jews and Christians belong would be incomplete. (2)

Muslim narratives in English are not only a literary phenomenon that was bound to emerge for demographic, historical, and cultural reasons but also as part and parcel of Muslims transacting with others in the global village in which English has become a lingua franca, a cyberlingua, and a major means of communication. The revelations of Prophet Muhammad have not only transformed the Middle East and major regions of Asia and Africa leading to the creation of the comparatively cohesive Islamic Ummah, but also have become one of humanity's defining moments that witnessed the emergence of a new dawn in spirituality, ethics, aesthetics, and scientific creativity. The Islam I have in mind, therefore, is not an exclusivist monolith: it rejects racism and combats cultural chauvinism of any stripe or orientation. It recognizes and respects the Other and celebrates the sanctity of living beings; hence, terrorism and the killing of innocent lives is an anathema to the essence of its message. Accordingly, Islam, as a religion, a culture, and a civilization, has been a positive, vital force in history and in contemporary reality, and shall remain so indefinitely, "for in the end, for us Muslims, Islam is another name for something better" (Sayyid 160).

With a resonant and prolific intellectual heritage, that began with the amazing word in the revelation to the Prophet Muhammad "Read," and with a tradition steeped in urging the pursuit of knowledge, the encouragement of reflection, and veneration of books and *the people of the book*, Islam should not be reductively identified with irrational prohibitionism, *auto-da-fé* orgies, or heinous terrorism. While Islam is lucid and specific in its doctrinal edicts concerning matters of this world and beyond, it promotes an appealing sophistication when it comes to matters of learning, metaphysics, and aesthetics. This can be seen in the flourishing of arts such as calligraphy, music, architecture, painting, and arabesques, where an organic union between spirituality and aesthetics operates. It can also be seen in various forms of classical narratives, prominent among which are the stories-within-stories of *The Thousand and One Nights*, poetry, and Sufic aphorisms. The spirit of such a variegated and tolerant tradition contrasts the inquisitorial, condemnatory mentality of the few who disdain dialogue, denigrate debate, and advocate violence.

# Notes

## INTRODUCTION

1. It needs to be pointed out here that a parallel phenomenon of Muslim writers in French exists involving authors such as Ahmadou Kouroma, Tahar Ben Jelloun, Driss Chraibi, and Assia Djebar, whose roots are from North and sub-Saharan Africa.

2. This fact alone refutes V. S. Naipaul's pathological obsession in desperately trying, in *Beyond Belief: Islamic Excursions Among the Converted Peoples*, to prove that Islam has damaged the culture of the so-called converted. Blinkered by a biased fervor, Naipaul fails to appreciate the richness and firm-rootedness of a vibrantly sophisticated, cross-cultural religion, functioning in diverse sites while being voluntarily espoused by adherents.

3. It should be noted here that the Arabic noun *Muslim* denotes the masculine gender; for the feminine it becomes *Muslimah*. However, my usage of the term is intended to be gender-neutral, embracing both men and women Muslim writers.

4. There exists two other significant "posts": postfeminism and post-Marxism. While they may be germane to the discussion here, their full impact is felt more acutely in the areas of social epistemology and political discourse. More importantly, these two "posts" are engaged in discourses and polemics other than the ones raised in the discussion here.

## CHAPTER THREE

1. The massacre of Karbala is retold and reenacted through elaborate passion ceremonies on the anniversary of the event, during the month of Muharram, in many parts of the Muslim world, especially in Iran, Iraq, Lebanon, the subcontinent, and in the immigrant Shi'a communities in Europe and North America. The commemoration reaches its peak on the 'Ashura, meaning the tenth day of the month. Moreover, professional religious mourners often conclude the memorial service for any deceased person of Shi'a affiliation with an elaborate passion narrative by recalling the events of Karbala. The idea behind the renarration of the Karbala massacre is, in my opinion, twofold. The first is to keep the memory of the martyrdom of al-Hussein alive, fulfilling the Shi'a slogan that

"Everyday is 'Ashura; Everywhere is Karbala." The second is psychological: to console the bereaved family that their loss cannot be greater or more traumatic than that of the pious descendants of the holy Prophet.

2. Farah's reference here to the three monotheistic faiths as "book religions" is a derivation from the Qur'anic reference to Jews and Christians as "Ahlul Kitab" (people of the book). Significantly, this term suggests to the majority of Muslim theologians that the "books," being already finalized or closed, would not sanction any flexibility to respond to new, unpredictable sociocultural realities. Within such a fixed texualist perspective, religious edicts and dogmas assume a terminality that is arrested in the Prophet's authoritative era of revelation. This line of interpretation allows no space for subsequent, altered and ever-altering conditions that continually emerge and reshape human reality.

## CHAPTER FOUR

1. I am grateful to my friend Khaldoun al-Nu'aimi for doing the diligent counting.

2. It is a sad fact that this major text of contemporary literature is still banned in Egypt and caused the almost fatal stabbing of its gentle, genial author in 1994.

3. There are many similarities between the story of Joseph in Genesis and the Qur'anic narrative of the prophet Yusuf such as Yusuf's piety, ascendancy from slavery to power, and reunion with his father and forgiveness of his brothers. However, there are several differences such as the mention of six dreams in Genesis (two by Joseph, two by the cupbearer and the baker, and two by the Pharaoh); in the Qur'anic narrative there are only four dreams by Yusuf, the baker, the cupbearer, and the Pharaoh. Also the Qur'an foregrounds Yusuf's male beauty, thus providing a motivation for the seduction attempt. The most distinguishing difference relates to Zulekha's dramatic tearing of Yusuf's shirt from behind, an incident that Gurnah capitalizes on effectively. In the Genesis story, Joseph, hurriedly fleeing the advances of the Potiphar's wife, simply "leaves his coat behind."

4. Gurnah's novels are set either in his native East African island of Zanzibar or in England, where he is a literature professor at the University of Kent. Departure, exile, and return to roots are salient motifs in his works.

5. Gurnah's three novels preceding *Paradise*—*Memory of Departure* (1987), *Pilgrim's Way* (1988), and *Dottie* (1990)—evince a similar cynicism associated with the torturous or unfulfilled life of his characters whether situated in East Africa or England. However, in the conclusion of his fifth novel, *Admiring Silence* (1996), one finds, in the tentative last short sentence, a hesitant hint at hope.

## CHAPTER FIVE

1. The Isma'ilis belong to a subsect of Shi'ism, one of the two great branches of Islam (the other being Sunnism).

2. The following passage illustrates the horror of the punishment; it also typifies Vassanji's style of fusing moods and modes, closing off in the fashion of magic realism:

German justice was harsh, swift and arbitrary. In return, you could leave your store unattended without fear of robbery. Thieves had their hands chopped; insubordination was rewarded with the dreaded khamsa ishrin, twenty-five lashes from a whip of hippo hide dipped in salt, which would never break however much blood it drew. It was said that the streets of Dar es Salaam were clean because even the donkeys feared to litter them—you only had to whisper those words "khamsa ishrin" into a donkey's ears and it would straightaway race to its stable to empty its bowels. (*Gunny Sack* 14)

3. In the short story "Refugee," the narrator presents a synoptic, sociopolitical report:

Now there were daily queues for bread and sugar; milk came in packets from the new factory, diluted, sometimes sour. There were rumours that boys would be recruited to fight Idi Amin, the tyrant to the north. And others that Amin would send planes to bomb Dar. The body of an Asian woman had been found on a beach, mutilated, hanging from a tree. Another, an elderly widow, had been hacked to death by robbers in her flat. (*Uhuru Street* 122)

In the tragic story ironically titled "What Good Times We Had," the emigrating heroine contemplates the sorry, frightened fate of the Asian community in Africa:

Life wasn't easy where she would soon be but it couldn't be so bad. There was a price for everything here. And after all that, there was no peace to be had even at night time for fear of robbers. They lived on the edge, not knowing if they would be pushed off the precipice the next day—or if the hand of providence would lift them up and transport them to safety. (*Uhuru Street* 93)

4. Like James Joyce's Dublin, Naguib Mahfouz's Cairo, and Salman Rushdie's and Rohinton Mistry's Bombay, M. G. Vassanji's Dar es Salaam endows the narrative with focus and imaginative referentiality.

## CHAPTER SIX

1. I remember distinctly a hijab-wearing student who dropped my senior English course, "Postcolonial Literatures," as soon she saw *The Satanic Verses* in the syllabus. Her contention was that, she, as a Muslim, could not read such a book, let alone study it and answer exam questions about it. What troubled her more was that the instructor teaching the course claims himself to be a "Muslim." This regrettable attitude reveals not only an a priori conviction (no pun intended), but also an incapacity to accord the text the right to present its point of view.

2. I wish to delineate three distinct aspects pertaining to the bizarre drama that is called "The Rushdie Affair." The first relates to *The Satanic Verses* as a complex literary text. The second relates to the concept of freedom of expression championed by liberal-humanists as well as the literati. The third relates to the death sentence against the author, a move that compounded an already-confusing situation and prompted the

swift, sensational media to get on the Islam-bashing bandwagon. The focus of this chapter is on the first aspect.

3. Abu Sufyan's wife, Hind, a strong-willed vengeful woman is reported to have eaten the liver of the Prophet's uncle, Hamza, after his martyrdom in the battle of Uhud (625 CE); Hamza had previously killed Hind's brother in an earlier altercation. Indeed, Rushdie does make a reference to this liver-chewing episode. Interestingly, Hind and Abu Sufyan's son, Mu'awiya, was the first to impose dynastic rule in Islam, thereby establishing the Ummayyad dynasty in Damascus.

4. As an illustration of such a culture-specific response, let me excerpt the statement by Syed Shahabuddin who rhetorically asks Rushdie, "You depict the Prophet whose name the practicing Muslim recites five times a day, whom he loves, whom he considers the model for mankind, as an impostor and you expect us to applaud you? You have had the nerve to situate the wives of the Prophet, whom we Muslims regard as the mothers of the community, in a brothel and you expect the Muslims to praise your power of imagination?" (3).

## CHAPTER SEVEN

1. For an analysis of Orientalist pictorial depiction of the world of Islam, see Rana Kabbani's *Imperial Fictions*. For a critique of French colonial fetish and fantasia about Algerian domestic life, see Malek Alloula's *The Colonial Harem*.

2. Haddad interprets what she terms the "resurgence of Muslim garb" among contemporary young Arab women as a protective, identity-affirming gesture: "This is done not only as a defense against what they see as the immorality and decadence of Western cultural patterns, but to appropriate anew God's guidance for family life in order to build a strong united nation committed to the ideology of Islam as the only road of salvation for the world" (70). On the other hand, Farzaneh Milani argues that "the veil can really be compared to a portable wall, a strategic mobile segregation" (21).

3. In Azhari's other book, *Mellor in Perspective*, she refers to herself as a modern *Tok Selampit*, "a traditional story teller who recounts tales orally in a sing-song manner" (4).

## CHAPTER EIGHT

1. Nawal El Saadawi gives a similar evaluation of Nasser. In a short article on the fortieth anniversary of the 1952 revolution, she wrote, "I stopped believing in Nasser's speeches about freedom and people's participation in power, but I used to sense that his loathing of imperialism was genuine" ("Fortieth Anniversary" 34).

2. This situation of intellectual hybridity echoes Naguib Mahfouz's declaration in his acceptance speech of the 1988 Nobel Prize for Literature: "I am the son of two civilizations that at a certain age in history have formed a happy marriage. The first of these, seven thousand years old, is the Pharaonic civilization; the second, one thousand four hundred years old, is the Islamic one" (220).

3. Interestingly, Soueif's first work of fiction, *Aisha*, is dedicated to her mother, the critic-academic Fatma Moussa-Mahmoud. On the other hand, the latter wrote Soueif's

biography in *The Bloomsbury Guide to Women's Literature* and translated *The Map of Love* into Arabic.

4. Asya's husband, Saif, does the same thing, except that his two "pet names"—"Princess" and "Sweetie"—sound more elegant.

5. While *The Map of Love* contains references to sympathetic Jewish figures, the discourse is decidedly against the organized Zionist colonization of Palestine in the 1900s culminating in the successful creation of the State of Israel in 1948; moreover, the novel's discourse is opposed to the suspect Israeli infiltration into Egyptian economic life in the 1990s. This political slant in the novel might have been a factor in not awarding the short-listed novel the 1999 Booker Prize. In an article published in *The Guardian*, John Sutherland, one of the Booker Prize judges, states that Soueif's novel "was by general agreement, the 'best read,' of the shortlist. . . . But its anti-Zionist sentiments made some members of the committee slightly uneasy."

6. The only treatment of circumcision/genital mutilation to be found in Muslim fiction in English is written by the Somali writer Nuruddin Farah in three of his novels: *From a Crooked Rib*, *Sardines*, and *Sweet and Sour Milk*. In French, Évelyne Accad's *L'Excisée* contains graphic and moving scenes about it; moreover, two male Muslim writers handle the issue quite effectively in their fiction: Ahmadou Kourouma in *Les soleils des indépendances* (The Suns of Independence) and Tahar Ben Jelloun in *La nuit sacrée* (The Sacred Night). In Arabic, the Egyptian physician-novelist Nawal El Saadawi deals with it from a feminist/psychiatric perspective in her collection of essays, *Al-Wajh Al-Makhfi LilMar'ah* (The Hidden Face of Eve). As well, Alifa Rifaat's moving short story "Bahiyya's Eyes" reveals the physical and psychic scars this practice engenders throughout the victim's life.

# Works Cited

## INTRODUCTION

Ahmad, Aijaz. *In Theory: Classes, Nations, Literature*. London: Verso, 1992.

Appiah, Kwami Anthony. *In My Father's House: Africa in the Philosophy of Culture*. New York: Oxford University Press, 1992.

Arkoun, Mohammed. "Artistic Creativity in Islamic Contexts." *The Postcolonial Crescent: Islam's Impact on Contemporary Literature*. Ed. John C. Hawley. New York: Peter Lang, 1998. 59–70.

Ashcroft, Bill et al. *The Empire Writes Back: Theory and Practice: Post-Colonial Literatures*. London: Routledge, 1989.

———. *Key Concepts in Post-Colonial Studies*. London: Routledge, 1998.

Badran, Margot. "Islamic Feminism: What's in a Name?" *Al-Ahram Weekly On-Line* 569 (2002): 27 August, 2002 <http://www.ahram.org/weekly/2002/569/cul.htm>.

Borges, Jorges Luis. *"The Thousand and One Nights." Seven Nights*. Trans. Eliot Weinberger. New York: New Directions, 1984. 42–57.

*Chimo: Newsjournal of Canadian Association for Commonwealth Literature and Language Studies* 31 (Fall 1995): 40.

Cooke, Miriam. *Women Claim Islam: Creating Islamic Feminism through Literature*. New York: Routledge, 2001.

Cragg, Kenneth. *The Pen and the Faith: Eight Modern Muslim Writers and the Qur'an*. London: Allen and Unwin, 1985.

Eco, Umberto. "Between Author and Text." *Interpretation and Overinterpretation*. Ed. Stefan Collini. Cambridge: University of Cambridge Press. 67–88.

Fanon, Frantz. *Black Skin, White Masks*. Trans. Charles Lam Markmann. New York: Grove, 1967.

———. *The Wretched of the Earth*. Trans. Constance Farrington. London: Penguin, 1990.

Faruqi, Isma'il Raji al-. *Toward Islamic English*. Herndon: International Institute of Islamic Thought, 1995.

Foucault, Michel. *The History of Sexuality. Volume I: An Introduction*. Trans. Robert Hurley. New York: Vintage, 1980.

Hart, William. D. *Edward Said and the Religious Effects of Culture*. Cambridge: University of Cambridge Press, 2000.

Hodgson, Marshall G. S. *The Venture of Islam: Conscience and History in a World Civilization. Volume One: The Classical Age of Islam*. Chicago: University of Chicago Press, 1974.

Huntington, Samuel. "The Clash of Civilizations?" *Foreign Affairs* 72.3 (Summer 1993): 22–49.

Jussawalla, Feroza, and Reed Way Dasenbrock, conds. and eds. "Nuruddin Farah." *Interviews with Writers of the Post-Colonial*. Jackson: University of Mississippi Press, 1992.

Kabbani, Rana. *Letter to Christendom*. London: Virago, 1989.

Kennedy, Valerie. *Edward Said: A Critical Introduction*. Cambridge, Eng.: Polity, 2000.

Macaulay, Thomas Babington. "Minute on Indian Education." *Selected Writings*. Ed. John Clive and Thomas Pinney. Chicago: University of Chicago Press, 1972. 237–51.

Majid, Anouar. *Unveiling Traditions: Postcolonial Islam in a Polycentric World*. Durham: Duke University Press, 2000.

Metcalf, Barbara Daly. "Toward Islamic English? A Note on Translation." *Making Muslim Space in North America and Europe*. Ed. Barbara Daly Metcalf. Berkeley: University of California Press, 1996. xv–xix.

Naipaul, V. S. *Beyond Belief: Islamic Excursions Among the Converted Peoples*. New York: Random, 1998.

Nkrumah, Gamal. "Ahmed Ben Bella: Plus ça change." *Al-Ahram Weekly On-line* 10–16 May 2001: 11 July 2001 <http://web.ahram.org.eg/weekly/2001/533/profile.htm>.

Rao, Raja. Foreword. *Kanthapura*. By Rao. 1938. London: Oxford University Press, 1947. N. pag.

Rhys, Jean. *Wide Sargasso Sea*. London: André Deutsch, 1966. 128.

Rushdie, Salman. *Imaginary Homelands*. London: Granta, 1991.

Said, Edward. "Figures, Configurations, Transfigurations." *From Commonwealth to Post-Colonial*. Ed. Anna Rutherford. Sydney: Dangaroo, 1992. 3–17.

————. "My Encounter with Sartre." *London Review of Books* 22.11 (2000): 12 July 2001 <http://web.lrb.co.uk./v22/n11/said2211.htm>.

————. *Orientalism*. New York: Vintage, 1978.

Salih, Tayeb. *Season of Migration to the North*. Trans. Denys Johnson-Davies. London: Heinemann, 1986.

Thiong'o, Ngugi wa. *Decolonizing the Mind: The Politics of Language in African Literature*. London: James Currey, 1987.

Young, Robert. *Postcolonialism: An Historical Introduction*. Oxford: Blackwell, 2001.

Zeleza, Paul Tiyambe. "Fictions of the Postcolonial." *Toronto Review of Contemporary Writing Abroad* 15.2 (Winter 1997): 19–29.

## CHAPTER ONE

Achebe, Chinua. *Things Fall Apart*. London: Heinemann, 1958.

Akbar, M. J. *Nehru: The Making of India*. London: Penguin, 1989.

Ali, Ahmed. *Ocean of Night*. London: Peter Owen, 1964.

————. *Of Rats and Diplomats*. Hayderabad, India: Sangam, 1985.

————. *Twilight in Delhi*. 1940. Bombay: Oxford University Press, 1966.

Anderson, David D. "Ahmed Ali and the Growth of a Pakistan Literary Tradition in English." *World Literature Written in English* 14 (1975): 436–49.

Desai, Anita. *Clear Light of Day*. 1980. New York: Penguin, 1986.

Forster, E. M. *A Passage to India*. 1924. Ed. Oliver Stallybrass. London: Edward Arnold, 1978.

Gowda, H. H. Anniah. "Ahmed Ali's *Twilight in Delhi* and Chinua Achebe's *Things Fall Apart*." *Alien Voice: Perspectives on Commonwealth Literature*. Ed. Avadhesh K. Strivastava. Lucknow: Print House, 1981. 53–60.

Hashmi, Alamgir. "Ahmed Ali: The Transition to a Postcolonial Mode." *World Literature Written in English* 29.2 (1989): 148–52.

Khairi, Saad R. *Jinnah Reinterpreted: The Journey from Indian Nationalism to Muslim Statehood*. Karachi: Oxford University Press, 1995.

King, Bruce. "From *Twilight* to *Midnight*: Muslim Novels of India and Pakistan." *The World of Muslim Imagination*. Ed. Alamgir Hashmi. Islamabad: Gulmohar, 1986. 243–59.

Macaulay, Thomas Babington. "Minute on Indian Education." *Selected Writings*. Ed. John Clive and Thomas Pinney. Chicago: University of Chicago Press, 1972. 237–51.

Mukherjee, Meenakshi. *The Twice Born Fiction: Themes and Techniques of the Indian Novel in English*. New Delhi: Heinemann, 1971.

Nehru, Jawaharlal. *An Autobiography*. 1936. London: Bodley Head, 1955.

Niven, Alistair. "Historical Imagination in the Novels of Ahmed Ali." *Journal of Indian Writing in English* 8.1–2 (1980): 3–13.

Raizada, Harish. "Ahmed Ali." *Indian English Novelists: An Anthology of Critical Essays*. Ed. Madhusudan Prasad. New Delhi: Sterling, 1982. 1–22.

Rao, Raja. Foreword. *Kanthapura*. By Rao. 1938. London: Oxford University Press, 1947. N. pag.

Rushdie, Salman. *Midnight's Children*. 1981. London: Picador, 1982.

————. *The Satanic Verses*. London: Viking Penguin, 1988.

Scholes, Robert. "Aiming a Canon at the Curriculum." *Salmagundi* 72 (1986): 101–17.

Sharkar, D. A. "Ahmed Ali's *Twilight in Delhi*." *Literary Criterion* 15.1 (1980): 73–80.

Stilz, Gerhard. "'Live in Fragments No Longer.' A Conciliatory Analysis of Ahmed Ali's *Twilight*." *Crisis and Creativity in the New Literature in English*. Ed. Geoffrey V. Davis and Hena Maes-Jelinek. Amsterdam: Radopi, 1990. 369–87.

Trivedi, Harish. "Ahmed Ali: *Twilight in Delhi*." *Major Indian Novels: An Evaluation*. Ed. N. S. Pradhan. Atlantic Highlands: Humanities, 1986. 41–73.

## CHAPTER TWO

Abdullah, Mena, and Ray Mathew. *The Time of the Peacock*. Sydney: Angus and Robertson, 1965.

Ali, Ahmed. "The *Raison d'Etre* of *Twilight in Delhi*." Introduction. *Twilight in Delhi*. By Ali. New York: New Directions, 1994. xi–xxi.

Alkali, Zaynab. "Important . . . but not the same." *West Africa* 11 July 1988: 1256.

————. *The Stillborn*. 1984. Essex, Eng: Longman, 1988.

————. *The Virtuous Woman*. Lagos: Longman, 1987.

Anand, Mulk Raj. "Attia Hosain: A Profile." *Sunlight on a Broken Column*. By Attia Hosain. New Delhi: Arnold Heinemann, 1979. iii–xvi.

Azad, Maulana Abul Kalam. *India Wins Freedom: The Complete Version*. London: Sangam, 1989.

Bhuchar, Suman. "Attia Hosain: 1913–1998." *Wasafiri* 27 (Spring 1998): 43–44.

Desai, Anita. Introduction. *Phoenix Fled*. By Attia Hosain. London: Virago, 1988. vii–xxi.

Gandhi, Rajmohan. *Eight Lives: A Study of the Hindu–Muslim Encounter*. Albany: State University of New York Press, 1986.

Ghazoul, Ferial J. "Halal Fiction." *Al-Ahram Weekly On-Line* 542 (2001): 7 August 2001 <http://www.ahram.org.eg/weekly/2001/542/bo4.htm>.

Gooneratine, Yasmine. "Mena Abdullah, Australian Writer." *Striking Chords: Multicultural Literary Interpretations*. Eds. Sneja Gunew and Kateryna O. Longley. Sydney: Allen and Unwin, 1992. 115–24.

Grewal, Inderpal. "Autobiographic Subjects and Diasporic Locations: *Meatless Days* and *Borderlands*." *Scattered Hegemonies: Postmodernity and Transnational Feminist Practices*. Eds. Inderpal Grewal and Caren Kaplan. Minneapolis: University of Minnesota Press, 1994. 231–54.

Hashmi, Alamgir. "Travails of Identity." *Commonwealth Novel in English* 6.1&2 (Spring and Fall 1993): 145–47.

Hosain, Attia. *Phoenix Fled*. 1953. London: Virago, 1988.

———. *Sunlight on a Broken Column*. 1961. London: Virago, 1988.

Hossain, Rokeya Sakhawat. *Inside Seclusion: The Avarodhbasini of Rokeya Sakhawat Hossain*. Trans. and ed. Roushan Jahan. Decca, Bangladesh: Women for Women, 1981.

———. "Sultana's Dream." *Sultana's Dream and Selections from The Secluded Ones*. Ed. and trans. Roushan Jahan. New York: Feminist Press, 1988. 7–18.

Hussain, Iqbalunnisa. *Purdah and Polygamy: Life in an Indian Muslim Household*. Bangalore: Hosali, 1944.

Jahan, Roushan. "'Sultana's Dream': Purdah Reversed." *Sultana's Dream and Selections from The Secluded Ones*. Ed. and trans. Roushan Jahan. New York: Feminist, 1988. 1–6.

Kalinnikova, Elena J. *Indian-English Literature: A Perspective*. Trans. Virendra Pal Sharma. Ed. K. K. Sharma. Ghaziabad, India: Vimal Prakashan, 1982.

MacDermott, Doireann. "*The Time of the Peacock*: Indian Rural Life in Australia." *Short Fiction in the New Literature in English*. Ed. Jacquelin Bardolph. Nice: Faculté des lettres, 1989. 203–09.

Mazrui, Ali A. *The Trial of Christopher Okibgo*. 1971. London: Heinemann, 1982.

Mernissi, Fatima. *Women and Islam: An Historical and Theological Enquiry*. Trans. Mary Jo Lakeland. Oxford: Blackwell, 1991. 194.

Ogunyemi, Chikwenye Okonjo. "Women and Nigerian Literature." *Perspectives on Nigerian Literature: 1700 to the Present*. Vol. 1. Ed. Yemi Ogunbiyi. Lagos: Guardian, 1988. 60–67.

Reddy, C. R. Foreword. *Purdah and Polygamy: Life in an Indian Muslim Household*. By Iqbalunnisa Hussain. Bangalore: Hosali, 1944.

Said, Edward W. "The Anglo-Arab Encounter." Rev. of *In the Eye of the Sun* by Ahdaf Soueif. *Times Literary Supplement* 19 June 1992: 19.

———. *Culture and Imperialism*. New York: Knopf, 1993.

Sheikh, Farhana. *The Red Box*. London: Women's, 1991.

Sollors, Werner. "Ethnicity." *Critical Terms for Literary Study*. Ed. Frank Lentricchin and Thomas McLaughlin. Chicago: University of Chicago Press, 1990. 288–305.

Spivak, Gayatri Chakravorty. *In Other Worlds: Essays in Cultural Politics*. New York: Methuen, 1987.

Suleri, Sara. *The Rhetoric of English India*. Chicago: University of Chicago Press, 1992.

Tharu, Susie, and K. Lalita. "Rokeya Sakhawat Hossain." *Women Writing in India: 600 B.C. to the Present*. Eds. Susie Tharu and K. Lalita. New York: Feminist Press, 1991. 340–42.


CHAPTER THREE

Adam, Ian. "The Murder of Soyaan Keynaan." *World Literature Written in English* 26.2 (1986): 203–10.

'Alawi, Hadi al-. *al-Ighitiyal al-Siyasi fil Islam*. Beirut: Centre for Research and Social Studies in the Arab World, 1987.

Cary, Norman R. "Islam in the Religious/Political Context of Modern Somalia: The Novels of Nuruddin Farah." *English and Islam: Creative Encounters 96*. Eds. J. U. Khan and A. E. Hare. Kuala Lumpur: International Islamic University, 1998. 115–21.

Cham, Mbye B. "Islam in Senegalese Literature and Film." *Faces of Islam in African Literature*. Ed. Kenneth W. Harlow. Portsmouth: Heinemann, 1991. 163–86.

Ewen, D. R. "Nuruddin Farah." *The Writing of East and Central Africa*. Ed. G. D. Killam. London: Heinemann, 1984. 192–210.

Farah, Nuruddin. *Close Sesame*. London: Allison and Busby, 1983.

———. *From a Crooked Rib*. 1970. London: Heinemann, 1978.

———. *Maps*. London: Picador, 1986.

———. *A Naked Needle*. London: Heinemann, 1976.

———. *Sardines*. London: Heinemann, 1981.

———. *Sweet and Sour Milk*. 1979. London: Heinemann, 1980.

Glassé, Cyril. *The Concise Encyclopedia of Islam*. San Francisco: Harper and Row, 1989.

Jussawalla, Feroza, and Reed Way Dasenbrock. "Nuruddin Farah." *Interviews with Writers of the Post-Colonial World*. Conds. and eds. Feroza Jussawalla and Reed Way Dasenbrock. Jackson: University of Mississippi Press, 1992. 42–62.

Kabbani, Rana. *Letter to Christendom*. London: Virago, 1989.

Mazrui, Alamin. "Mapping Islam in Farah's *Maps*." *The Marabout and The Muse: New Approaches to Islam in African Literature*. Ed. Kenneth W. Harrow. Portsmouth: Heinemann, 1996. 205–17.

Pajalich, Armando. "Nuruddin Farah Interviewed by Armando Pajalich." *Kunapipi* 25.1 (1993): 61–71.

Phillips, Maggi. "The View from a Mosque of Words: Nuruddin Farah's *Close Sesame* and *The Holy Qur'an*." *The Marabout and The Muse: New Approaches to Islam in African Literature*. Ed. Kenneth W. Harrow. Portsmouth: Heinemann, 1996. 191–204.

Turfan, Barbara. "Opposing Dictatorship: A Comment on Nuruddin Farah's *Variations on the Theme of an African Dictatorship*." *Journal of Commonwealth Literature* 24.1 (1989). 173–84.

Wright, Derek. "Going to Meet the General: Deeriye's Death in Nuruddin Farah's *Close Sesame*." *Journal of Commonwealth Literature* 29.2 (1994). 23–30.

Zakaria, Rafiq. *The Struggle within Islam: The Conflict between Religion and Politics*. New York: Penguin, 1988.

## CHAPTER FOUR

Ali, Abdullah Yusuf. *The Holy Qur'an: Text, Translation and Commentary*. Qatar: Presidency of Islamic Courts and Affairs, n.d.

Bardolph, Jacqueline. "Abdulrazak Gurnah's *Paradise* and *Admiring Silence*: History, Stories and the Figure of the Uncle." *Contemporary African Fiction*. Ed. Derek Wright. Bayreuth, Germany: Bayreuth University, 1997.

Bloom, Harold. *The Western Canon: The Books and School of the Ages*. New York: Riverhead, 1994.

Conrad, Joseph. *Heart of Darkness*. 1902. New York: Norton, 1971.

Cragg, Kenneth. *The Event of the Qur'an: Islam in Its Scripture*. 1971. Oxford: Oneworld, 1994.

Gurnah, Abdulrazak. *Admiring Silence*. New York: New, 1996.

———. *Dottie*. London: Jonathan Cape, 1990.

———. *Memory of Departure*. New York: Grove, 1987.

———. *Paradise*. London: Penguin, 1994.

———. *Pilgrim's Way*. London: Jonathan Cape, 1988.

Mahfouz, Naguib. *Children of the Alley*. Trans. Peter Theroux. New York: Doubleday, 1996.

Salih, Tayeb. *Season of Migration to the North*. Trans. Denys Johnson-Davis. London: Heinemann, 1969.

Schwerdt, Dianne. "Looking in on Paradise: Race, Gender and Power in Abdulrazak Gurnah's *Paradise*." *Contemporary African Fiction*. Ed. Derek Wright. Bayreuth, Germany: Bayreuth University, 1997.

Vassanji, M. G. *The Book of Secrets*. Toronto: McClelland and Stewart, 1994.

———. *The Gunny Sack*. Oxford: Heinemann, 1989.

## CHAPTER FIVE

Achebe, Chinua. *Things Fall Apart*. 1958. London: Heinemann, 1985.

Ahmed, Akbar S. *Jinnah, Pakistan and Islamic Identity: The Search for Saladin*. 1997. London: Routledge, 2000.

Azad, Maulana Abul Kalam. *India Wins Freedom: the complete version*. London: Sangam, 1989.

Badawi, Jamal. *Bridgebuilding between Christian and Muslim*. Halifax, NS: Islamic Information Foundation, n.d.

Birbalsingh, Frank. "South Asian Canadian Writers from Africa and the Caribbean." *Canadian Literature* 132 (1992): 94–106.

Bissoondath, Neil. "True Expatriate Love." *Saturday Night*, June 1991, 44–46.

Blaise, Clark. "Voyages of Discovery." *Globe and Mail*, 4 May 1991: E1.

*Chimo: Newsjournal of Canadian Association for Commonwealth Literature and Language Studies* 31 (Fall 1995): 40.

Conrad, Joseph. *Heart of Darkness*. 1902. New York: Norton, 1971.

Cooke, Miriam. *Women Claim Islam: Creating Islamic Feminism through Literature*. New York: Routledge, 2001.

Farah, Nuruddin. *Sweet and Sour Milk*. London. Heinemann. 1980.

Gugelberger, George M. "Postcolonial Cultural Studies." *The Johns Hopkins Guide to Literary Theory and Criticism*. Ed. Michael Groden and Martin Kreiswirth. Baltimore: Johns Hopkins University Press. 1994. 581–84.

Kanaganayakam, Chelva. *Configurations of Exile: South Asian Writers and Their World*. Toronto: TSAR, 1995.

Khan, Adib. *Seasonal Adjustments*. St. Leonards, NSW Australia: Allen and Unwin, 1994.

Liberman, Serge. "Strength from Confusion." *Australian Book Review* 160 (May 1994): 12–13.

Moten, Abdul Rashid. "Nationalism, Elite Politics, and the Break-up of Pakistan." *Muslim World* 88.1 (1998): 93–101.

Murdoch, Iris. *The Bell*. London: Chatto and Windus, 1958.

Richards, Thomas. *The Imperial Archive: Knowledge and the Fantasy of Empire*. New York: Verso, 1993.

Rushdie, Salman. *Imaginary Homelands*. London: Granta. 1991.

———. *Midnight's Children*. 1981. London: Picador. 1982.

Sarvan, Charles Ponnuthurai. "M. G. Vassanji's *The Gunny Sack:* A Reflection on History and the Novel." *Modern Fiction Studies* 37 (1991): 511–18.

Smith, Stephen. "Stories Not Yet Told." *Books in Canada* 21.5 (1992): 26–29.

Sorensen, Rosemary. "Seasonal Adjustments." *Australian Book Review*, 160 (May 1994): 14–15.

Spivak, Gayatri Chakravorty. *Outside in the Teaching Machine*. New York: Routledge, 1993.

Spurr, David. *The Rhetoric of Empire: Colonial Discourse in Journalism, Travel Writing, and Imperial Administration*. Durham: Duke University Press, 1993.

Vassanji, M.G. *The Book of Secrets*. Toronto: McClelland and Stewart, 1994.

———. *The Gunny Sack*. London: Heinemann, 1989.

———. *No New Land*. Toronto: McClelland and Stewart, 1991.

———. "The Postcolonial Writer: Myth Maker and Folk Historian." *A Meeting of Streams: South Asian Canadian Literature*. Ed. M. G. Vassanji. Toronto: TSAR, 1985. 63–67.

———. *Uhuru Street*. Toronto: McClelland and Stewart, 1992.

## CHAPTER SIX

Ali, Maulana Muhammad. *The Holy Qur'an: Arabic Text, Translation and Commentary*, 4th ed. Lahore, Pakistan: Ahmadiyyah Anjuman, 1951.

Ahmed, Akbar S. *Postmodernism and Islam: Predicament and Promise*. London: Routledge, 1992.

Akhtar, Shabbir. *Be Careful with Muhammad: The Salman Rushdie Affair*. London: Bellow, 1989.

Brennan, Timothy. *Salman Rushdie and the Third World: Myths of the Nation.* New York: St. Martin's, 1989.

Carlyle, Thomas. *On Heroes, Hero-Worship, and the Heroic in History.* Ed. Achibald MacMechan. Boston: Ginn, 1901.

Fanon, Frantz. *The Wretched of the Earth.* Trans. Constance Farmington. London: Penguin, 1963. 169.

Goonetilleke, D. C. R. A. *Salman Rushdie.* New York: St. Martin's, 1998.

Harrison, James. *Salman Rushdie.* New York: Twayne, 1992.

Hospital, Janette Turner. "Angels in the Skies above England." *Globe and Mail,* 22 Oct. 1988: C17.

Hutcheon, Linda. "Challenging the Conventions of Realism: Postmodernism in Canadian Literature." *Canadian Forum* (April 1986): 34–38.

———. "The Postmodern Problematizing of History." *English Studies in Canada* 14.4 (1988): 365–82.

Jussawalla, Feroza. *Family Quarrels: Towards a Criticism of Indian Writing in English.* New York: Peter Lang, 1985.

———. "Rushdie's *Dastan-e-Dilruba*: *The Satanic Verses* as Rushdie's Love Letter to Islam." *Diacritics: A Review of Contemporary Criticism* 26.1 (1996): 50–73. Rpt. in *Critical Essays on Salman Rushdie.* Ed. M. Keith Booker. New York: G. K. Hall, 1999. 78–106.

Kirchhoff, H. J. "From Daddy to Rushdie, It's All Germane to Greer." *Globe and Mail,* 5 Aug. 1989: C2.

Mahfouz, Naguib. *Children of the Alley.* Trans. Peter Theroux. New York: Doubleday, 1996.

Mazrui, Ali A. "Is *The Satanic Verses* a Satanic Novel? Moral Dilemmas of the Rushdie Affair." *Michigan Quarterly Review* 28.3 (Summer 1989): 347–71.

Nasr, Seyyed Hossein. *Islam: Religion, History, and Civilization.* New York: HarperCollins, 2003.

Rushdie, Salman. "In Good Faith." *Imaginary Homelands: Essays and Criticism, 1981–1991.* London: Granta, 1991. 393–414.

———. "Interview: Salman Rushdie Talks to the London Consortium about *The Satanic Verses.*" *Critical Quarterly* 38.2 (Summer 1996): 51–70.

———. *Midnight's Children.* 1981. London: Picador, 1982.

———. "One Thousand Days in a Balloon." *Imaginary Homelands: Essays and Criticism, 1981–1991.* London: Granta, 1992. 430–39.

———. "Outside the Whale." *Granta* 2 (1984): 125–38.

———. *The Satanic Verses.* London: Viking Penguin, 1988.

———. *Shame.* London: Jonathan Cape, 1983.

———. "Why I Have Embraced Islam." *Imaginary Homelands: Essays and Criticism, 1981–1991.* London: Granta, 1991. 430–32.

Ruthven, Malise. *A Satanic Affair: Salman Rushdie and the Wrath of Islam.* London: Hogarth, 1991.

Said, Edward. "Intellectuals in the Post-Colonial World." *Salmagundi* 70–71 (1986): 44–64.

———. *Orientalism.* 1978. New York: Vintage, 1979.

Shahabuddin, Syed. "You Did This with Satanic Foresight, Mr. Rushdie." *Times of India,* 13 Oct. 1988, sec. 2: 3.

Singh, Khushwant. "A Riot Has Been Averted." *Times of India,* 30 Oct. 1988, Sunday Review: 1.

Spivak, Gayatri Chakravorty. *In Other Worlds: Essays in Cultural Politics.* New York: Methuen, 1987.

Stewart, Philip. Translator's Introduction. *Children of Gebelawi.* By Naguib Mahfouz. Trans. Philip Stewart. Washington, DC: Three Continents, 1988. vii–ix.

Suleri, Sara. *The Rhetoric of English India.* Chicago: University of Chicago Press, 1992.

Thorpe, Michael. "Risky Deconstruction: The Rushdie Affair." *World Literature Written in English* 31.1: 21–32.

Watt, W. Montgomery. "Carlyle on Muhammad." *The Hibbert Journal: A Quarterly Review of Religion, Theology and Philosophy* 53 (1955): 247–54.

Wolpert, Stanley. *A New History of India.* New York: Oxford University Press, 1977.

## CHAPTER SEVEN

Accad, Evelyne. "Sexuality and Sexual Politics: Conflicts and Contradictions for Contemporary Women in the Middle East." *Third World Women and the Politics of Feminism.* Ed. Chandra Talpade Mohanty. Bloomington: Indiana University Press, 1991. 237–67.

Alloula, Malek. *The Colonial Harem.* Trans. Myrna Godzich and Wlad Godzich. Minneapolis: University of Minnesota Press, 1986.

Azhari, Che Husna. *Mellor in Perspective.* Bangi, Malaysia: Furada, 1993.

———. *The Rambutan Orchard.* Bangi, Malaysia: Furada, 1993.

El Saadawi, Nawal. "Women and Islam." *The Nawal El Saadawi Reader.* London: Zed, 1997. 73–92.

Farah, Nuruddin. "Mapping the Psyche: Robert Moss Interviews Somali Writer, Nuruddin Farah." *West Africa* 3600 (1 September 1986): 1827–828.

Forster, E. M. *Aspects of the Novel.* 1927. London: Edward Arnold, 1958.

Gusdorf, Georges. "Conditions and Limits of Autobiography." *Autobiography: Essays Theoretical and Critical.* Ed. James Olney. Princeton: Princeton University Press, 1980. 28–48.

Haddad, Yvonne Yazbeck. *Contemporary Islam and the Challenge of History.* Albany: State University of New York Press, 1982.

Harlow, Barbara. Introduction. *The Colonial Harem.* By Malek Alloula. Trans. Myrna Godzich and Wlad Godzich. Minneapolis: University of Minnesota Press, 1986. ix–xxii.

Hofmann, Murad. *Islam 2000.* Beltsville: amana, 1996.

Kabbani, Rana. *Imperial Fictions: Europe's Myths of Orient.* 1986. London: Pandora, 1994.

Mernissi, Fatima. *Beyond the Veil: Male–Female Dynamics in a Modern Muslim Society.* New York: Schenkman, 1975.

———. *Doing Daily Battle: Interviews with Moroccan Women.* Trans. Mary Jo Lakeland. New Brunswick: Rutgers University Press, 1989. Trans. of *Le Maroc raconté par ses femmes.* Rabat: Société Marocaine de Éditeurs réunis, 1984.

———. *Dreams of Trespass: Tales of a Harem Girlhood.* 1994. New York: Addison Wesley, 1995.

———. *The Forgotten Queens of Islam.* Trans. Mary Jo Lakeland. Minneapolis: University of Minnesota Press, 1993.

————. *Scheherazade Goes West: Different Cultures, Different Harems*. New York: Washington Square, 2001.

————. *Women and Islam: An Historical and Theological Inquiry*. Trans. Mary Jo Lakeland. Oxford: Blackwell, 1991.

————. *Women's Rebellion and Islamic Memory*. London: Zed, 1996.

Milani, Farzaneh. *Veils and Words: The Emerging Voices of Iranian Women Writers*. Syracuse: Syracuse University Press, 1992.

Minai, Naila. *Women in Islam: Tradition and Transition in the Middle East*. New York: Seaview, 1981.

Olney, James. "Autobiography and the Cultural Moment: A Thematic, Historical, and Bibliographical Introduction." *Autobiography: Essays Theoretical and Critical*. Ed. James Olney. Princeton: Princeton University Press, 1980. 3–27.


CHAPTER EIGHT


Accad, Évelyne. *L'Excisée: The Mutilated Woman*. Trans. David Bruner. Washington, DC: Three Continents Press, 1989. Trans. of *L'Excisée*. Paris: L'Harmattan, 1982.

————. *Veil of Shame: The Role of Women in the Contemporary Fiction of North Africa and the Arab World*. Sherbrooke, Québec: Naaman, 1978.

Ahmed, Leila. "A Woman Caught Between Two Worlds." *Washington Post* 13 June 1993, Book World: 6.

————. *Women and Gender in Islam: Historical Roots of a Modern Debate*. New Haven: Yale University Press, 1992.

Arteaga, Alfred. "Another Tongue." *Another Tongue: Nation and Ethnicity in the Linguistic Borderlands*. Ed. Alfred Arteaga. Durham: Duke University Press, 1994. 8–33.

Bakhtin, M. M. *The Dialogic Imagination: Four Essays*. Trans. Caryl Emerson and Michael Holquist. Ed. Michael Holquist. Austin: University of Texas Press, 1981.

————. *Problems of Dostoevsky's Poetics*. Ed. and trans. Caryl Emerson. Minneapolis: University of Minnesota Press, 1997.

Ben Jelloun, Tahar. *The Sacred Night*. Trans. Alan Sheridan. New York: Ballantine, 1991. Trans. of *La nuit sacrée*. Paris: Seuil, 1987.

Bhabha. Homi K. *The Location of Culture*. New York: Routledge, 1994.

Booth, Marilyn. Rev. of *In the Eye of the Sun*, by Ahdaf Soueif. *World Literature Today* 68 (1994): 204–05.

de Beauvoir, Simone. *The Second Sex*. Trans. H. M. Parshley. New York: Vintage, 1974.

El Saadawi, Nawal. "The Fortieth Anniversary." *Al-Adab*. (Sep./Oct. 1992): 32–35.

————. *The Hidden Face of Eve: Women in the Arab World*. Trans. and ed. Sherif Hetata. London: Zed, 1980.

Farah, Nuruddin. *From a Crooked Rib*. London: Heinemann, 1970.

————. *Sardines*. London: Heinemann, 1981.

————. *Sweet and Sour Milk*. London: Heinemann, 1979.

Fernea, Elizabeth Warnock. *In Search of Islamic Feminism: One Woman's Global Journey*. New York: Doubleday, 1998.

Foucault, Michel. *The History of Sexuality, Volume I: An Introduction*. Trans. Robert Hurley. New York: Vintage, 1980.

Génette, Gérard. *Narrative Discourse: An Essay in Method.* Trans. Jane E. Levin. Ithaca: Cornell University Press, 1983.

Ghazoul, Ferial J. "Halal Fiction." *Al-Ahram Weekly On-Line* 542 (2001): 7 Aug. 2001 <http://www.ahram.org.eg/weekly/2001/542/bo4.htm>.

Ghosh, Amitav. *In an Antique Land.* London: Granta, 1992.

Ibrahim, Sonallah. "Je ne sense pas de danger intégriste." *Le Monde* 20 May 1994, Des Livres: viii.

Kabbani, Rana. *Letter to Christendom.* London: Virago, 1989.

Kermode, Frank. "Asyah [*sic*] and Saif." Rev. of *In the Eye of the Sun*, by Ahdaf Soueif. *London Review of Books* 25 June 1992: 19–20.

Kourouma, Ahmadou. *The Suns of Independence.* Trans. Adrian Adams. London: Heinemann, 1981. Trans. of *Les soleils des indépendences.* Montréal: Les Presses de l'Université de Montréal, 1968.

Mahfouz, Naguib. "Nobel Lecture, 8 December 1988." *Georgian Review* (Spring 1995): 220–23.

Mantel, Hilary. "Double Identity: *In the Eye of the Sun.*" *New York Review of Books*, 40.15 (23 Sep. 1993): 28–29.

Mohanty, Chandra. "Under Western Eyes: Feminist Scholarship and Colonial Discourse." *Feminist Review* 30 (Autumn 1988): 61–88.

Montrose, Louis. *The Purpose of Playing: Shakespeare and the Cultural Politics of the Elizabethan Theatre.* Chicago: University of Chicago Press, 1996.

Moussa-Mahmoud, Fatma. "Turkey and the Arab Middle East." *The Bloomsbury Guide to Women's Literature.* Ed. Claire Buck. New York: Prentice-Hall, 1992. 210–16.

Mukherjee, Bharati. "Mimicry and Reinvention." *The Proceedings of the Triennial Conference of CACLALS*, Pt. 2. Ed. Uma Parameswaran. Calcutta: Writers Workshop, 1983.

"Omdurman, Battle of." *The New Encyclopaedia Britannica: Micropaedia.* 15th ed. 1998.

Pakravan, Saideh. "An Interview with Ahdaf Soueif." *Edebiyat* 6 (1995): 275–86.

Rifaat, Alifa. "Bahiyya's Eyes." *Distant Views of a Minaret and Other Stories.* Trans. Denys Johnson-Davies. London: Heinemann, 1985. 5–11.

Rushdie, Salman. *Imaginary Homelands: Essays and Criticism 1981–1991.* London: Granta, 1991.

Said, Edward W. "The Anglo-Arab Encounter." Rev. of *In the Eye of the Sun*, by Ahdaf Souef. *Times Literary Supplement* 19 June 1992: 19.

———. *Culture and Imperialism.* New York: Knopf, 1993. 336.

———. *Orientalism.* New York: Vintage, 1978.

Shohat, Ella. "Antinomies of Exile: Said at the Frontiers of National Narrations." *Edward Said: A Critical Reader.* Ed. Michael Sprinker. Cambridge: Blackwell, 1992.

Soueif, Ahdaf. *Aisha.* London: Jonathan Cape, 1983.

———. *In the Eye of the Sun.* London: Bloomsbury, 1992.

———. *The Map of Love.* London: Bloomsbury, 1999.

———. *Sandpiper.* London: Bloomsbury, 1996.

Sutherland, John. "The Booker Turns a Leaf." *Guardian Unlimited* 26 Oct. 1999. 17 May 2004 <http://www.guardian.co.uk/booker/Story/0,2763,201683,00.html>.

Young, Robert J. C. *Colonial Desire: Hybridity in Theory, Culture and Race.* London: Routledge, 1995.

## CONCLUSION

Minh-ha, Trinh T. *Woman, Native, Other.* Bloomington: Indiana University Press, 1989.

Nasr, Seyyed Hossein. *Islam: Religion, History, and Civilization.* New York: HarperCollins, 2003.

Rumi, Jalâluddîn. *The Mevlevi Order.* Home page. The Threshold Society. 15 May 2003 <http://www.sufism.org/society/mevlev.html>.

Said, Edward. *Covering Islam: How the Media and the Experts Determine How We See the Rest of the World.* New York: Pantheon, 1981.

Sayyid, Bobby S. *A Fundamental Fear: Eurocentrism and the Emergence of Islamism.* London: Zed, 1997.

Young, Robert J. C. *Postcolonialism: An Historical Introduction.* Oxford: Blackwell, 2001.

# INDEX